D0940692

1495

DEATH ON THE GALLOWS

New Mexico Roads and Settlements 1910

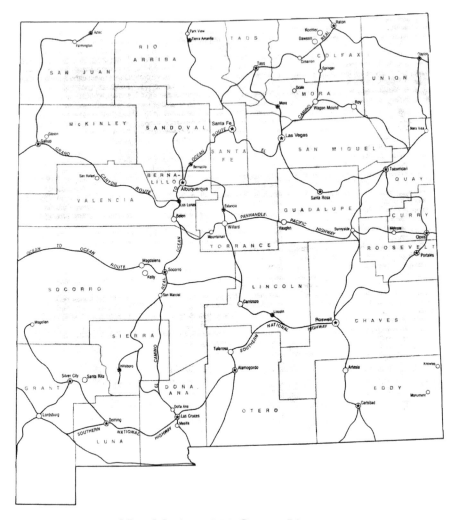

New Mexico 1910 County Lines

Source: Dept. of the Interior, General Land Office, 1910

DEATH ON THE GALLOWS

The Story of Legal Hangings In New Mexico 1847-1923

By West C. Gilbreath

High-Lonesome Books
Silver City, New Mexico

Copyright © 2002 by West C. Gilbreath

ISBN # 0-944383-57-2

Library of Congress Card Number 2002103968

First Edition May 2002

Dedication:

To my mother, Eileen
And
My wife, Sabrina
For all your love and support.

High-Lonesome Books
P.O. Box 878
Silver City, New Mexico 88062

Table of Contents

List of Illustrations

Special Thanks to:

Rio Grande Historical Collection, NMSU, Las Cruces, New Mexico
Palace of the Governors, Santa Fe, New Mexico
State Records Center and Archives, Santa Fe, New Mexico,
    Archives Chief Daphne S.O. Arnaiz-DeLeon
Historical Museum of Lawmen, Doña Ana County Sheriff's Department
Grant County Sheriff's Department

Preface

The punishment of executing criminals by hanging was a method first used in Europe. In the twelfth century, the gallows consisted of a post with a crossbeam. The condemned person was forced to climb up the ladder to the crossbeam, whereby the noose was placed over the neck. An assistant would then twist the ladder out from under the victim who then strangled to their death.

Execution of criminals carried over into the new world, with the first executions in the United States dating back to 1608. New Mexico's first executions occurred in 1847. New Mexico law required the execution to take place in the county where the crime occurred. The task of securing and executing the prisoner fell on the County Sheriff who received fifteen dollars in fees for serving the court order. The gallows built in New Mexico consisted of a platform and two upright posts with a crossbeam. A spring lever would be pulled to release the bolt under the trap door, or a person could cut the rope with an axe for the trap to fall. Milton Yarberry was the only person who was executed by the use of weights and pulleys. The paper referred to this method of execution as being "jerked to Jesus." In his case, when the 400 pounds of weights were dropped, the 200 hundred pound man was jolted forcibly into the air. If the sudden force upward 6 feet into the air did not break the neck, the downward fall would. Paula Angel may have been the only person in New Mexico executed from a tree limb as the wagon she stood upon was moved out from under her.

Prior to an execution, the rope, being of a fine hemp fiber, would be ordered. As in the case of Thomas Ketchum, in 1901, the rope ordered cost an overwhelming $20.70. Once the rope was received, it would be pre-stretched with sands bags to the desired length and to remove any elasticity. The hangman's noose had either 8 or 9 coils and was placed behind the left jawbone under the left ear at the hollow area of the neck. The length of the drop was calculated depending on the weight and physical condition of the person. The drop usually varied between 4 to 7 feet. The slack in the rope was either adjusted on the right side above the person, or allowed to lie on the right side.

Except for Don Antonio Maria Trujillo and Thomas Ketchum, all the people listed in this book were convicted for the crime of murder in the first degree, and had a sentence of death imposed. Don Trujillo was convicted of treason against the United States, and Thomas Ketchum was convicted of assault upon a railroad with the intent to commit a felony, a capital offense at that time. During the 19th century, executions were a public event with souvenirs being offered and photographs of the deceased being sold. Businesses closed for the day, and the women prepared lunches and dressed in their finest clothes. The spectators and newspaper reporters expected a show of bravery with no emotions from the condemned shown. The same was expected of the Sheriff. He was expected to hang a man without suffering, or decapitation, and was praised afterwards for handling his duties properly. A successful execution resulted if the victim's neck had been broken.

In later years, New Mexico enacted laws that restricted the viewing of execution to 20 persons. A list of witnesses would be prepared by the Sheriff and approved by the District Court Judge. Afterwards, the Sheriff would issue invitations to this approved list of witnesses. An additional requirement ordered that an enclosure be built which surrounded the gallows and kept it from public view. Today in New Mexico, all executions are carried out at the New Mexico State Penitentiary in Santa Fe. Capitol punishment can be sentenced upon the conviction of first-degree murder or murder with aggravated circumstances. The law requires the Warden to be present during the execution. The Warden is directed to invite a physician, State Attorney General, and twelve citizens. The condemned is allowed to invite five witnesses. Those five can include friends, family or a peace officer. Two ministers or clergy may be present. Once the condemned person is secured in the death chamber, the law directs the execution to be carried out by administrating a "continuous, intravenous injection of lethal quantity of an ultra-short acting barbiturate in combination with a chemical paralytic agent."

Although more states are turning towards execution by lethal injection, some states still use the gas chamber or electric chair as methods. Montana, New Hampshire and Delaware are the only states to still use hanging. Idaho and Utah have the firing squad as a option.

This book details the execution of sixty-two men and one woman in New Mexico from 1847 to 1923, to include information about the criminal activity and arrest that lead to the death sentence. Other persons were convicted and sentenced to death. Because New Mexico did not complete construction of the penitentiary in Santa Fe until 1885, many prisoners escaped from the Sheriff's holding facility and were never recaptured, or worse yet, were lynched! Other prisoners were commuted to life in prison and sent to the Kansas State Penitentiary, while some chose suicide as a last resort. After 1923, execution in New Mexico for a time was done by the electric chair, and most recently by lethal injection.

Kansas was contracted by New Mexico to house its inmates at twenty cents a day per inmate until the penitentiary was built and began accepting its own prisoners in 1885. Once built those inmates were returned to New Mexico to serve the remainder of their sentence. The Governor usually offered female inmates the option of an early release from the Kansas penitentiary on the condition she was not to return to New Mexico. Today, it is estimated that it cost's taxpayers $25,000 to $38,000 per year for each inmate housed, depending on the state.

On November 6, 2001 at 7:10 p. m. , 45-year-old, Terry Clark became the first man in New Mexico in 42 years to be put to death. Clark was executed for the 1986 rape and murder of a 9–year–old girl at Squaw Canyon

Ranch, sixty miles from Artesia, New Mexico. Men prior to Terry Clark who were waiting for their scheduled appointment with death, were commuted to life imprisonment by Governor Tony Anaya prior to him leaving office. Early law required the condemned to be executed thirty days after trial. An appeal stayed the execution for another thirty days to allow the Supreme Court to review the case. Once the sentence was upheld the Supreme Court then ordered the execution date. Today, it takes an average of 14 years to exhaust all appeals for the execution to be carried out. The legal cost from trial and through the appeal process can cost from $800,000 to $2,000,000 dollars. The families of victims today are frustrated with the legal system, as they were in the past. In the early days, citizens had little trust in the legal system. Fearing the suspected offender may escape, be acquitted or win an appeal, citizens sometimes took matters upon themselves as they saw fit by lynching the accused. Such towns as Socorro and Las Vegas, New Mexico openly approved of lynching by organizing vigilante groups as a deterrent and warning to all criminals. Appendix A lists 153 lynchings from 1851 through 1893. Although lynchings were unlawful and should have been considered as a murder, in most cases little if anything was done by lawmen to identify, arrest or convict the parties who were responsible.

During the 76 years that hanging was the only method of execution in New Mexico, Grant and Santa Fe Counties performed the most with ten each. Luna County, with a total of six, held the most executions in both one month and one year. Santa Fe County and Luna County, with a total of four each, had the most executions held in a single day.

This book will fascinate the armchair historian by the details of the crimes committed, sentencing from the judges, and the actual newspaper accounts on the day of the execution. At times the reader may note certain discrepancies. Sometimes different newspapers would report different accounts of the same crime and execution. Some town newspapers only printed once a week. Much of the information the editor received was old or third hand. By the time the story was printed about a crime the facts of the incident had changed. It further depended on the editor of a particular newspaper what information he chose to use as facts and the credibility of the information he had obtained. In this book, newspaper accounts of each incident of crime and punishment are printed verbatim, with the exception of correction of obvious errors in spelling, capitalization or typography. For authenticity, the sometimes archaic stylistic trends of newspapers of the time are maintained. The author's narrative relative to each incident is taken, however, from a variety of newspapers and sometimes other sources, in an attempt to best summarize the information available. Newspaper editors of the time had no vision their newspapers would be preserved on microfilm and their words revealed later to give us a singular view of crime and punishment in the Old West.

West Gilbreath,
Las Cruces, New Mexico

Chapter 1

Bernalillo County

Milton J. Yarberry	February 9, 1883
Dionicio Sandoval	September 24, 1896
Jose P. Ruiz	June 1, 1900
Demecio Delgadillo	May 16, 1913

Milton J. Yarberry

Albuquerque was a small Spanish village, founded on the banks of the Rio Grande in the center of the Territory in 1706. The Atchison Topeka and Santa Fe railway reached Albuquerque on April 10, 1880. The town at the time was unincorporated and had no town government. After the arrival of the railroad the town quickly expanded and the need for law and order was obvious.

The town held its first election on February 1, 1881. Milton J. Yarberry, became the first Constable of Albuquerque, elected to Precinct 12. Constable Yarberry was originally from Walnut Ridge, Arkansas. He was about 37 years old and had steel gray eyes.

About two months after becoming the Constable, Milton Yarberry was involved in his first shooting as a law officer. The shooting occurred on Sunday evening of March 27, 1881, and resulted in the death of Harry Brown. Less than three months after killing Mr. Brown, Constable Yarberry was involved in another shooting in Albuquerque that took a life on June 18, 1881. The deceased was a thirty-two-year-old carpenter by the name of Charles D. Campbell who was employed by the Atlantic and Pacific Railroad. It was for Campbell's death that Milton Yarberry was tried and convicted of first-degree murder.

Milton Yarberry believed politics played a role in convicting him of murder since Harry Brown was the nephew of Ex-Governor Neil S. Brown. Milton Yarberry's execution date was first scheduled to take place on June 15, 1882, but was delayed when lawyers appealed the case to the Territorial Supreme Court. For security, Milton Yarberry was kept in the Santa Fe County jail.

On September 9th, Yarberry escaped from jail after he and two other prisoners overpowered a guard. Yarberry was recaptured after three days on the run and returned to the Santa Fe County jail. His execution date was rescheduled for February 9th, 1883 between the hours of 11:00 a.m. and 3:00 p.m. Milton Yarberry at first tried to control his nervousness each day by playing the fiddle. As the day of his execution became closer, his nervousness and anxiety increased. He ate heartily, but slept very little. A reporter asked Yarberry how his health was. Yarberry replied, "Oh, I'm feeling first rate, take my meals regular. Do I look like a man who is sick or scared?" The reporter commented that he looked pale. "That may be, but I ain't sick and I ain't scared either. Hell, I wouldn't get scared if they walked me out on the scaffold right now."

But nervous and scared Yarberry did become, for he begged Sheriff Romero to supply him liquor for his nerves. Sheriff Romero purchased a half-gallon of whiskey and wine for the condemned man. Yarberry was given a full glass of wine with each meal and one before going to sleep. The citizens felt it would have been inhumane to deny such a request and approved of the Sheriff's action. Sheriff Romero spoke with a reporter and described Milton Yarberry as at times "displaying some symptoms of animal fear that his life is insecure and limited to only a few days. Yarberry is so illiterate and devoid of any evidence of kindly, human parental rearing that he does not conceive the immensity of his crime or the doom before him. He asserts his belief he will never die at the hands of the public hangman. He persists that he shot at Campbell under the belief that he was executing his duty and believed his own life in imminent peril."

A week prior to Yarberry's scheduled execution, Sheriff Romero foiled a second escape attempt. While making an inspection of the jail, the Sheriff discovered the cell door that secured Yarberry had been tampered with. A large iron bar fastened to the cell door slid over a hook that was then padlocked. The sheriff discovered the large flattened riveted heads missing and holes of the rivets had been filled with soap. The exterior of the door was smeared with dirt and soot, which gave the door its normal appearance. Upon Yarberry seeing that the Sheriff had discovered his escape plan he angrily said "I curse the ---- ---- who gave me away!" Sheriff Romero replied, "Nobody gave you away, I'm on the lookout for these things." Yarberry, having a "hang-dog look in his eyes," said: "Well, under the circumstances who wouldn't have done it. I'm sentenced to be hanged – you would have done it too."

On the morning of the execution, Milton Yarberry was transported on an Atchison Topeka and Santa Fe train to Albuquerque. Security was tight for Governor Sheldon ordered fourteen armed soldiers from Company E (Governor's Rifles) to board the train. The Governor ordered Companies H and F to the Albuquerque train depot, armed with rifles and 20 rounds each of ammunition, while officers were armed with pistols.

The Albuquerque *Morning Journal* dated February 11, 1883, told the history and execution of Milton Yarberry.

THE LAST CHAPTER

IN MILTON L. YARBERRY'S EVENTFUL CAREER.
HE SHOWS THEM HOW TO DIE GAME.

THE TRIP FROM SANTA FE TO ALBUQUERQUE
ON A SPECIAL TRAIN.

HIS LAST MOMENTS ON EARTH
HIS SPEECH DELIVERED FROM THE GALLOWS
JUST BEFORE THE DEATH SIGNAL.

HIS DENIAL OF EVER KILLING ANYONE BE-
FORE LIVING IN ALBUQUERQUE.

The crime

The crime of which Yarberry now stands convicted is one sickening to the sensibilities of all those who are acquainted with its particulars. It was committed at a time when Albuquerque was the liveliest and perhaps the most lawless town in New Mexico. Milt Yarberry ran the town being clothed with the authority of constable having been appointed to the position by the county commissioners.

Upon the fatal night of June 18, there was a party of men in R. H. Greenleaf's restaurant on Front Street,

DRINKING AND CAROUSING.

At about 9 o'clock some one fired a shot in the house, after which every thing was thrown into a high state of excitement. Who fired that shot has never appeared. Immediately after this occurrence Charles D. Campbell started toward Stover, Crary & CO's wholesale store. At the same time Milt Yarberry, attracted by the pistol shot started toward Greenleaf's from the Maden House, accompanied by a gambler well known in the city at that time named Frank Boyd. Yarberry's attention was directed toward Campbell and he and Boyd started after him. They advanced nearly across the street. Boyd considerably to the north of Yarberry, when a volley of shots was heard and Charles D. Campbell fell to the ground,

PIERCED BY THREE BULLETS.

Yarberry gave himself up to Sheriff Armijo and was taken to the Sheriff's Office, which at that time was located in old town. Boyd, who had as much to do with the killing as Yarberry, remained in town forty-eight hours after the shooting, but from then to the time of his death nothing was heard of him by the authorities at Albuquerque. Campbell's remains were picked up and carried to Tom F. Phelan's office, which at that time was located just three doors north of Zieger's saloon on Front Street. Frank Reese, who was coroner impaneled a jury, and an inquest was held. As the testimony given at the

CORONER'S INQUEST

Had the merit of being taken so shortly after the murder, it must have been as nearly correct as it was possible for it to have been. At the time Capt. R. C. Hawley testified as follows:

"I was talking with Tom Park on the platform at the side of Stover & Co.'s store, when I heard a pistol shot on the opposite side of the street. Immediately afterwards I saw the officers and others going that way. I stepped down the steps by the office and one minute after I saw the deceased

COMING TOWARD ME

And a distance of twenty or thirty feet behind him were two men who appeared to be in pursuit. One of them said, "Throw up your hands." Instead of obeying the order he reached as if for a revolver. I did not see him draw a pistol. He turned a little but continued his course. Don't know whether the deceased fired or not. After I heard the first shot I left for shelter in the store. About ten or twelve shots were fired altogether. The man said something in answer to the officer's challenge, but I did not understand what. The men who followed him did not state that they were officers. I do not know

WHO FIRED THE FIRST SHOT,

But believe it was Mr. Yarberry. The man did not quicken his pace when ordered to halt but rather seemed to stop. A crowd soon congregated after he was down. I was about ten or fifteen feet from the man when the firing commenced."

Major T.W. Park testified: "Mr. Hawley and myself were sitting on Stover & Co.'s platform when we heard a shot near Maden's. In about a half a minute a dog came running into the store. Mr. Hawley said some one had shot at the dog. Shortly after a crowd was seen walking toward the store. Mr. Hawley walked toward the office, and when he got about to the door I heard some one say:

'HOLD UP YOUR HANDS,'

and simultaneously with the order shots were fired. Mr. Hawley came in the store. I thought the shots were fired at Mr. Hawley. The deceased did not fire at the officers. The shots were fired by those who gave the order, 'Throw up your hands.' I would have taken the challenge as coming from robbers and not officers, from the manner in which it was given."

J. M. Platt, night watchman at the Atchison, Topeka & Santa Fe depot, said: "I heard the order 'Throw up your hands' given and in a second or two after the shots. I thought that the person who gave the order intended to rob the deceased. The man who was killed did not fire. I did not recognize the man who did the firing because of the darkness. I know that because of the darkness. I know that

TWO MEN DID THE SHOOTING.

"A man would not have had the time to put up his hands after the order was given, before the shot was fired."

Drs. Gilkey and Howard who examined the wounds in Campbell's body testified that he was shot in three places, twice in the back and once in the left side. Each ball passed clear through the body and either would have caused death.

The jury returned a verdict that Charles D. Campbell came to his death from pistol shots fired by Milton Yarberry and another person, whose name is unknown. The morning after the murder a reporter for the Journal called at Sheriff Armijo office, and Milt Yarberry made the following statement:

"I was sitting in a chair in front of the Maden Hotel. While sitting there I heard a pistol shot around the corner about a block south of the Maden's. I walked down the street and Frank Boyd was with me. I met two fellows close to old man Greenleaf's on the sidewalk. I thought the shooting might be in Greenleaf's and Boyd who was with me, asked one old gentleman who was sitting on the sidewalk, if he knew where the shooting was. He pointed out two men on the street. They had separated, and one went up the street toward Maden's and the other struck across toward Stover's.

The old gentleman said,

'THERE GOES THE MAN'

pointing to the one who went toward Stover's. I started into Greenleaf's and Boyd spoke to me saying, "Milt, this gentleman says there goes the man who fired the shot. I started after him and told Boyd to come ahead. I got within ten steps of the man and ordered him to hold up his hands, that I wanted him. When I said that he turned and said, 'You hold up yours, GOD damn you.' Then he shot at me as soon as he got out his pistol. Then he shot five or six times at me and I shot five at him. He shot two or three times

AFTER HE WAS DOWN.

Then I went over to Maden's and shortly after surrendered myself to the Sheriff."

Yarberry took particular pains to exhibit to the reporter on that visit a revolver which a friend of his found near where Campbell was killed the morning after the tragedy. For the next few days after the killing Albuquerque was the scene of the

GREATEST EXCITEMENT.

Meetings of indignant and excited citizens were frequent, but cool heads and wise council did much toward quieting the hot headed populace, and this together with the brave and determined stand taken by Sheriff Armijo prevented Yarberry from being tried in Judge Lynch's court.

Monday morning Campbell's funeral took place from the platform of Moore, Bennett & Co.'s store – now Putney & Trask – and the street was crowded with men, mostly employees of the Atlantic & Pacific Railroad Company. The body was encased in a fine metallic coffin bought by the railroad men, a telling sermon was delivered by Rev. N. H. Gale. The funeral procession was a long one, and was composed of

MEN ON FOOT,

Carrying banners on which were mottos expressing the feeling of the bearers. No demonstration was made, however, and the crowd dispersed quietly.

A very unnecessary delay was made in hearing Yarberry's preliminary examination. He objected to appearing before Justice Sullivan for personal reasons, and the prosecution objected to having the hearing before Alcalde Martin on the same grounds. Finally

THE EXAMINATION

Took place in Martin's court, July 5, and Yarberry was held to await the action of the grand jury. He was sent to Santa Fe for safe keeping, and remained in jail there until the grand jury met. He was indicted, but not soon enough for his case to come to trial during that term, and he was again sent to Santa Fe and lodged in jail. Last May he was brought to this city for trial, and on May 15 his case was called, and he pleaded not guilty. The trial commenced on the 18th, and lasted three days, when the jury, after being absent only an hour

RETURNED A VERDICT

As charged in the indictment. During the trial the court room was crowded, there being many ladies present. The prosecution was conducted by William Breeden and Arnet R. Owen, and the defense by L. S. Trimble and Col. Frank Chaves. The prosecution exerted every effort to bring witnesses here, and perhaps if it had not been for the opportune arrival of Major T. W. Park, who is a resident of Missouri, Yarberry would be free man to-day. He appeared perfectly cool upon the announcement of the verdict and was carried off to jail in irons. On the 23rd he was again brought into court and

SENTENCED TO BE HANGED

Friday, June 15. He appeared not in the least affected until the last words of the judge, "And may god have mercy on your poor soul" were pronounced. When his face suddenly turned to a livid hue and his cold gray eyes flashed out darts of malice toward the judge as he said: "Judge, I have not had a fair trial: You have not treated me justly: The men in New Town who tried to hang me have falsely sworn my life away."

He was again taken to jail in Santa Fe, but his lawyers appealed the case to the Supreme Court, and he was thus given an extension of life.

THE ESCAPE.

Not withstanding the fact that Yarberry was to have another chance for life, he did not have any very great confidence of receiving his liberty from the courts, and made up his mind to escape if possible. The jail at Santa Fe is not one that is easily broken, and the undertaking was a formidable one. He formed a plan with Billy Wilson, George Pease and one Harris, which worked to perfection one evening of Sept. 9. It seems that the guard opened the cell door to lock up a prisoner who was allowed the range of the placita during the day, when the moment the door opened, they threw a blanket over his head, knocked him down, and escaped by rushing up the stairway, and passing through the guard's room on the roof, from whence they easily

JUMPED TO THE GROUND.

The other guard on duty fired several shots without effect, as it was dark. Pease was recaptured quickly, but the others made good their escape. In some manner the prisoners obtained possession of a file with which they removed their shackles, not withstanding the fact that they were in constant view of the guards, whose room was immediately overhead, having an aperture in the floor for the purpose of watching the movements of the prisoners.

Yarberry was recaptured after only three days of liberty, by Frank Chaves, chief of police of Santa Fe, in the Arroyo Gallesto. He was traveling along a wagon road, when the men rode down upon him and took charge of his person and his effects. The latter consisted of six dollars, which was found in his pockets. Yarberry had separated from his companions, it being considered more safe to scatter. He was returned to his

OLD QUARTERS

At the jail where he remained without any occurrence of note until the Supreme Court refused to reverse the decision of the lower court, and the day of his death was again set.

CAMPBELL'S CAREER

Of Charles D. Campbell but little is known previous to his residence in Albuquerque, and his naturally quiet and reserved disposition prevented even his best and most intimate friends from knowing but little. He never received any letters and neither letters nor papers that could cast any light upon the identity of his parents or relatives were found upon his person. At the time of his death he was about thirty-two years of age. He was born and grew to man's estate in some small town in Tennessee. Of an adventurous nature he was induced to go to Dodge City, Kansas, in 1875, where he was engaged in the occupation of

CATTLE HERDING

And buffalo hunting. While there he was in the company of his brother Henry whose whereabouts are now unknown. At the time of the famous Leadville excitement he started for that place and remained there until the winter of 1879-80, when he came to Albuquerque and went to work for Joe Hampson, a bridge contractor, at that time on the Atchison, Topeka & Santa Fe railroad. He succeeded in getting a little money ahead, and next went to Deming (NM) where he engaged in the restaurant business. Here it is said he killed a Chinaman, but his friends here denied this assertion, and say that the cause of his leaving Deming was because of trouble he had with

THE RUSTLERS

Who, at that time were having things all their own way. However this may be he returned to Albuquerque about three weeks before his murder, and went to work at his trade, that of a carpenter. He finally obtained work in the carpenter shop of the Atlantic & Pacific Railroad Company, where he was employed on the fatal 18th of June. Those who knew him say he was quiet and inoffensive, and did nothing worse than drink whiskey.

THE FATE OF FRANK BOYD.

Frank Boyd, the man who assisted Yarberry in the murder of Campbell, knew that he had committed a crime, which, if he received his deserts, would result in his being hanged. And not being foolhardy enough to risk the chances of remaining in Albuquerque, he took the wise course of leaving town. He made his way west over the line of The Atlantic & Pacific Railroad and took his place with the

ROUGH ELEMENT

That is always to be found at the front of all western roads. He did nothing to bring him into prominent notice until the afternoon of Oct. 5 between the hours of 4 and 5 o'clock.. At that time he was at Martin's ranch, near Holbrook (AZ), where he met two unarmed and defenseless Navajo Indians on horseback. Grasping the bridle of one of them, he held the horse firmly, while he drew his revolver and shot the rider, killing him instantly. The remaining Indian put his horse to the best speed and dashed away over the prairie. Boyd also made himself scarce. At sundown

FORTY NAVAJO INDIANS

Appeared at Armstrong's ranch, near Holbrook, and demanded to know the whereabouts of the murderer of their comrade. A white volunteered to go with them and guide them in the direction taken by Boyd. A short, hard ride soon brought the avengers to the Frank Davis ranch where Boyd was seen just about to mount his horse. He was identified as the murderer and at a signal from the leader every Indian in the party leveled his rifle at the cowardly cur, and his body was literally riddled with bullets and left upon the plains to rot. The Indians were perfectly satisfied with their revenge. A life for a life was all that was wanted.

THE KILLING OF HARRY BROWN.

The first man whom Yarberry killed in Albuquerque was Harry Brown, on the evening of the last Sunday in March, 1881. This trouble grew out of a woman named Sadie Preston, of whom both Yarberry and Brown were enamored. The two men had it in for each other, and had come to words at different times before the fatal meeting. On that evening Brown, together with the woman, went to Girard's restaurant which was then located where Zeiger's wholesale liquor store now stands. They were driven there in a hack by a colored man named John Clark.

THE WOMAN

Was inside eating her supper and Brown stood upon the sidewalk in front of the house when Yarberry came up the street leading the little daughter of the woman. He took the child, about fours of age, in the restaurant, ordered some supper for it and then came out when Brown accosted him saying, "Milt, I want to talk with you." There were no witnesses to their conversation except the hackdriver Clark, who heard Brown say, "I want you to understand I am not afraid of you and would not be even if you were marshal of the United States."

Clark said he then heard a pistol shot, and turning, saw Brown reeling, and at the same time saw

YARBERRY FIRE AT HIM,

And saw the bullet strike Brown's breast, by the dust that flew from his coat. Yarberry fired two more shots at Brown after he had fallen. Only four shots were fired altogether, and four shots entered Brown's body.

Yarberry claimed that Brown attempted to draw his revolver from his scabbard and that if he had not shot at the time he did, he would have been killed himself.

Yarberry was arrested, taken before Alcalde Martin for a preliminary examination, and

WAS DISCHARGED

from custody. Nothing more was done about the matter until the next session of the grand jury when an indictment was found against him and his case brought to trial. He produced witnesses who testified that Brown had sworn to kill him on sight and the jury returned a verdict of not guilty.

BROWN'S HISTORY.

Harry Brown, at the time of his death, was about 25 years of age. He was the youngest son of Ex-Gov. Neil S. Brown, of Tennessee, and at one time minister to Russia, and a nephew of Ex-Gov. John C. Brown, quite well known in New Mexico as general western solicitor for Jay Gould's railway system. In 1876 Harry started west, having secured a position as messenger for the Adams express company, on a run over the Atchison, Topeka & Santa Fe railroad. About a year after he took his place, his car was entered one night at Kinsley, Kansas, by four robbers, among whom was Dave Rudabough. The youngest messenger took the situation at a glance, and putting out the light in the car,

COMMENCED FIRING

at the intruders. He killed two of them and wounded a third. Rudabaugh alone escaped. This act made him a privileged character with the Adams Express Company, and do as he would he knew he was always certain of his position. From the date of that occurrence he grew reckless and whenever he became intoxicated was very quarrelsome and continually drawing his six-shooter on someone. He made numerous bad gun plays in Albuquerque, but his friends always kept him out of trouble. When he was sober he was a perfect gentleman and was well liked by all. His remains were shipped to Tennessee for burial.

ARRIVAL IN ALBUQUERQUE

The announcement in THE JOURNAL yesterday morning that the Yarberry special train would arrive in Albuquerque between the hours of 10 and 12 o'clock had the effect of attracting a large number of people to the depot. It is estimated that no less than 2000 persons were congregated on the platform. The southbound emigrant train pulled in at 10:20 o'clock, and directly behind it was the looked for special, which stopped at precisely 10:23. The guards were in waiting, and formed a hollow square, facing the north, with the north side left open. Yarberry walked out of the car under the guard of four members of the Governor's rifles, and Col. Max Frost. They walked up in front of the guards who

CLOSED UP

About the prisoner and then the entire procession marched toward the street railway track. The line of march took them directly over the ground where Campbell met his death. When the fatal spot was reached, Yarberry, who stood head and shoulders above all those surrounding him, was seen to raise his head and glance sharply about him as if rapidly taking in the changes that had taken place since he stood there before. Three street cars were in waiting at the end of the track to carry the party to the west end. Yarberry and a number of the guards entered the rear car and the two forward ones were

RAPIDLY FILLED

By curious people anxious to be on the ground and witness the legal tragedy. At the depot Yarberry nodded recognition to several friends and shook one or two of them by the hand. He seemed

PERFECTLY COOL

And but little affected by the thought of the trying ordeal through which he will pass. He kept his composure until after he entered the street car when he weakened and gave way to his feelings. He wept at intervals and used expressions which denoted the thoughts which were running through his brain concerning his crime.

"I did just what any sane man would have done under the circumstances," he said. Several other similar remarks were made by him but were not addressed to any one in particular. The car on which Yarberry was riding stopped at the street leading to the jail and the party alighted and marched to the gallows yard.

AT THE JAIL.

Upon the arrival at the jail Yarberry was placed in a cell, and immediately his old friends and acquaintances in Albuquerque were applying for admission. He expressed a desire to see a number of them, principally among whom were Elwood Maden, Al Connors, Frank Fagaly, Matt Bradely "Doc" Munroe and John Burke.

Father Persone, S. J. and Father Fede baptized Yarberry

IN HIS CELL

and administered spiritual consolation. At the last minute the miserable man expressed to the reverend gentleman his belief that a respite would yet arrive from Washington in time to save his life. He expressed a belief in the Catholic faith and made confession.

Yarberry wore when he arrived here a brown, seedy looking suit of clothes and a clean white shirt without any collar. His friends, to do him a last act of kindness, purchased a new suit of black clothes for which he exchanged the old ones that he was wearing. From 2 o'clock until he was led from his cell to the gallows, Yarberry exhibited his anxiety and uneasiness by frequently asking the time of day; excepting for this he was perfectly cool.

THE EXECUTION.

At just twenty minutes before 3 o'clock the guards were ordered to the posts and the crowd was pushed back to a line east of the gates leading to the yard. The sheriff brought some pieces of rope from the box near the scaffold and carried them to the cell in which Yarberry was, and tied the prisoner's hands behind him. The procession then started from the cell door across the yard to the gallows. It was headed by Sheriff Armijo, followed by Yarberry, supported by Chief Howe and Deputy Sheriff George Munroe. The Governor's Rifles came just behind and formed in line

IN FRONT OF THE SCAFFOLD.

At fifteen minutes before 3 o'clock Chief Howe read the death warrant. Yarberry during the reading kept his eye on the officer constantly, and seemed not at all affected by it. After it had been concluded he stood erect and eyeing the crowd that faced him, spoke as follows:

"You are going to hang Milt Yarberry. You are going to hang him not for the murder of Campbell, but for the killing of Brown. There is Col. Bell (pointing him out among the crowd) what did he say? Come around Bell. So I can see you, don't hide your face. What did he say to Sheriff Whitehall when he asked him what was done with the Deputy Sheriff that killed Campbell. Bell said he is in the Santa Fe jail, and the s—n of a b----

OUGHT TO HANG!

Whitehall told him that they ought to give Yarberry a reward for killing such a character. Brown struck town as a bad man. Bell is a brother of the judge. He said you go ahead and hang Yarberry, he killed Ex-Gov Brown's son. I was perfectly justified in killing both men and there are several men right here who know that. Several citizens told me, Brown is going to kill you, look out for him. I wanted to evade difficulty with him, but I was not going to hide in a back room. What did Tom Phelan say in the preliminary examination? It's all right now. He said to Judge Trimble if he would dip into the affair in as much, they would hang him up. 'Milt.' he said, 'you killed ex-Gov. Brown's son and we will help to hang you.' I can point out several who know in their heads I was justified. Whitehall telegraphed to Mr. Sheldon about Campbell killing the chinaman. He shot him and his bowels ran out. That's the word. One night Campbell was at his boarding house here,

BOUGHT A 45 SIX- SHOOTER

And when some asked him what he was going to do with it, said: 'I'm going to take in the town—this is my night out.' Yarberry went on and told about the Campbell murder until he was informed that the time was growing short. "Let me finish," he said, coolly and continued with his narrative. At precisely half a minute before 3 o'clock his hat was taken from his head, his feet having been previously bound together, the noose was adjusted and he was compelled to stop speaking. The black cap was drawn down over his face by Archie Hilton. A second before the signal was given Yarberry said, "Well, you are going to hang

AN INNOCENT MAN."

Scarcely had these words escaped his lips when the signal was given. The rope which held the weight was cut, and Yarberry shot into the air. The jerk was so sharp and sudden that his head nearly struck the cross beam of the scaffold and he again dropped until he took the slack in the rope, and remained dangling in the air. The man's neck was broken by the shock. The cracking of the joints could be plainly heard.

As soon as the body swung from the ground DRS. J.J. Derr and Z. B. Sawyer, of Albuquerque, and Dr. John Symington, of Santa Fe, rushed to the gallows and

CUTTING LOOSE THE ROPE

which bound the hands of the hanging man, felt his pulse, which was found to be beating as follows: At the end of the first minute, 100; At the end of the second minute; 104: Third minute; 128; fourth minute; 108; fifth minute; 130; sixth minute; 140; seventh; 184. Death ensued at the ninth minute.

At ten minutes past 3 o'clock all that was mortal of Milt J. Yarberry was cut from the scaffold and placed in the narrow box and the black cap was removed from his face. His eyes were open and glared up at the crowd with a blank stare, and his jaw had dropped down on his breast. The lid was nailed on and the corpse was carried to the cathedral where the funeral services were held. The remains were then taken to the Catholic cemetery and laid away beneath the ground.

The Albuquerque *Morning Journal* made these final comments:

"No one can deny that Yarberry died game".
"There were plenty of Yarberry's enemies on the grounds as well as friends".
"The Governor's Rifles was composed of sixteen men and three officers".

"Yarberry wanted Sheriff Bowman of Colfax County, to execute him, but he staunchly refused".

"Yarberry was surprised that he did not have to mount. He was not up to the new fangled arrangements."

The Albuquerque *Evening Review* dated February 8, 1883 had the following information about the type of scaffold that was used. Other papers referred to the scaffold method as being "Jerked to Jesus."

IN ALBUQUERQUE

The enclosure and scaffold, near the jail, are complete. The rope, fifty feet long, one-and-a-quarter inch, has been prepared and stretched to a thickness of five-eighths of an inch. Yarberry is to be hung on the "Jerk on New York plan," an improvement on the old drop plan. A four hundred pound weight hangs six feet from the ground. Attached to a rope running through pulleys, the noose being around the criminal's neck, and two feet of slack line occurring between the noose and the upright beam where the rope is first supported. A small rope, holding the weight to its position, is cut, and the weight falls, jerking the man six feet into the air. The two feet of slack then gives him a dead drop of two feet and his neck is broken. The plan always works with success and as every precaution has been taken in this case there is little reason to apprehend a failure.

The Albuquerque *Morning Journal* dated Thursday, Feb 1, 1883 provided additional information about the construction of the gallows.

Plans of scaffold are being examined and the best and cheapest of those submitted will probably be erected. The Scientific American recently printed a cut and description of a gallows, a counterpart of which will probably be used. It consists of two upright posts, well braced, and connected at the top by a cross-beam. At one end of this beam is a pulley, and another one is in the center. The rope runs over these pulleys, and at one end is attached a heavy weight. The other end comes down over the pulley in the center of the cross-beam, and is attached to the doomed criminal's neck, who is standing upon the ground. An arrangement on one of the posts is so made that upon pulling a pin the weight is allowed to fall with a jerk. As the weight goes down the man goes up, and the weight is so heavy that it is thought the drop will break a man's neck. This is one of the simplest and at the same time most effectual contrivances that can be imagined, and will give Yarberry's soul a good start on the road to glory.

The Albuquerque *Evening Review* dated Feb 9, 1883, also provided a full detailed story with large headlines as *The Morning Journal* did on Feb 11, 1883.

"I must have whiskey," he said. This was supplied to him and he drank frequently during the day. The liquor barely kept him from sinking but did not stimulate him.

The paper described Yarberry as he was being led to the gallows. "The Militia formed a double line, allowing some ten feet space for the prisoner to march through to the scaffold. His elbows were hitched together at the back by ropes and his wrists handcuffed. When the noose was attached to his neck, the extra rope supporting the balance weight was cut. He was jerked into the air so that his head came within a foot or two of the cross beam at the top, then dropped a distance of three or four feet. His neck was broken either by the upward or downward jerk, and there was no perceptible movement after the drop."

The *Daily Review*, Saturday, February 10, 1883, made some accusations that people had said Yarberry was drunk from the time he had gotten off the train in Albuquerque and up until he had given his speech. While in the jail he was given a pint of whiskey just prior to his execution. Sheriff Armijo, Colonel Frost and Chief Howe said, "Yarberry was not affected by the drink, it only strengthened his nervous condition, and gave him a manner of firmness and ease which he could not otherwise have possessed."

Yarberry, at the last instant, just as the black hood was being outstretched to cover the head, and while the words of his narrative were yet on his lips, raised his eyes toward the dome of heaven with a far-away expression which cannot be described.

The paper wrote that Captain Borradaile issued 110 witness tickets to the execution. It was said another thousand people watched the execution from rooftops and trees. It was rumored people paid as much as one dollar to witness the execution from the rooftops. Milton Yarberry's was one of the most publicized executions in the Territory. The newspapers even competed against each other. Milton Yarberry refused to speak about his past, family members or to allow photographers to take a picture of him. Albuquerque's first Constable was hung, and he was the only Law Officer ever hung in the Territory for committing a crime.

Sources:

The Albuquerque *Morning Journal*, February 1, 11, 1883
Santa Fe *Daily New Mexican*, February 3, 4, 8,10, 1883
Albuquerque *Evening Review*, February 8, 9, 1883
Daily Review (Albuquerque), January 29, February 10, 1883
PC News, Vol. 10, Number 12, December 1992

Dionicio Sandoval

Dionicio Sandoval and Victorian Tenorio were sheepherders employed by J. M. Sandoval. Both men were responsible and in charge of separate flocks owned by their employer. On the evening of July 29, 1895, near San Ysidro in Bernalillo County, Dionicio arrived at Victorian's camp. Soon after Dionicio's arrival, an argument ensued over statements made by Victorian as to Dionicio having more lambs than he should. The argument ended when Dionicio shot and killed Tenorio.

Dionicio Sandoval was tried before Judge Collier on November 29, 1895. Pedro Gallegos and Enrique Salazar, who were present when Victoriano was killed, testified and gave their account of the killing. Dionicio Sandoval testified and was the only witness for his defense. Sandoval told the jury that both Tenorio and himself were in charge of different flocks of sheep belonging to County Commissioner J. M. Sandoval. Dionicio learned Mr. Sandoval was intending to inspect the flocks and he only went to Tenorio's camp to tell him he needed to take his sheep to the corral. At the camp Tenorio and he began calling each other liars. Dionicio claimed Tenorio rushed upon him and grabbed the rifle he had with him. During the scuffle over the weapon, the rifle went off and accidentally shot Tenorio.

On November 30th, Judge Collier instructed the jury that they must find Dionicio Sandoval guilty of murder in the first degree, or innocent by accidental killing. It took the jury only 45 minutes to return a verdict of murder in the first degree. Judge Collier sentenced Dionicio Sandoval to hang on January 3, 1896. The execution was stayed while attorneys appealed his case to the Territory Supreme Court. The case went before the Supreme Court on August 13th. On September 22nd, the court rendered their decision which affirmed the District Court and the execution was set for September 24, 1896. Dionicio's attorneys asked Governor Thornton to commute the death sentence to life in prison on the grounds that Dionicio Sandoval was mentally defective. Governor Thornton appointed the Territory's three leading physicians to examine Dionicio and provide a report to his office. Doctors J. P. Kaster, W. G. Hope and James H. Wroth prepared the report to Governor Thornton which read; "We are satisfied he is an uneducated man, but we see no sign of such mental depression as would warrant us in calling him below the average person in his station and avocation. We find nothing that will warrant our considering him to be so deterrent in intelligence as to be irresponsible." Upon finding no mental illness, Governor Thornton refused to interfere or commute the sentence to life.

The gallows was erected about a half mile behind the jail near the southwest end of the fair grounds. The scaffold was 12 feet square with 2 trap doors being nine feet above the ground when closed. From the platform to the above beam there was a distance of 8 feet, 6 inches. The rope had been specially ordered from the east and stretched by Sheriff Hubbell with 200 hundred pound sacks of sand. The drop was calculated at six feet.

On the morning of September 24, Dionicio was awakened at 6 o'clock. His spiritual advisor, Father Durant arrived at 6:25 and remained with him until 7 o'clock. During his confession, he maintained the killing was accidental. Dionicio said he had no ill will toward anybody and asked to be forgiven by everybody who had anything against him. He told Father Durant, "I am ready to meet God, if it's the will of God, I will die. If I had no religion I would now despair; with it I die gladly. God will receive me in heaven. There is no mercy for me on earth, but there is mercy in heaven."

At 7 o'clock, Sheriff Hubbell brought the condemned man his breakfast, which consisted of steak, eggs, toast, potatoes, tomatoes, fruit and chocolate. At the end of his breakfast, Dionicio was dressed in his new clothes and driven to the scaffold. At 7:25 Sheriff Hubble read the death warrants. The first warrant being from the Governor and the second from the clerk of the Territory Supreme Court. After the reading, Dionicio said, "I am ready to die and have nothing to say." At 7:40 Dionicio was lead out of his cell and walked out to an awaiting hack. At 7:47 Sheriff Hubble arrived at the gallows and Dionicio walked up the steps of the scaffold. After a prayer was said in Spanish, the noose was thrown over his head at 7:52 with the "hangman's knot" resting on the back of the left ear. Sheriff Hubble asked someone to check whether the pin was removed from the bar below the trap door, and this was done. The Sheriff pulled the lever of the trap and "the body dangled between heaven and earth at 7:55." Dr. J. F. Pearce held the left hand feeling a pulse for eight minutes. Four minutes later, Doctor Pearce pronounced Dionicio dead. The neck was broken and the Sheriff cut the rope above the knot and turned the remains over to Undertaker Strong.

The body was laid on a bench and the straps and black cap was removed. The body was then displayed for public view and several hundred people gazed over the lifeless body. Sheriff Hubble kept the hangman's knot so that he could present it to Dr. Kaster for his collection at the Atlantic & Pacific hospital.

The Albuquerque *Morning Democrat* had the following story.

SWUNG INTO ETERNITY
_____

Murderer Sandoval Paid the Pen-
Alty With His Life for Hav-
Ing Killed Tenorio.

A SUCCESSFUL EXECUTION
_____

The Prisoner Was Calm and Self Possessed
Throughout – Upwards of 1,500 People Present

Dionicio Sandoval was hanged yesterday morning at Old Town for the murder of Victorian Tenorio. The trap was sprung by Sheriff Hubbell at 7:50 o'clock and twelve minutes afterward Dr. J. F. Pearce pronounced the prisoner dead. The body was then taken in charge by undertaker Strong. Services will be held today at 8 o'clock from the Catholic church of Old Town and the remains will be interred in San Ignacio cemetery.

Sandoval's last night on earth was restless one, as Jailer Jones said he did not sleep more than three hours. As early as 6:15 o'clock Father Durant was closest with the prisoner and remained until 7 o'clock, administering to his spiritual needs. A substantial breakfast was then served, of which Sandoval ate sparingly, simply partaking of a little fruit and chocolate.

The prisoner was then dressed and made ready for the execution. A complete new outfit had been furnished for him to wear, and after being dressed he jokingly remarked: "I'm going out of here mighty high toned." The hat selected did not fit his head very well and he insisted on wearing his old sombrero. The prisoner was the least affected of any one present while the preliminaries were being arranged. Half a dozen persons were in the adjoining room, every one of whom was impressed with the solemnity of the occasion, while Sandoval was calm and unconcerned, and even saluted a passerby from the window with a smile and a wave from the hand. At this juncture Sheriff Hubbell read the death warrant to the prisoner, who sat upon a cot twirling his thumbs, apparently indifferent to the fate that awaited him. The shackles were brought in and the prisoner helped the officers adjust them to his hands, after which he was lead from his cell to a carriage, and in company with Sheriff Hubbell, Jailer Jones and Father Durant, driven to the place of execution. The prisoner alighted and with a firm and steady step mounted the gallows. His legs were strapped together below and above the knees and his arms were pinioned from behind. During all this time Father Durant was praying for the welfare of his soul, after which he pressed a crucifix to the prisoner's lips. The rope was then placed around the his neck, the black cap was drawn over his head, and without a moment's delay the sheriff touched the lever and Sandoval swung into eternity.

Sandoval had evidently given the future some thought, for he told Turnkey Masters he would pray for him in the other world. To a lady who called to see him he said no mercy had been shown him on earth but it would be in heaven.

After the trap fell not a muscle of the prisoner was seen to move, his neck being broken in the fall. When the rope was cut and the body placed on a stretcher, the remains were viewed by several hundred people. Everything passed off decently and in order and from 1,200 to 1,500 people witnessed the hanging, two thirds of whom were the native population.

This is the first hanging that has taken place in this county for fourteen years. A history of the crime is as follows:

Dionicio Sandoval was indicted at the October, A. D. 1895 term of the District Court for the county of Bernalillo, charged with having killed one Victoriano Tenorio, on the 29th day of July, 1895, at San Ysidro, in Bernalillo county, with a rifle. He was tried November 29, and convicted of murder in the first degree, and sentenced to hang on January 3.

The evidence for the Territory consisted of the testimony of two witnesses, Pedro Gallegos and Enrique Salazar, and showed that on the evening of the killing Sandoval came to the sheep herd of the deceased, Tenorio, and sat down upon a keg. Tenorio asked him to take a seat upon some sheep skins, which he declined. A quarrel then arose between them regarding some statements Tenorio had made concerning Sandoval. Sandoval asked deceased why he had said that he, Sandoval, had on his account so many lambs in his fold without rams or mothers – meaning that he had stolen the lambs from the herd of Tenorio. Tenorio answered, "I didn't say that; what I did say was you didn't deliver to me all of my sheep." Then Sandoval said, "you are a liar," and Tenorio answered, "I don't lie," and then Sandoval shot.

The defendant was the only witness on behalf of the defense, and he claimed that upon their calling each other liars, the deceased, Tenorio, "jumped up as though to strike him, and then he got hold of the rifle and in the twist they gave it in getting up, the gun went off and the deceased was shot. That he did not do it intentionally." The parties were employed and were working for the same man, J. M. Sandoval, but were in charge of different flocks of sheep.

Upon this state of facts the court instructed the jury that the killing was either murder in the first degree or accidental, and that their verdict should be either murder in the first degree or not guilty.

The case was appealed to the Supreme Court of the territory and the execution of the sentence stayed until its determination in that court. The defendant's attorneys claimed that the court should have instructed the jury as to murder in the second and third degrees, and allowed the jury to consider verdicts of these degrees in determining the case upon the evidence as adduced at the trial. The case was argued in the Supreme Court by E. L. Medler, one of the attorneys for the defendant, August 13, and the Supreme Court ordered, a few days later, that the sentence of the District Court be carried out which has been done.

Sources:

Santa Fe *Daily New Mexican*, November 30, 1895
Albuquerque *Morning Democrat*, September 23, 24, 25, 26, 1896

Jose P. Ruiz, alias Jose Romero

The senseless killing of an innocent child, and subsequent hanging of the killer, one Jose P. Ruiz, was described by the Santa Fe *New Mexican*, June 1, 1900.

JOSE P. RUIZ HANGED

The Murderer Suffered the Penalty of Death at Albuquerque This Morning.

GOVERNOR OTERO REFUSED A PARDON

Special to the *New Mexican*.

Albuquerque, June 1. - Jose P. Ruiz, who shot and killed Patricio O'Bannon, 5 years old, was hanged in Old Town this morning at 9 o'clock. He mounted the scaffold as unconcerned as if he was not to suffer the death penalty. The noose was adjusted by a physician, the black cap pulled over his face by a deputy sheriff, and a colored man sprung the trap. He was dead in 23 minutes and his body was turned over to his father. He, with a companion, was here on May 28th 1898, and while drunk, riding through the town, fired at some children playing in the O'Bannon yard, killing the O'Bannon child and wounding another. He was convicted in October 1898. The case was taken to the territorial Supreme Court, and in January last, the latter court sustained the verdict of the lower court, fixing the hanging for Friday, June 1st.

WHY A PARDON WAS REFUSED.

In this matter many petitions for clemency were presented to Governor Otero, who examined the records in the District Court and in the Supreme Court very carefully and thoroughly. He found nothing in the records to justify executive clemency, and no extenuating circumstances outside of the record were presented. He concluded that unless there were recommendations for clemency filed by the prosecuting officers, the trial court and the justices of the Supreme Court, all familiar with the facts, he would be compelled to let the law take its course and the sentence be carried into effect. The petitions presented were given due and full weight and consideration, but it was a case which demanded extreme punishment, and such was accordingly meted out to Ruiz, who expiated his crime on the Gallows.

The crime of murder for which Jose P. Ruiz was executed on June 1, 1900, occurred outside Albuquerque, in the late afternoon of May 28, 1898. On this day, Jose Ruiz had been drinking with Donacian Garcia. In the afternoon, the two men continued to drink as they rode their horses out of town. Jose Ruiz's drunkenness turned into a shooting rage directed at anyone who came into his path. The Albuquerque *Journal* described the shooting rampage and the capture of both men.

Horrible Murder

The Most Wonton Murder that has Sullied Albuquerque's Fair Name. Fiends in Human Form Shoot Down Two Innocent and Helpless Children. The Murderers are now in Jail.

The Most Wanton and Cold Blooded Murder that has ever Been seen in Albuquerque.

6:00 o'clock p.m., last evening, a 8 year old boy shot and almost instantly killed. Another about 6 years of age is having surgery and may be dead before this is read.

Donacian Garcia and Jose Romero (Ruiz) were in Albuquerque yesterday and both succeeded in getting very drunk. A little before 6:00 o'clock they took their horses and started for the west side of the river. As soon as they were outside the city, Romero began to spur his horse to make it buck and flourish his pistol over his head in the approved dime novel style. As they passed down the river road, they came across Bunicio Anaya and who was saddling his horse to return home.

Romero drew down on him and snapped his revolver twice but for some unreason it failed to go off. About 50 yards further two little boys, Patricio O'Bannon and Arturo Garcia and a little son of Ysidro Aragon were playing marbles under the shade of trees of Felipe O'Bannon's house. As soon as the drunken horsemen came up on them, Romero stopped and fired. He shot twice, one shot striking O'Bannon in the left shoulder coming out above the collarbone severing the jugular vein. The little boy died in his mothers arms a minute or two later. The second shot struck the little Garcia boy in the back of the neck near the base of the skull slightly injuring the spinal column and passing near the spinal cord.

After leaving the scene, Romero fired two more shots before crossing the bridge. Authorities were notified immediately. Within twenty-nine minutes, Sheriff Hubbell, Deputy NewComber, and Marshal Fornoff were in pursuit. About a mile on the other side of the river they came upon the camp of a couple of Mexicans and noticed a very sweaty horse in which the saddle had recently been removed which was recognized as Garcia's. The owner was soon located and when told to surrender, did so without the least resistance and beginning to cry and protesting his innocence. The party continued until the sand hills were reached on a road to Rio Puerco and on the crest of this hill, Romero was overtook and jerked off his horse by Marshal Fornoff.

In the mean time almost the entire population near where the shooting occurred had joined in the pursuit and when the murderer struck the ground fully fifty guns were pointed at him and it looked as if he would answer for his crime right there had it not been for the three officers. The sheriff spoke to the people in Spanish stating that Romero's worthless carcass was reserved for the gallows. Both prisoners were taken to the county jail. The boy was almost 8 years of age. His father was Felipe O'Bannon, an employee of the Southern Pacific shop. The 6-year-old boy lived. It was reported that after Romero crossed over the river, Romero fired another shot at a child in front of the house of Manuel Antonio Jaramillo, the bullet cutting through the little ones clothing, but doing the child no harm.

Both Romero and Garcia are known as toughs and utterly worthless desperados and professional sheep and cattle thieves. Donacian Garcia is about 38 years of age, married and the father of a large family. He did not fire a shot, but at the same time made no effort to restrain his murderous companion. Witnesses said he encouraged Romero to do his awful act.

Jose Romero is 24 years of age and is from Rio Puerco county and is known as a worthless desperate character. Unmarried but living with a unmarried woman, his face shows no signs of intelligence nor courage. He is a brute pure and simple. Neither men had any arms and it is believed they threw them away when being pursued.

Romero and Garcia were interviewed by the Democratic reporter late last night. Romero was awakened by the reporter, still stupid from his drunkenness. He denied all knowledge of the shooting and evidence. No admission what so ever. 24 years of age, unmarried, and claims to been around Albuquerque for the past five days. Said he got drunk in Old Town. Garcia said to be 41 years of age, father of three boys. He denied any knowledge of the shooting. He said he had come to old town to attend a celebration at a church and met Romero and proceeded to Ruberto's were they both got drunk. Bought a bottle of whiskey and started home. Said he was too drunk to know what happened after that.

Sources:

Santa Fe *New Mexican*, June 1, 1900

Demecio Delgadillo

Demecio Delgadillo was a native of Chihuahua, Mexico, who arrived in Albuquerque in 1912. In Albuquerque, he obtained work as a laborer at the American Lumber Mill. A pretty twenty-six year old woman named Soledad Sarracino de Pino caught Demecio's attention and the two dated for a short time. Demecio fell in love with Ms. Sarracino and became overly possessive and frightened the woman by his actions. Ms. Sarracino ended the courtship and continued dating a Frank Lucero who she was in love with. Angrily, Demecio told Ms. Sarracino that if she continued to date Frank Lucero, he would kill her. Concerned by the threat made, Ms. Sarracino told her uncle she was in fear of Demecio. Ms. Sarracino was advised to pay no attention to what Demecio said and the uncle gave it no further thought. Frank Lucero soon proposed marriage and he and Ms. Sarracino decided to marry on Monday, September 23rd.

On Friday night, September 21, 1912, the happy couple went out on a last date just before their marriage. After Ms. Sarracino returned home, Demecio who had been waiting, approached her. The two talked, and Ms. Sarracino was last seen, alive, speaking with Demecio. The next morning, Ms. Sarracino's body was found inside her home with a bullet wound to the heart. Demecio quickly became the suspect of the murder and could not be found. The evidence at the scene led the authorities to believe Ms. Sarracino was held up against Demecio's chest when the fatal bullet was fired. Undersheriff Dick Lewis learned during his investigation that Demecio had been consuming alcohol during the entire night. It was believed Demecio initially intended to kill Ms. Sarracino and Frank Lucero together. After killing Ms. Sarracino witnesses saw Demecio drunk in Old Town Albuquerque searching for Frank Lucero until eleven at night.

Undersheriff Lewis notified all surrounding agencies of Demecio Delgadillo's description and to be on the lookout for the wanted man. The Undersheriff learned Demecio Delgadillo might have earlier fled Flagstaff, Arizona, after committing a murder under the assumed name of Agapito Delgadillo. Two nights after the Albuquerque murder, from the description given, Deputies at Los Lunas arrested the wanted man. When arrested, Demecio was in possession of a .38 caliber revolver having one spent cartridge.

The following day, Monday, September 24, Demecio Delgadillo was indicted for murder in the first degree. The two-day trial ended on October 22nd with the jury finding Demecio Delgadillo guilty of the murder. On November 7, 1912, Judge Herbert F. Raynolds sentenced Demecio to hang on November 29th, but the execution was delayed by the appeals filed before the State Supreme Court. The high court affirmed the District Court's conviction of Demecio on April 25th, and reset the execution for May 16, 1913.

An eleventh hour plea for clemency by attorney J. Benson Newell was made before Governor W. C. Mc Donald. Attorney Newell had obtained 2,000 signatures on a petition and delivered the petition to the Governor at 9 o'clock at night. After two and half hours of considering the attorneys arguments, Governor Mc Donald said he would not interfere with a decision already made by the Supreme Court. At midnight the Governor made the following statement.

"I have given most careful consideration and the most thorough investigation to the case of Demecio Delgadillo. This matter was taken up, shortly after the man was convicted, by the state department at Washington at the request of the Mexican embassy. I made a report on the case or had it made, which apparently was satisfactory to those people. About that time parties came here in the interest of Delgadillo. They gave me a transcript of the testimony which I have had for some months and have carefully considered. Yesterday, I received from Judge Raynolds a message not only refusing to intercede in any way, but saying that he did not consider this a case for clemency. One of the attorneys for the defendant said to me that the appeal probably would not be perfected because there was no chance to get a reversal from the Supreme Court.

"I have acted finally with a full sense of responsibility, understanding my duty, as I believe it to be, to the people of this state. The evidence has convinced me beyond a doubt that the man is guilty. Nothing has come to me in any manner which would, to my mind justify interference with the degree of the court or further delay in this case."

At 3:30 a.m. in the morning Demecio was awakened quietly without any of the other prisoners knowing. Demecio was then dressed in black trousers, shirt, necktie and blue coat. After eating breakfast, Demecio was escorted to the gallows by two officers. Sheriff Jesus Romero asked, "Delgadillo are you guilty?" Demecio answered, "I did not kill that woman." Once on the scaffold, the customary question was asked regarding whether Demecio had any last words. Demecio replied, "No, I have nothing to say." Prayers were resumed in Spanish and his spiritual advisor told Demecio "to put his trust in Christ, the savior and source of mercy." Father Tommasini took out a small silver crucifix and raised it to Demecio lips. Demecio kissed the cross and finished his prayer. At 5:07 the lever was pulled. The 6-foot drop broke the neck on the condemned man and ten and a half minutes later the body was cut down. The Albuquerque *Morning Journal* had the following headlines and story.

Demecio Delgadillo Hanged at 5:07
This Morning; Denies Guilt to Last

PAYS EXTREME PENALTY FOR MURDER OF WOMAN

Condemned Man Exhibits Sto-
icism to Final Moment,
Eating Hearty Breakfast
Before Going to Scaffold,

DEATH INSTANTANEOUS DROP BREAKING NECK

Execution Devoid of Any Un-
toward Features, Few, People Except Witnesses Being
Aware of Hour of Occurrence

Demecio Delgadillo was hanged at 5:07 o'clock this morning in the jail yard at Old Albuquerque for the murder of Mrs. Soledad Sarracino de Pino. The prisoner maintained his innocence to the last minute. He declared as he entered the stockade surrounding the scaffold that he did not kill the woman. When he was asked on the scaffold if he had any statement to make he simply said: "No," in Spanish.

Father Tommasini, spiritual advisor, arrived at the jail at 4:30 o'clock this morning. He spent thirty minutes with the prisoner, hearing his confession and administering his last communion. Delgadillo then ate breakfast. He ordered steak and potatoes. He ate heartily. As soon as he had finished eating, the officers strapped his hands in front of him.

The witnesses already were inside the enclosure when the prisoner was led in. He evinced no fear whatever walking erectly but with his eyes cast down. He mounted the steps, followed by the officers and Father Tommasini. The officers strapped his legs and arms securely when he stood on the trap. Have you any statement to make was asked.

No, said Delgadillo. The cap was then placed over his head, and next the rope. In the meantime Delgadillo kept repeating after Father Tommasini,. "Jesus y Maria." Those were the last words as the lever was thrown. It was just 5:07 o'clock. The neck was broken by the drop through the trap, death being practically instantaneous. Dr. Charles A. Frank, county physician, stepped under the platform and placed the stethoscope at his breast. The body did not even quiver, but hung as a dead weight. The heart continued to beat for ten and one half minutes. Dr. Frank then pronounced him dead.

The body was then taken to Fred Crollott's undertaking rooms. Funeral services are to held in this morning in the Church of the Sacred Heart. Burial is to be in San Jose cemetery, friends having charge of the funeral. Delgadillo's characteristic stolidity did not desert him yesterday. At times, however, when prisoners, friends of his who knew him before he was transferred from jail to Santa Fe penitentiary, talked with him in the afternoon his attention appeared to lapse, but this was the only sign of mental strain.

The prisoner arose at 6 o'clock yesterday morning. He was cheerful and showed interest in the menu offered by the jail cook. He ate heartily and, as he did Wednesday night he talked jestingly with the guards. J. Benson Newell, his attorney, visited him yesterday morning with undersheriff Dick Lewis. Delgadillo reiterated his statement that he was innocent of the murder of Mrs. Soledad Sarracino de Pino, who was found dead with a bullet hole through her head in her house at Old Albuquerque, September 21. Father P. Tommasini of the San Felipe de Neri Jesuit mission was with Delgadillo in the morning for a short time and returned again in the afternoon when he heard the prisoner's confession. The prisoner occupied the northwest cage on the first floor of the jail yesterday. He was transferred from the small cell up to the second floor to the large room in the morning which over looked the scaffold. When the noose was tested Delgadillo heard the crash of the trap. The officers dropped the rope over an iron weight being 175 pounds. One of the officers pushed the lever forward and the iron shot downward with a crash and the timbers creaked under the strain. The rope stood the test. Delgadillo gave no sign that he heard the crash, although he surely understood its meaning. A few hours more and the same sound would be the signal of his death, but he gave no outward sign of terror. Delgadillo, according to the officers had not shown "the white feather" since the time of his arrest at Los Lunas.

The hour set for the execution was kept secret from other prisoners. Delgadillo occupied the cage alone and none of the other prisoners knew that he had been led to the scaffold unless the dropping trap awakened them. The scaffold was surrounded by a high board fence yesterday. A large number of applications for admission to the stockade and the crowd coming and going all day led the officers to believe that a mob would occupy nearby roofs before daylight this morning, so the high fence was erected to screen the execution. The enclosure, about 20 x 20 feet was large enough only for the witnesses, officials and newspaper men who were admitted by passes issued by Sheriff Romero. The total number of persons who saw the execution was twenty.

About 100 men, women and children clamored at the jail door for admission to see the scaffold yesterday. One woman carried a baby in her arms. The scaffold was built in the yard west of the building. The platform stood six feet above the ground and although Delgadillo was not above average stature, a pit two feet deep was dug directly under the trap. The officials took precautions to prevent an accident, besides carefully testing the trap and rope. Delgadillo was allowed a 6-foot drop, considered sufficient to break his neck and effect a painless death. When the body dangled at the end of the rope the top of the black cap was level with the platform.

Practically every one of Delgadillo's visitors yesterday went on official business. An alien, he had few friends in Old Albuquerque where he lived. No relatives were here. M. C. Ortiz, an attorney, took a list of relatives from the prisoner whom he wished to have notified of his death.

Sources:

Albuquerque *Morning Journal*, September 24, 1912; April 26, May 16, 1913
Santa Fe *New Mexican*, May 16, 1913

Chapter 2

Chavez County

Antonio Gonzales   September 24, 1894

Antonio Gonzales

Chavez County had its only legal execution in the county's history on September 24, 1896. Antonio Gonzales was hanged in Roswell, New Mexico for the cold-blooded murder of Charles Van Sickle, which Eugenio Aragon and he committed on February 12, 1894.

Antonio Gonzales rested the night before the execution and was said to be in good spirits. After awakening, he declined to eat any breakfast and he appeared eager to have the job over. He then dressed himself in a new black suit of clothes provided to him by the county. At 6:55 a.m., Gonzales walked firmly to the scaffold. On the platform, he addressed the sixty spectators who had gathered to witness the execution. He told those present he had forgiven his enemies, and hoped they had forgiven him. He asked forgiveness from God, and concluded by saving he now stood on the gallows to pay the penalty for the laws he had broken.

His arms and legs were strapped and the black cap and noose were adjusted over his head. At 7:00 a.m., the trap was sprung and the fall broke Gonzales' neck. Six minutes later his pulse ceased to beat and life was pronounced extinct. It was said Gonzales death came quick and easy in the bright light of a New Mexican morning. The following story was printed in the Roswell *Register,* Albuquerque *Daily Citizen* and Albuquerque *Weekly Citizen.*

LAUNCHED INTO ETERNITY

ANTONIO GONZALES HANGED at ROSWELL – HISTORY of the CRIME,

From Roswell Register, Sept, 26.

Thursday morning, at 7 o'clock, in the presence of about 100 spectators, Sheriff Haynes complied with the order of the court and edict of the people of Chaves County by launching the soul of Antonio Gonzales into eternity from the end of a hemp rope.

We feel safe in the assertion that never was there more unanimity of opinion existing in an entire community in regard to a legal execution than that of the people of this county in the execution of Gonzales. A brief synopsis of the story adduced from testimony:

Antonio Gonzales and Eugenio Aragon stood convicted of the midnight murder of Charley S. Van Sickle, on Feb.12, 1894. Van Sickle was foreman for the Seldom Ridge and Pebble Sheep Company, and lived alone at their headquarter ranch for Chavez County, known as Zubar ranch. About a week before his death he met Aragon, who was hauling some hay, and discovering some lumber about the wagon that he knew to be the property of his employers, he ordered its return, and threatened to prosecute Aragon unless said order be complied with. On the following Saturday night, Aragon, accompanied by his brother–in–law, Marcelino Sanchez, went to the Zubar ranch with the intention of killing Van Sickle, but finding that he had company, made no attempt. Marcelino, who is only about 16, got scared and would not go again, so a trade was made with Antonio Gonzales, and on Monday, Feb. 12, he and Aragon went to Zubar ranch, and Aragon leaving Gonzales outside, went in and talked matters over with Van Sickle. The outcome of the conversation was that Aragon promised to return the lumber, told Van Sickle he was sorry for having taken it, and Van Sickle had in turn told him that it was all right, and no prosecution would be made, and that he was freely forgiven just as soon as the lumber was returned. At this juncture Gonzales knocked on the door and Van Sickle, suspicioning some foul play, picked up his pistol and stepped to the door to admit whoever it might be. Just as he opened the door and peered into the darkness to see who sought admission, Aragon shot him from behind, the ball passing through the left hemisphere of the brain and tearing out the left eye. Aragon then compelled Gonzales to shoot the prostrate body.

About eight days after Van Sickle's death, Mr. Newman, who came to relieve him, (Van Sickle was preparing to start to his old home in Missouri on a visit to parents and friends), and not finding him at the ranch started to Fred Keyes, but met Keyes, Albert Forest and Balentine Garcia coming to see about Van Sickle as Aragon had confessed to Garcia that they killed Van Sickle. Deputy John Legg and posse placed the murderers under arrest, and brought them and the dead body of Van Sickle to Roswell, where the body was interred.

A mis-trial at the October term of court saved the necks of the criminals for a few months, but a special term was held by Judge Bantz in July, 1895, at which evidence, mostly circumstantial, was adduced agreeing completely with statement as now published here. A verdict of death was the result. Attorney Allen, of the defense, carried the case to the Supreme Court, which in August '96 confirmed the verdict of the lower court and the execution was set for Sept. 4. On September 9, Eugenio Aragon, who had managed to conceal a spoon in his cell and had whetted the handle into a knife, saved the Sheriff any further trouble by cutting his throat from ear to ear. After Aragon's death Gonzales made a full and complete confession of not only the murder of Van Sickle but of all other criminal acts of his own and Aragon's so far as he knew of those of the latter.

Sources:

The Albuquerque *Daily Citizen*, September 30, 1896
Albuquerque *Morning Democrat*, October 1, 1896
Albuquerque *Weekly Citizen*, October 3, 1896

Chapter 3

Colfax County

William Breckenridge	May 8, 1877
Damian Romero	February 2, 1993
Theodore Baker	May 6, 1887
David Arguello	May 25, 1906
John Medlock	May 25, 1906

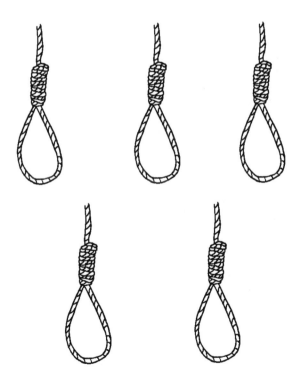

William Breckenridge

William Breckenridge was a black man sentenced to hang for the double murder he committed on March 23, 1877 of William Maxwell and his son Emmet. The following article was published in The *Daily New Mexican* dated May 14, 1877.

Public Execution in Cimarron
Cimarron, N.M., May 9th, 1877.

Most of our readers will remember the circumstances attending the murder of William Maxwell and his son Emmet near the Palo Blanco in Colfax county on the 23d of March last, and the subsequent capture of the murderer in Trinidad (CO), a Negro named William Breckenridge, who was tried and convicted at the last term of court in Taos and sentenced to be hung on the 8th day of May.

The hanging of the Negro was an all absorbing topic from the date of his sentence up to the time of his execution. By noon yesterday the town was full of people from all parts of the county and at a few minutes before 1 o'clock p.m., the doomed man was led from the jail and placed in a wagon upon his coffin and followed by a large crowd, was taken to the gallows, which had been erected about one-fourth of a mile west of town.

At ten minutes past one he mounted the gallows, accompanied by Sheriff Burlison and deputies Goodlet and Beardsley. Through the whole proceeding the murderer had exhibited no sign of emotion, but was quietly engaged in chewing a large quid of tobacco. The Sheriff read the death warrant and the condemned man proceeded to make a statement of the killing of Mr. Maxwell and his son.

He had previously, while in jail, made a confession of the crime to Rev. Lougheed, but up to the time he was taken out to be executed he had denied having robbed either of his victims or molested their bodies in any way. On the scaffold, however, he acknowledged that he robbed the elder Maxwell of $58.50. He said that he shot at Mr. Maxwell three times, hitting him twice, one in the breast and once in the head. He shot at the boy only once, hitting him in the head and killing him instantly.

At half-past two he finished his confession, having talked in a wandering, broken way for more than an hour, closing with a long prayer, after which Rev. Mr. Lougheed made an appropriate prayer, and the Sheriff than bound his arms and feet, upon which he said good-bye to all. Up to this time the hardened wretch had shown no sign of weakness. He appeared perfectly calm and unaffected until the black cap was drawn over his head, when a perceptible tremor shook him and his knees appeared to be getting weak.

At 2:31 the drop fell, and the soul of Wm. Breckenridge was launched into eternity saddled with as great a crime as was ever perpetrated. After hanging 8 minutes, Drs Ludium and Tipton pronounced life extinct, and at 2:45 the body was cut down and placed in the coffin for burial.

The execution was witnessed by about 400 people and the most perfect order and quiet prevailed throughout the whole affair. No expressions of sympathy were to be heard, and though the condemned man spoke for more than an hour I do not think he awakened a spark of sympathy in the breast of any of his hearers. The universal feeling among the citizens of Cimarron and of Colfax County, is, that hanging was too good for him. The scaffold and its appointments were perfect, and reflect great credit upon Sheriff Burlison and his assistants.

Sources:

The Daily New Mexican, May 14, 1877
Weekly New Mexican, May 15, 1877
The New Mexican, May 15, 1877

Damian Romero

Damian Romero by all accounts was a well-mannered eighteen-year-old man. Damian was born into a poor family consisting of his Mexican father, Navajo mother, and his four sisters. Although he had only had six months of schooling in his life before the age of twelve, Damian could read and write the basics. He also could speak English, Spanish and the Navajo language.

It is still a mystery why Damian killed his employer and friend, William Brocksmidt on Wednesday, January 12, 1882. He had other previous opportunities in the past for greater amounts of money and property. Brocksmidt's body was not found until the following Sunday. With the disappearance of Damian, suspicion immediately focused on him. A determined Mora County Deputy Sheriff by the name of Petro Sanchez pursued Romero capturing him in Rio Arriba County. Upon his capture Damian confessed he had shot Brocksmidt in the head with a Winchester rifle while Brocksmidt stood in the doorway of his home. Damian followed up by shooting two more bullets into the torso. He then dragged the body into the house and removed valuables and clothing from the victim. He made the same confession to a reporter, but named an Indian by the name of Juan Antonio Rael as his accomplice. Damian later recanted both confessions. Sheriff Bowman believed Rael was an accessory to the murder, but he was never charged. Six miles north of Mora, members of the Silva gang later killed Rael in 1894.

Damian's execution was witnessed by between 550 to 1,000 people. As the Sheriff prepared for his first execution, Damian told him on the scaffold, "Good bye, old boy, I hope to meet you in heaven." When the trap was sprung, Damian's neck did not break. While protesting his innocence, Damian strangled to his death for fifteen minutes. After Damian's body was lowered, the sheriff gently placed Damian's head on his lap as he cut the rope from around the neck. Sheriff Romero later told the Governor that hanging Romero was the hardest task of his career for Romero had once been a trusted employee of his family.

The following is the complete story as it was printed in the Santa Fe *Daily New Mexican*, Saturday Morning, Feb 3, 1883

Romero Roped,
Damian Romero, the youthful mur-
Derer, pays the penalty of
His crime,
Being Hanged at Springer in the
Presence of a Large Con-
Course of People,

History of the Crime, trial, Sentence,
Imprisonment and Exe
Cution.
The Prisoner Walks to His Doom
With a Firm Step and With
Perfect Calmness.

He Protests His innocence to the Last
His Speech on the
Scaffold.

Graphic Description of the Closing
Scenes in the Life of the Mis-
Guided Boy.

Springer, Feb 2. – Springer, the County seat of Colfax County is located on the Atchison, Topeka & Santa Fe (RR), seventy-one miles north of Las Vegas. The town is essentially an American settlement and has within the past year grown at a rapid pace. The great commercial house of Porter & Clouthier is located here and an extensive trade has grown up with the stockmen of the neighboring ranches. Present appearances indicate that at no distant day Springer will be a town of considerable importance as a commercial center. The courthouse, recently completed and built entirely of brick, is beyond doubt the finest edifice of the kind in the territory. The rear wing of the building is the county jail, and within its gloomy portals, until 12:20 p. m. to-day, Damian Romero has spent over a year awaiting, until recently, the verdict of the tribunal of last resort and more recently the hour set by the Governor for his execution.

The personal history of the deceased can be summed up briefly: Born at Mora, the county seat of the county of that name, on July 4, 1864, he to-day

CLOSED HIS CAREER,

Which lasted only eighteen years, six months and twenty-eight days. His parents were Savino Romero, of Mora county, who died four years ago, and Clarita Lavato de Romero, of the county of Rio Arriba, now living with four daughters – Damian being the only son-at Cañoncito Ocate, this county.

Owing to lack of means on his parents part, the boy only spent six months of his life at school, but in that short time he learned the rudiments of reading and writing which he afterwards improved by study while not at work. When twelve years of age he began working for one W. M. Corbett, a stockman of Mora County. From there he took a situation with one Francisco Roy, doing odd jobs around a sawmill which his employer owned, in the vicinity of Mora. He only remained there one month, at the expiration of which time he returned home and stopped for several months. He next entered the employ of William Schaffer, a father in law of Sheriff Mason T. Bowman, of this county. Romero remained with Mr. Schaffer until the latter sold his ranch to the father of William Albert Brocksmidt, the man who

FELL A VICTIM

of the cupidity of his trusted employee. Romero was then engaged by Brocksmidt and remained with him until the time of the murder. Of the antecedents of his victim but little is known, save that he came here to manage the sheep ranch of his father. A prominent and wealthy citizen of Iowa, who for many years was auditor of the Iowa Central Railroad Company, he was handsome in person and agreeable in manner. A dashing horseman and owing one of the fastest animals in Colfax, the Silver Tail, who figured so prominently in the trial, young Brocksmidt soon won many friends and was at the date of his untimely death a general favorite throughout this section of the country. Between him and Romero there always existed the kindest relations, and to use the expression of the latter on the night preceding the execution, they stood more in the relation of brothers than that of master and servant. Romero taught his young employer the Spanish language and the latter instructed him in English, and at the time of the murder each spoke the other's language very fluently. In appearance Romero was

DECIDEDLY BOYISH,

Looking not over sixteen years of age, his face beardless, his height just five feet four and half inches, and his figure slight, but his frame well knit. His complexion was rather light, his hair short, thick and black, his feet and hands small and well shaped, his mouth rather large and somewhat repulsive, and a large roman nose, completing his appearance. As he sat on his cot on his last night on earth, talking cheerfully of his fate and expressing a readiness to meet his creator, his worst feature was his eyes, black as the crime with which his hands were stained. There was a restless, furtive look about them which was not calculated to inspire confidence. In conversation he would smile constantly, but betrayed a certain amount of restlessness which plainly showed that it took all the courage which he could muster to keep from breaking down.

THE CRIME

The crime which young Romero to-day expiated with his own life, was committed in Colfax County on the 12th day of January, 1882. A day or two before the murder, Brocksmidt had gone over to Springer and received a package of money containing $150 and the knowledge of his victim having this in his possession was the immediate cause of death at the hands of

Romero. The evidence brought out at the trial was entirely circumstantial, but it fixed the guilt beyond doubt upon the accused. It is surmised that Romero first shot his employer in the head, and then not entirely satisfied that his bloody work had been completed, he shot him twice again; one ball entering the breast and the other breaking the right arm. Immediately

AFTER THE TRAGEDY

Romero mounted his employer's horse first securing all the money and valuables about the premises, and rode off in the direction of Rio Arriba County, wearing the victim's cap, coat and watch.

As soon as the body of Brocksmidt had been found, the disappearance of Romero fastened suspicion upon him and a reward of $500 was offered for his capture by Gov. Sheldon. He was finally caught on the 5th of February at Upper Chama, in the county of Rio Arriba by Pedro Sanchez, a deputy sheriff. When arrested Romero had in his possession the watch, coat, and cap of the deceased. He was taken to Chama to Espanola and from there to Santa Fe, being transferred from that city to Springer to await trial. While at Espanola, in response to inquiries from his captors regarding the killing; Romero stated that

HE FIRED THE FIRST SHOT,

Hitting Brocksmidt in the head, and that the other two wounds were inflicted by an Indian named Juan Antonio Rael, who had been stopping at the ranch for a day or two. He further stated that he had fired when commanded by the Indian, who had threatened him with death, if he disobeyed. After the killing, according to the first account given by the accused, he and Rael divided the money found on Brocksmidt, amounting to $120; and mounted, the Indian his own animal and Romero to Brocksmidt's. They left the scene of their crime, leaving the dead man lying on the floor of his own dwelling, his clothes saturated with the blood which continually flowed from his three death wounds.

After going for some distance together, the Indian and Romero departed company and did not meet again until the trial. This story Romero denied when testifying in his own behalf, affirming that all of the shots were fired by the Indian.

THE TRIAL

Romero was indicted for murder by the grand jury of Colfax County, at the April term, 1882, and his trial opened at Cimarron, then the county seat on April 5th. The accused being unable to employ counsel, the court appointed Frank Springer, Esq, of Cimarron, and Judge W. D. Lee, of Las Vegas, to act in that capacity. A large number of witnesses were brought forward on behalf of the territory, and the testimony showed clearly that the crime had been committed by but one man, and that man was prisoner at the bar. The Indian when placed on the stand, gave a straightforward story of his stay at the ranch and his departure, averring that when he left Brocksmidt was

ALIVE AND WELL.

He maintained this position under a rigid cross-examination and after the close of his evidence but little hope remained for the prisoner. Romero then took the stand and stated that he had been directed by Brocksmidt to go out and milk the cows, and while he was engaged in this duty Brocksmidt and the Indian were shooting at a mark. When he entered the house, he was met by the latter, who told him that he must prepare to leave the place, and on Romero's expressing surprise, he was informed by Rael that he had killed his employer, and threatened by him (Rael) with the same fate if he dared to disobey. These are about the main points in the testimony produced at the trial, and in the light of these facts the jury, on April 6th, returned a verdict of

GUILTY AS INDICTED.

The court then assessed the penalty at death, fixing the 10th day of May, 1882, as the date for the execution. A motion for a new trial was made by the prisoner's counsel, but this was denied by the court. An appeal was then taken to the Supreme Court, the case coming up at the term just ended.

This tribunal, after listening to all of the grounds advanced by the counsel for the defendant why the case should be remanded for a new trial, claiming that the court below erred in giving some and omitting to give other instructions and that the evidence did not justify the verdict, decided to affirm the decision of the District Court, and on receipt of the papers in the case, Gov. Sheldon fixed Friday, February 2d, 1883, between the hours of 10 a. m. and 2 p. m. as the date on which the majesty of the law was to be vindicated and justice satisfied, even though done at the expense of human life.

A Heartrending Scene.

About 10 o'clock Thursday morning, the day preceding his execution, the doomed man was visited in his cell by his mother and two of his sisters. The meeting was a very affecting one. The aged mother, bowed down with grief at the awful death rapidly dawning on her only boy, clasped him in the arms which had nursed him in childhood and wept, though the cup presented to her lips was more bitter than she could drink. The two sisters clasped his manacled hands and mingled their tears with those of their mother. Damian, alone unmoved, not a tear dimming the luster of his bright eyes, implored his mother to realize, as he did most fully, that all hope for him in this life was at an end, but that having made peace with heaven and being conscious of his entire innocence of the crime for which he was to suffer, he was prepared to step over into the unknown land without a tremor of fear. Even his cheerful manner could not check her grief, however, and the look which she gave her ill-fated son on taking leave of him left an impression on those who witnessed the scene which will not soon be effaced. In that look were blended a depth of love and affection which only a mother's heart can give, with the most

AGONIZED DESPAIR

and anguish to which human eyes can give expression. Later on in the morning, Romero expressed a wish to have his photograph taken and his request was at once complied with by Sheriff Bowman, who endeavored to soothe the last moments of the prisoner with every comfort which could be suggested. Romero was attired in a short time and conducted to the court room, where everything was in readiness and a number of good pictures were taken. Here he was again joined by his mother and sisters and a group was taken at his request, with Romero and his mother sitting with one of the sisters on either side.

Sheriff Bowman's Views.

While Romero was sitting for his picture Sheriff Mason remarked to the reporter that Romero's face could not strike anyone as that of a hardened criminal, and added that he had maintained his cheerfulness during the entire period of his incarceration. The Sheriff then went on to state that when first confined Romero weighed 122 pounds. During the whole of the past year he has never been sick, never gloomy, has always had a good appetite and during that time, while

CONFINED IN A NARROW CELL,

He had only lost seven pounds of flesh. The Sheriff then went on to state what he knew of Damian's history. He was evidently impressed with the story of the prisoner and considered that the Indian was at least an accessory to the crime. He could not see, he said, what could have induced Romero to murder Brocksmidt for the paltry sum he had in his possession at the time, when, if he had been capable of perpetrating such a crime from a desire for money, many better opportunities had presented themselves, when Brocksmidt had in his possession a much larger sum than he had on the day of his murder. Again, the Sheriff went on to explain, when Romero was employed by Schaffer, the latter often left him on the ranch alone with Schaffer's wife and children, having in the house at the time large sums of money, at one time as much as $1,000, and Romero knew of it being there and yet never attempted any

VIOLENCE OR ROBBERY.

In fact everyone who ever knew the prisoner bears testimony of his industry and general excellence of character, and those who knew him the best are loth to believe him guilty of the offense charged at his hands.

Romero's Statement.

In response to an inquiry from the reporter of the New Mexican for his version of the murder, Romero said, speaking in his mother's tongue: "On the night preceding the murder Brocksmidt and myself were both in bed, when we heard a loud rap at the door. On opening it I saw the Indian Juan Antonio Rael. He asked me if the house of Lota Padilla was in the neighborhood, and I told him it was about a mile and half distant. He then said his horse was worn out and requested shelter for the night. Here Brocksmidt called out to me to let him in, which I did. The Indian then stretched himself on the floor before the fire and was soon asleep. In the morning after breakfast the Indian left us, but returned again about 4 p. m. A little before 5 o'clock Brocksmidt directed me to milk the cows. When I left the house on this errand, he and the Indian were standing at the door, shooting at a mark. This was the last time I ever

SAW BROCKSMIDT ALIVE.

On my return the Indian met me in the kitchen and said: 'You must go with me.' I said 'Why?' He said, 'You must go with me because I have killed him,' meaning Brocksmidt. In my fright I dropped the bucket of milk which I had in my hand, and rushed to the front entrance where I saw the dead body of Brocksmidt. In the yard were two horses, Silver Tail and the Indian's pony saddled and hitched to a wagon which was standing there. The whole thing was so terrible and so sudden that I lost control of myself and could only obey what the Indian told me. We united the horses and the Indian, who had collected a lot of Brocksmidt's clothes, then gave me the dead man's cap, coat, and watch. We walked down the road for about a mile, leading our horses. Here the Indian stopped and pulling out

A LOT OF MONEY

And gave me $60, which I took. Brocksmidt had on his person when he was killed, nearly $300. After going some distance further together, we parted, and I didn't see him again until the trial." The reporter then inquired of Romero why he did not go at once to Springer, and inform the Sheriff of the murder. To this he replied: "I was too frightened to do it. I did not think of anything except to get out of the way of the Indian. I was afraid he would kill me."

"Why did you not hide or dispose of the clothing of Brocksmidt you had in your possession? Did you not realize that when you were discovered with them it would fasten suspicion on you?"

"No, I did not think of this. I knew I was innocent of crime and I did not stop to think that any one would suspect me of murder. I loved Brocksmidt very much. He was just like a brother to me."

"Did you not say when captured in Rio Arriba that you fired the first shot at Brocksmidt, the one which struck him in the head?"

"No, I did not."

"Have you made preparations for death, and are you contented to go?"

"Yes, I am trying to prepare myself to meet my death.

I KNOW I AM INNOCENT

and am not afraid to die. I do not want any one but the Sheriff to put the rope around my neck. He has been very kind to me. I know he will not treat me roughly." The condemned man then went on in a religious strain. He affirmed his belief in a God and in a future state. He said he had ceased to think of bodily pain and suffering and was trying to prepare his soul to meet its maker. At this point the conversation was brought to a close by the appearance of the Rev. Father Accorsint,. Romero's spiritual adviser, who requested all present to withdraw, as he desired to hear the last confession of his charge and give him such spiritual comfort that he might be enabled to go to peace to his eternal Father. When he had finished his ministrations, the reporter returned but found the prisoner so engrossed in his religious duties that further conversation for the night was deemed out of place, and Romero was left alone in his cell. He retired about 9 p.m. and spent, according to his own account, a very good night.

THE FATAL MOMENT

Romero arose a little after 6 a.m., and then displayed the first and only sign of weakness he has evinced. He could not eat any of the breakfast prepared for him and showed considerable restlessness. At 8 a.m. the priest called and administered the last sacraments, and from that time Romero never showed a sign of fear. A little later his mother and sisters appeared at the grating and were admitted. They only remained a few moments and did not see Romero again until he was a corpse.

At 10 a.m. Dr. North, county physician, called and found the prisoner's pulse to be 128. This showed that he was laboring under great excitement, but his demeanor was quiet and composed.

At 11:30 Sheriff Bowman brought from his own house a very nice dinner, which had been prepared at Romero's request, consisting mainly of pies, cakes and other delicacies. This he devoured in haste and with much relish. The reporter of the *New Mexican*, who spent nearly the entire morning with Romero, here asked him if he felt any fear, to which he replied: "Why should I? I am entirely innocent and am

NOT AFRAID TO DIE."

Preparations were then made for the march to the scaffold. The engine of death was erected on the north side of the jail, almost adjoining the building. It was a very substantial structure and the mechanism was perfectly arranged, the drop being about six feet. The sheriff stated to the prisoner that he would place a handkerchief in his hands, and when he was ready to die, to drop it. Romero expressed satisfaction at the arrangements and said: "I am glad that everything is so well fixed. I want the work done quickly and well."

At 12:30 a crowd of about 550 people, mainly Americans, had collected about the gallows, around which a rope was stretched to keep the crowd back. Precisely as 12:45 the death march was begun from the southern door of the jail, as follows: First, Sheriff Bowman and the prisoner, whose hands and feet had been freed from the irons; then Deputies Budeson and Deacy, while the New Mexican representative, accompanied by the Optic reporter, brought up the rear. Romero mounted the scaffold with a firm tread, accompanied by the parties mentioned above.

When he had taken his stand on the trap the sheriff said: "Damian Romero, have you anything to say before the death warrant of Governor Sheldon is executed upon you?" To which Romero replied speaking English in a loud, clear voice:

THE SPEECH.

"Well, gentleman, all I have to say is that I am not afraid to die, Because I am not guilty. Good bye."

As he stood on the threshold of eternity, thus protesting his innocence, he was dressed in a dark blue coat, black vest, dark pants, standing collar, black cravat and light broad brimmed hat. He smiled and waived his hand to the sea of upturned faces below, not a trace of fear being visible on his countenance. At this moment Father Accorsini appeared and remonstrated with the sheriff for having nearly hung Romero before he received the last benediction. The sheriff replied that the law must take its course and that he had waited as long as he could. Romero then knelt down and received the blessing of the Holy Father, at the same time kissing the crucifix which was placed to his lips. The reverend father then withdrew.

Just here the mouth of the prisoner twitched nervously, but this passed in a moment and he regained his self control, which he maintained to the end. He then shook hands with the sheriff, deputies and reporters. When he took the hand of the New Mexican representative he said in a clear voice, "Good bye," smiling and appearing absolutely content to meet his awful fate. He then handed the sheriff his hat and his arms and legs were pinioned, the black cap placed on his head and the noose adjusted, and the sheriff placed the handkerchief in his hand. All then left the scaffold, the prisoner standing alone. Just before the trap was sprung Romero used these

REMARKABLE WORDS,

shouting them out at the top of his voice: "Good bye all. I am going to Mora to-night, but will come back soon." This led many present to think that his mind was wandering. He seemed to forget the sheriff's instructions about the handkerchief, but when Bowman said: "Damian, are you ready? If so, drop it," he dropped it instantly, and the trap was sprung at just seven minutes past 1 p.m.. The body fell six feet and for five minutes the contortions were very severe, and he appeared to be suffering dreadful agony. The body raised several inches and then dropped again; the legs and arms twitched convulsively and it was plain that he was dying by strangulation, and that the neck had not been dislocated. From the moment he dropped the pulse was very faint and the heart beat rapidly, but soon subsided, and at 1:22 Dr. North pronounced life extinct and the deceased was placed in the coffin, which was brought out of the jail. Some difficulty was experienced in getting the noose from around the neck and when this was done and the black cap removed,

A GHASTLY SIGHT

Was revealed. The face was much swollen and terribly discolored, while the rope had made a great jagged, purple line about the neck. The eyes were staring and the mouth wide open. When the face had been arranged the coffin was closed and the body turned over to the mother of the deceased.

Tonight a number of friends of the family held a wake over the body according to the custom of the church. The remains will be taken from here to the home of Mrs. Romero, at Cañoncito Ocate, and there

LAID AT REST.

The best order prevailed throughout the execution and every arrangement was carried out by the sheriff with dispatch, and without a hitch or jar being discernible in the proceeding.

Romero was going to meet his victim, and weather he was innocent or guilty will probably never be disclosed. In this connection a significant fact was learned this afternoon by the reporter. At the time of the preliminary examination held here, the Indian Rael came very nearly being lynched. And this coming to the ears of Father Accorsini a short time ago, he remarked, in the presence of several witnesses, that it was fortunate that this did not occur, as, had the Indian been lynched, an innocent man would have been murdered. In spite of this, however, the feeling is strong that although Romero met a well deserved fate, the Indian was equally guilty and should have shared it with him.

Sources:

Santa Fe *Daily New Mexican*, February 3 and 4, 1883
The Albuquerque *Morning Journal*, February 3, 1883
Albuquerque *Evening Review*, February 2, 1883

Theodore Baker

Frank S. Unruh was a young German who arrived in the United States in 1878. When not working as a government surveyor, he worked for the Prairie Cattle Company in Trinidad, Colorado. In Colfax County, near the town of Springer, Fred Unruh purchased a small cattle ranch as he planned to start a family. He had been corresponding with a woman in Pennsylvania and returned there in 1880 to marry her. Afterwards he returned to the ranch with his new bride, Kate. Kate Unruh was a pretty 22-year-old woman with blue eyes and fair colored hair. In 1882, their only son was born. By all accounts, they shared a happy and prosperous marriage until 1885.

In July of that year, Frank Unruh was going into Springer for supplies when he saw Theodore Baker, an old acquaintance he knew from Arizona. His friend told him he was looking for property in the vicinity to invest in the cattle business. Fred Unruh invited his friend to stay with him and his family while he looked for a homestead near him.

As a government surveyor, Frank Unruh was away from home a great deal. In his absence, Theodore Baker began paying a lot of attention to Mrs. Unruh along with helping her with her household chores. While working to seduce the woman, Theodore told Mrs. Unruh of her husband's numerous relationships with women in Arizona. He further told Kate it was the opinion of the people in the county that she was too good for Frank, and that he was generally hated. In the two months he lived at the Unruh home, Theodore convinced Kate to divorce her husband and marry him.

It was near this time that Frank Unruh and his wife began having arguments; he suspected the marital problems were the result of Baker and told his wife so. Kate told Baker her husband was watching them. Trouble continued to grow between Frank Unruh and Baker, and yet Baker was allowed to remain in the home. With the tension growing, Baker told neighbors of the problems he and Unruh were having and remarked that if "Unruh did not behave himself he would take a six shooter and beat Unruh's head off."

On Monday, December 14, 1885, Frank Unruh overheard his wife and Baker whispering to each other. He angrily went to his cellar and consumed a large quantity of wine. Drunkenly, he yelled out loudly enough for his wife to hear that he intended to, "Knock the Hell out of the bitch." Baker told Kate that her husband intended to kill all of them. Fearing her husband, Mrs. Unruh removed his revolver from their bedroom and gave the gun to Baker who placed the pistol in his room.

At dusk, Baker went outside to tell Frank Unruh supper was ready. After both men sat down at the dinner table, Frank angrily said he "ought to cut Baker's heart out and hang it on a pole." Without saying a word, Baker left the dinner table to go to his room. When he returned words were exchanged and both men wrestled with one another. The fight took them both into Baker's room where a shot was fired. Frank Unruh cried out, "My God, Kate, I am shot!" When a second shot was fired, Frank Unruh ran out of the house and into the darkness running about 800 yards before collapsing. Theodore Baker at first chased after Frank, but returned to his room to get the other pistol. Now armed with two pistols, he followed the trail of blood left by Frank Unruh. Finding his victim sitting on the ground, he shot Frank Unruh in the head, arm and side with the victim's own gun. Afterwards, Baker returned to Kate and told her Frank was dead. Fearing he might still be alive, Baker returned and fired two more shots into the body.

Both Baker and Kate Unruh were arrested and lodged in the Springer jail. On the night of December 23rd, an angry mob forced themselves into the jail and removed Baker from his cell. A noose was quickly tightened around Baker's neck and the rope thrown over a telegraph pole. The vigilantes hoisted Theodore up in the air and left him for dead. A Sheriff's Posse arrived on the scene and cut his body down. Baker was not dead; he was revived and secretly placed on a train and transported to the New Mexico Territory Penitentiary in Santa Fe for safe keeping until trial.

South entrance of the New Mexico Penitentiary in Santa Fe, circa 1912. Courtesy Museum of New Mexico, Neg. No. 61406. Photographer, Jesse L. Nusbaum. Theodore Baker was a guest at the Territory Penitentiary in 1885 for his own safety. A vigilante group in Springer, NM had lynched him once, unsuccessfully.

Kate Unruh was offered her freedom in exchange for her testimony as prosecuting witness. Shortly after testifying against Theodore Baker, she went back to Pennsylvania with her three-year-old son. Theodore Baker's verdict was guilty of murder in the first degree and he was sentenced to hang after Judge Elisha Long imposed the sentence on September 6, 1886. Judge Long not only condemned the man to death, but also in the sentencing:

"The evidence discloses that the deceased, took you, a wanderer, and gave you a home within his own family, with the opportunity to reside there and eat at his table. His business necessarily called him much of the time away, often for days and weeks. At such times the friend who had given you shelter, gave into your keeping the honor of his family. Did you ever think of the sacred character of that trust? Instead, the evidence proves that you poured into not unwilling ears, stories, that you might win and debauch his wife while she was in the highest sense of manly honor entrusted to you. It may be said she should have turned away from you. That is true. It is however, the weak and defenseless who need protection and not the strong and powerful. Does it lessen your wrong that she was weak and listened to you? Who but you and she know of the words of love and admiration expressed to her, in violation of your trust, to lead her to the path of dishonor. What a spectacle -- A woman dishonored, her paramour in the very presence of the husband, aware of his humiliation, disarmed and powerless in his own home, converted by your act into a house for his enemies, the darkness of night approaching with secret whispering and consultations between you and your paramour. It was a condition to invite murder."

It was said terror struck Theodore Baker as he heard the sound of the hammer and saws building the scaffold in the jail yard: "He is prostrated, completely cowed, and speaks to those about him only when he is spoken to." A fence twenty feet high and seventy-five feet square was built surrounding the jail yard and gallows to shut out any unwanted spectators. Admission tickets were issued and 67 witnesses watched the execution. Theodore Baker was lead from his jail cell to the scaffold. He professed his innocence and said Mrs. Unruh committed the murder.

The Santa Fe *Daily Democrat* had the following headlines and story.

Baker's Bluff
At the Portals of Death
He Says the Wo-
Man Did it.

He Gamely Gives the Signal "Let
Her Go," to the Sheriff and
Leaps into Eternity.

Special to the Democrat.

Las Vegas, May 6- Baker spent a quiet but wakeful night. Four ministers and about thirty Christian men and women held religious service with him last evening. He seemed submissive but not penitent, protesting to the last the truth of the account furnished by him to the reporter, in which he declared Mrs. Unruh killed her husband, and he was to swear that he did it in self-defense to save her and himself, and she was to confirm the statement. He was quite hopeful up to the middle of the afternoon yesterday, when a telegram was received from Governor Ross, refusing to further interfere. He did not give up to despair, having a superstitious faith that as he once already had been hung for this offense something would impose to save him at the last moment. All the clergy of the city telegraphed the Governor this morning for another respite.

The execution took place in the jail yard at seven minutes to 4 o'clock and only sixty-seven persons were permitted to be present. The condemned was clad in a plain but genteel suit of grey, furnished by the county, as was also the plain coffin in which he was buried. He has a brother in Newark NJ, in good circumstances, and a brother in the state of Arkansas, but neither of them gave him any assistance at any time since the murder.

On the scaffold he told the story already told. When the sheriff put the black cap over his face he said: "Gentlemen, I am sorry it ends thus." Then addressing the sheriff he added: "Let her Go." The drop was sprung and he did not make a motion or a quiver. After seven minutes his pulse ceased and after seventeen minutes he was cut down.

Theodore Baker was hung for the murder of Jacob Unruh on December 14, 1885. The evidence introduced at his trial showed that his victim had invited Baker to become an inmate of his house, that he might be enabled to enter a piece of land near Unruh's ranch. In doing so he took a viper to his bosom which when warmed by the heart turned and stung him.

Unruh was a surveyor and frequently away from his home. During his absence Baker pitted the wiles of the seduced and succeeded in ruining his benefactor's wife. Damning evidence convinced Unruh that the destruction of his domestic happiness had been accomplished, and charged Baker with the deed, which resulted in nothing more than a heated war of words. During the afternoon Unruh's wife secured her husbands revolver and secreted it until an opportunity was presented to give it to her paramour. On the same evening the quarrel was renewed in Baker's room and blows were exchanged, a shot was fired. Unruh came running out of the room, desperately wounded in the intestines. He ran through the dinning room and out of the door, Baker pursuing and shooting at him. At the door Baker turned and returned to his room, secured another revolver and continued the pursuit of the victim. Finding Unruh seated on the ground 340 yards from the house, the determined manslayer deliberately shot his victim twice, once through the head and once in the thigh. The deed accomplished, he returned to the embraces of his victim's wife.

So incensed was the community at the atrocious murder, that on December 23, 1885, a mob seized and hanged him to a telegraph pole, but he was cut down by officers of the law in time to save his life for the halter. He was born in Newark, NJ, April 12, 1857, and consequently was 30 years old last month.

Sources:

Santa Fe *Daily New Mexican*, May 6, 1887
Albuquerque *Morning Democrat*, May 7, 1877
The *Daily Optic*, May 4, 1887

David Arguello and John Medlock

On Friday, May 25, 1906, David Arguello and John Medlock were hanged minutes apart at Raton, New Mexico, for separate murders.

David Arguello lived in Bowen, Colorado, with his wife and children. Mr. Arguello was described as a good father and husband, and a religious man with a good reputation. In June, 1903, Mrs. Celia Dassart and her family arrived in Bowen, Colorado, and moved into a house near the Arguello's home. Celia Dassart was a pretty 19-year-old girl who David Arguello immediately had affections for. Mr. Arguello's continued persistence for her affections became harassing. In an attempt to stop Mr. Arguello's behavior, Mrs. Dassart told Mrs. Arguello of her husband's actions. The Santa Fe *New Mexican* told what happened next on July 23, 1903.

Early on the morning of the crime, Arguello had gone to the Dassart home. The Dassart's were living in house No.5 directly across from the Bowen saloon. His attractions were again repulsed, and again Mrs. Dassart sent word to the wife of Arguello's actions. When Arguello returned, it is said, his wife upbraided him for his actions and struck him over the head with a big sugar bowl in the presence of Mrs. Dassart, who had come to witness the quarrel. Arguello became enraged, and procuring his pistol, left the house. Mrs. Dassart returned to her home and a few minutes later Arguello followed her into her home. He was seen by the people across the street in the saloon to open the front door, go inside and close the door behind him. In a few minutes three shots were heard and Arguello came outside and walked off into the hills.

Mrs. Dassart's brother ran to the house and found his sister lying on the floor dead, with a bullet wound through her heart. The woman had evidently turned to run into a back room and was shot down in the doorway as she was lying on her face, and the bullet had entered her back.

An armed posse started in pursuit of Arguello, keeping him in sight for several miles, but he was well armed and was able to stand them off with a fusillade of bullets, himself being uninjured by their shots. He finally got away and became a fugitive from justice, living in remote places, under assumed names, and working as a sheep herder, ranch hand or anything which offered employment. During this time he assisted in the support of his family and was with them a portion of the time. More than two years were spent in this way, Arguello evading arrest all this time, although the officials of Las Animas County, Colorado, were constantly on the watch for him. A reward of $300 was offered by the county for his capture, dead or alive, and it was known he was a fugitive from justice. The husband of the woman, too, offered a reward of $300 for his capture.

Early in October 1905, Francisco Garcia informed Sheriff Davis of Trinidad (CO) that he believed he could discover the murderer, and was deputized to make the arrest. He found that the family of Arguello had been living for a year or more east of Johnson's mesa (Colfax County, NM), and that Arguello had worked for sometime as a sheepherder for Jerome Troy. On Thursday, October 19, Garcia called at the Floyd ranch, on Johnson's mesa, and found Arguello there. Garcia was not prepared to arrest his man at this time, being unarmed. Arguello shot him after a short scuffle. In his dying statement Garcia stated that he had not expected to find Arguello at the Floyd ranch, but had come there on other business. It is probable that he only sought to locate his man and intended to return later with assistance, as Arguello was known to be a desperate character and it was believed by the Trinidad officers that he would resist arrest.

Medlock's Life and Crime.

John Medlock was born in Tennessee and came to New Mexico some years ago. He was engaged as a miner at Gardiner at the time of his crime. Carrie Boyd, or Mckinley, was living at Gardiner with a Negro named Mckinley, and Medlock began paying attentions to her. After some time she left Mckinley and went to live with Medlock. The woman proved fickle and left Medlock after a few weeks. The murder occurred at the saloon in Gardiner. Medlock went to the house where the woman was stopping and failing to gain admittance, left. That night he found her at the saloon, and without warning, shot her. As she fell someone attempted to lift her up. Medlock exclaimed, "Let her alone; I want to see her drop." Several persons were in the saloon at the time and Medlock cleared the room, waving his pistol in a threatening manner. When the room was cleared he rushed out and escaped in the darkness. Search was made for him and every effort was made for his capture, but he escaped to Oklahoma. There in a short time he was arrested for the attempted murder of another woman, tried, convicted and sentenced to the federal penitentiary at Leavenworth for three years. At the expiration of this sentence he was brought to Raton to answer to the charge of murder. Last July, Medlock in company with a number of other prisoners sawed out of the jail, which was then badly over-crowded, and unfit for desperate prisoners, and escaped. He was traced to Pueblo, there captured and returned by Sheriff Littrell. His case did not come up at the September term of court, and therefore he has been in jail in Raton for more than a year. In a mine explosion some year since, Medlock suffered the loss of one eye and this peculiar mark rendered his identification easy.

The Santa Fe *New Mexican* dated Friday, May 25, 1906 had the following story and headlines.

ARGUELLO, AND
MEDLOCK DIED
GAME ON THE SCAFFOLD

———

Both Had Killed Women in Cold Blood
As Result of Unrequitted
Affections.

———

"Do not follow
IN MY FOOTSTEPS"

———

As the Parting Advice of One Prisoner to His Life Long
Friend ---Hanging Took Place in Raton --- trap
Sprung First at 10:15 a. m.

———

Special to the *New Mexican.*

On May 25. - David Arguello and John Medlock arose at a very early
hour this morning. Medlock was in good spirits. He had retired an hour later
after Arguello who retired at 12:30. He slept well the remainder of the night
until breakfast which was served shortly before 7 o'clock this morning.
Medlock ate a good breakfast, but Arguello spent the time in bed and ate
nothing. Medlock joked and sang about the cell as guards grabbed up and put
away the dishes from the morning meal. Both men appeared nervous last
evening as the sun marked their last day. John Medlock was the first to be
lead to the scaffold. Before being lead to the scaffold, John Medlock confessed
to his crime and said he regretted it. Medlock made a statement which was
read from the scaffold in which he thanked Sheriff Littrell for his kindness
during his imprisonment, and thanked Reverend Jacobs for religious
consolation, affirming repentance for his crime and his hope of heaven. His
statement contained a warning to young men to shun bad companions and
abstain from drink and he attributed his condition today to these evil
influences. His statement closed with a prayer from the Lutheran Church
service. Marshal Howe adjusted the noose and Medlock swung at 10:15. His
pulse continued to beat for thirteen minutes after the drop, but there was no
struggle, not even a tremor, and he was cut down at 10:35. His neck was not
broken, but strangulation was perfect.

Arguello made the following statement, which was also read: "I am
getting ready to meet God today. I am sorry for breaking the law and also
sorry for my past". He also made a short prayer before the drop was sprung.

Arguello was brought from his cell at 10:45 and his bearing was apparently as calm as was that of Medlock. The drop was sprung at 10:53. Arguello's pulse continued to beat for seven minutes and he was cut down at 11:05. His neck was broken.

MEN DIED GAME.

By Associated Press.

Raton, N. M., May 25. - John Medlock, colored, and David Arguello, a Mexican, were hanged here today for murder. Both men died game. Arguello was a double murderer, killing Mrs. Celia Dassart at Bowen, Colorado, and Deputy Sheriff Francisco Garcia, who attempted to arrest him for the crime. Medlock killed a Negro woman at Gardiner this county.

Sources:

Santa Fe *New Mexican*, July 23, 1903; May 25, 1906

Chapter 4

Doña Ana County

F.C. Clark   May 13, 1881
Santos Barela   May 21, 1881
Ruberto Lara   April 30, 1885
Jesus Garcia   November 6, 1896
Toribio Huerta   April 26, 1901

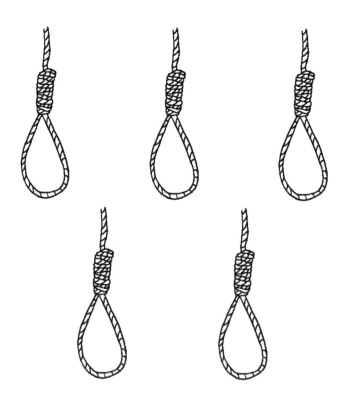

Frank C. Clark

Not much is known about F.C. Clark who was hung in Mesilla, on May 13, 1881. Clark was tried and convicted for the murder of Robert R. (Luint) Mann in January, 1881. Mr. Clark was quoted as saying: "I knew Luint Mann well and would kill Mann again under the like circumstances." The papers did not record what the circumstances were.

On the day of his execution, while being led out of his cell, Clark stopped and spoke with Santos Barela in the adjoining cell. Santos Barela was awaiting a scheduled May 21st execution for murder. Clark told Barela, "Your time will soon come, be prepared to meet your creator. I hope you well be as well prepared to meet him as I am". To the next prisoner he suggested to him to "try to amend and make a man of yourself". Sheriff Southwick, Father Morin, and guards then led Clark out of the building to an awaiting farm wagon which would take them to the scaffold. Clark sat down erect next to his coffin. While being driven to the scaffold, he commented on what a nice ride the wagon was. The paper wrote during their journey, "As the procession moved along beneath giant cottonwoods, the air was redolent with the perfume of flowers." Once reaching the scaffold, Clark was again permitted to speak briefly with his sisters who had followed the procession. Afterwards, Clark mounted the gallows with a firm step. At precisely 1:24 p.m., the trap was sprung and F.C. Clark was pronounced dead at 1:54 p.m. The Mesilla Valley *Independent* had the following story dated May 14, 1881.

The Unknown F.C. Clark, So Called,
Legally Hanged At Mesilla, New Mexico
Remarkable Nerve!
Officers Done Well In There Part.

At about 1:00 PM, Sheriff Jim Southwick and a guard lead Mr. Clark to the scaffold. Clark would not speak with reporters about his age, other than he was born in Ohio and was mostly a gambler by trade.

Sheriff Southwick did allow Clark to have a few minutes to say his goodbyes to his three sisters who were waiting in a carriage. Afterwards at the scaffold, Mr. Clark asked the sheriff: "How much drop you got?" Sheriff Southwick said "about three feet". Mr. Clark replied: "I think that ought to be drop enough". When Mr. Clarks legs were tied together, Clark said: "Down a little lower Jim, it's not necessary to tie them so tight". When Sheriff Southwick placed the noose around the neck, Clark stated: "That's right, put the noose around my ear so that when I drop I don't slip." After the sheriff placed the hood over Clark's head, Sheriff Southwick started down the steps and gave Deputy Dave Wood the signal with a white handkerchief to cut the rope to the double trap doors. Clark's neck was broken and he never moved or jerked once.

The body was then taken to the Catholic Church and placed in a coffin where it was taken to the cemetery for burial. The officers received general praise for performing their duty so well.

The Las Vegas *Optic* in its headline of the execution indicated the hanging was not so smoothly done:

Clark Choked

A Doña Ana Murderer goes to
The Gallows

And kicks Himself to Death in
The Light Air

Sources:

Mesilla Valley *Independent*, May 14, 1881
The Las Vegas *Daily Optic*, May 14, 1881

Santos Barela

Santos Barela was publicly hanged in Mesilla on May 21, 1881. The Rio Grande *Republican* had the following headlines.

Santos Barela pays the price of lust and murder.
The second swinging in Mesilla within 8 days.
Scenes at the scaffold – a successful execution.

Santos Barela was described as being approximately 21 years of age, and a native of the area. At the time of his crime, he was employed as a teamster on a railroad grading contract near the town of Colorado (now Rodey, New Mexico). During the time Santos was working in Colorado, he met Jose Jojola and Mr. Jojola's wife. The Jojola family was described as a respectable family. Mrs. Jojola was described as being about 25 years of age and "her fair proportions seemed to have aroused in the beast, a most hellish desire."

On the evening of February 18, 1881, the Jojola couple spent the evening with Santos Barela at his home. At the end of their visit, they both left to return to their home. Santos is said to have immediately left his house to follow them, "led on by demon lust". After arriving home, Mr. Jojola laid down on his bed while his wife went to light a candle. Santos Barela approached Mr. Jojola's bedside with a .45 caliber pistol in his hand. As Mr. Jojola lay resting, Santos Barela quietly placed the end of the barrel to Mr. Jojola head, and fired the pistol.

At the sound of the shot, Mrs. Jojola ran out of the house and into the street screaming for help. A few yards down the street Santos caught her and threw her to the ground. While he held her down with his knee, Santos threatened to kill her with the same pistol he had killed her husband with if she did not submit. A man named Guerena, hearing the disturbance, went out to investigate to find Santos on top of Mrs. Jojola. Instead of rescuing the helpless woman, Guerena held down Mrs. Jojola while Santos raped her.

When Santos was arrested, he was asked who killed Jose Jojola. Santos replied coolly and carelessly: "I killed him because I liked his wife and I had money to pay for it." In April, Santos was indicted for murder in the first degree. The trial lasted for two days. Three days after the trial, Santos was sentenced to death. The judge ordered the execution to take place in one month to give Santos time "to make peace with his creator".

On May 21, 1881, sixty people gathered to watch the execution. Sheriff Southwick tried to keep the execution as private as possible. At 12.45 p.m., Santos was removed from the cell. Colonel Albert J. Fountain read the death warrant in Spanish to Santos. As he was lead to the gallows, he bade farewell to his fellow prisoners. Walking up the steps of the scaffold, it appeared to reporters that Santos was weakening rapidly.

Once at the scaffold, Santos took off his hat and threw it down in front of him. While kneeling, Santos received Father Morin's last blessing. Afterwards both of his arms and legs were tied together. Santos asked that his arms be tied in a manner that he could reach the crucifix with his hands. After the rope was adjusted and the black cape drawn over his face, Santos began to lean heavily to one side. As he was about to fall over, Sheriff Southwick pulled out a white handkerchief from his pocket. This was the signal to Deputy Wood to use the sharp hatchet to cut the rope that held the trap door in place. Deputy Wood did cut the rope with one quick blow. Santos Barela's body dropped through the trap at 12:52 p.m. The body hung motionless for 13 minutes while his pulse was being monitored to zero. Then it hung for another 7 minutes before being cut down and placed in a coffin.

The Newspaper wrote, "Much credit was given to Sheriff Southwick and his efficient Deputy Wood for their skillful and successful manner in which both this execution and that of Clark was conducted."

Sources:

Rio Grande *Republican*, May 21, 1881

Ruperto Lara

Ruperto Lara was sentenced to death for the murders of George Nedsmith, his wife and their 8-year-old adopted daughter. The murders occurred in the desert near present day Tularosa on August 17, 1882. The bodies of the Nedsmith family were located three weeks after the murders when two men noticed a couple of wolves and buzzards attracted to a wagon. Because the bodies were in such a state of decomposition, the Nedsmith's were unrecognizable. His silver watch identified George Nedsmith's body. The wagon contained several articles in a trunk that belonged to the family, but George Nedsmith's overcoat was missing along with the horses.

When word of the murders got out, people in the small village of Doña Ana, north of Las Cruces, remembered seeing a Mexican wearing an overcoat like the one George Nedsmith owned. Two men identified as Ruperto Lara and Maximo Apodaca fled to Mexico, and did not return to the area for four years when they were both apprehended. Maximo Apodaca confessed to his part in the murders and turned states evidence and became the prosecutor's witness in the trial against Ruperto Lara.

The Rio Grande *Republican* dated May 2, 1885, was the best source of information as to the crime, and the execution of Ruperto Lara, who was hung on April 30, 1885. Below is the story as it was printed in the newspaper.

> When the sun set last Wednesday night Ruperto Lara knew that he would never live to see another, yet he slept in his cell as usual, indifferent to his fate. In the morning when asked by Sheriff Van Patton what he wanted to eat, Lara being a Pueblo Indian requested some frijoles con chili, which was done.
>
> At 11:00 am on Saturday Pat Coghlan and Perry Kearney who worked for Coghlan made the trip to the jail. Both men claimed they had never seen the condemned man to their knowledge. Lara was further taken out of jail and was asked to identify the two who were among 25 others. Without hesitation, Lara pointed out Dave Woods as the man who bribed him, and pointed out H.J. Cuniffe as Coghlan.
>
> At precisely a quarter past two he was brought out of the cell and his arms were bound. While still in the jail he was asked if he wished any liquor. Lara replied that he did not need it but would drink it anyway. Then a procession was formed with Lara at the head between the Sheriff and deputy Ascarte.
>
> Once up on the trap the prisoner coolly surveyed the crowd of about 1200 people who had assembled to witness the avenging of the murder of the Nedsmith family. Sheriff Van Patton read the death warrant, translating it

into Spanish. Afterwards Lara was asked if he had anything to say, and it was evident that he was very eager to accept the invitation.

Lara then made the short statement that he was offered $1,000 dollars by Coghlan to commit the murder and repeated the story of the crime as he had given in his confession. Late on Saturday, prior to his execution, the Sheriff was informed that Lara desired to make a confession for the crime for which he had been convicted.

Because District Attorney Wade was absent, Col. Fountain was called in. He suggested putting the statement in writing and this was done. The confession read:

"I Ruperto Lara am a prisoner in the jail at Las Cruces, under a sentence of death for the murder of George Nedsmith and his family. My time is very short, and I have not long to live. Before I die, I want to tell all about the murder. I thought I had some friends who I thought would help me in this trouble as they had promised, but it appears they have abandoned me to my fate. It is right that I should speak the truth. What I now say I declare to be the whole truth in the presence of GOD who will soon judge me for my deeds. There is a man who lives in Tularosa who I have the right to look to for assistance; he should have been my friend for it was him who got me in this trouble. His name is Pat Coghlan and he keeps a store in Tularosa. A short time before the Nedsmith murders, I was at Coghlan's store in Tularosa. There at the store was Coghlan and a man whose name I do not know. I bought some provisions and started off. When I was getting on my horse, Coghlan came out of the store and asked me if I knew George Nedsmith. I said no. He told me Nedsmith lived on a ranch at 3 rivers and was trying to jump a ranch at 3 rivers. He said if I would kill Nedsmith he would pay me for it.

He said he would give me 1,000 dollars to kill Nedsmith. He also offered me a wagon and a pair of horses which he said were worth about 300 dollars. He did give me a saddle out of the store. He also gave me 10 dollars in gold, and that is all the money that I received from Coghlan out of the 1,000 dollars that he offered me. I never received the wagon and horses, but did receive the saddle.

Maximo Apodaca was with me. At White River we made the acquaintance with Nedsmith. The child and woman were with him. About sun down, I rode up to the side of the wagon and fired. I don't know if I hit Nedsmith or not, but he raised up and hallooed. Maximo got up on the seat and shot Nedsmith in the breast and he fell. The shots were fired in such quick succession that I could not bring my horse close to the wagon. The woman crawled under the seat. Maximo placed the rifle under her arm and shot her through. The child was crying. Maximo raised up and put the rifle at her head and shot her. We then turned off the road and Maximo drove the wagon until the wagon was out of sight.

From there we went to Organ and bought some meat at the store. About that same time a ambulance with soldiers passed by. From there we went to El

Paso and traded the Nedsmith horses for others. I then returned to Tularosa and told Coghlan that they were all dead. Coghlan refused to pay me, unless Maximo was present. I offered to show Coghlan where the bodies were at. Instead, he gave me a bottle of whiskey and told me he would settle up once Maximo returned with me".

This was the confession Lara swore on April 28, 1885, and what he told the public on the scaffold on May 2, 1885. After a time he told the Sheriff in Spanish, to tell the crowd that he did not fear death at all. One of the guards asked him in an undertone if he felt bad about dying, and Lara replied he was not troubled. A glass of liquor was brought to him and he drank by raising his head and having it poured down. Sheriff Van Patton requested the priest to ask him: "Have you been asked by any persons to make a confession?" Lara answered: "I have not been advised by anyone to say what I have said".

Immediately afterwards the priest concluded the religious ceremonies and Lara's legs were bound securely. During this operation he looked down and examined the trap door. A black velvet cap with a hood attached was handed to the Sheriff who proceeded to adjust it with a noose. Up to the time the hood was pulled down over Lara's head, his face had not changed in its expression. The rope with which he was hung was an inch manila, and the hangman's knot was tied in a scientific manner. As it was adjusted, Lara took one deep breath. Four seconds later the Sheriff stepped off the trap and gave a signal by dropping a handkerchief. As an answer to this signal there was a quick blow. The rope of Ruperto Lara was dropped into the space, breaking his neck and causing instant death.

The time was sixteen minutes before three o'clock. Two and a half minutes later Doctor Wood still felt a pulse beating. The doctor felt at intervals until thirteen minutes later he pronounced him dead. The coffin was placed in position and at three o'clock, just sixteen minutes after the trap was sprung, Lara was cut down and placed in the coffin. Shortly afterwards the coffin was taken to its final resting place.

The paper went on to say that: "From first to last there was no hitch. Sheriff Van Patton deserves credit for the neatness and perfect manner in which the execution was dispatched". It was the newspaper's belief that Lara's implication of Mr. Coghlan was pure fabrication, because Lara wanted revenge against Coghlan, or he was aware that Coghlan offered Jim Lloyd 500 dollars if he captured the men responsible for the Nedsmith murders. Jim Lloyd received the reward by tricking Lara to return to the United States from Mexico to join a cattle rustling operation that he was supposedly going to start. Little belief was given to Lara's confession implicating Coghlan for there was no further investigation as to his involvement.

Maximo Apodaca received a death warrant as well. The Governor commuted Maximo's sentence to life in prison for his cooperation. Maximo Apodaca however spent little time at the New Mexico territory prison, for on

November 4, 1885, he committed suicide. It was said he killed himself because he had heard the child's crying ever since he killed her.

Sources:

Rio Grande *Republican*, May 2, 1885

Jesus Garcia

Jesus Garcia was accused of the senseless shooting and murder of a woman who lived in the village of Loma Parda, New Mexico. The Rio Grande *Republican* provided the following information.

Rio Grande *Republican*, July 31, 1896

Jesus Garcia was brought down from Loma Parda and confined in the county jail on the charge of attempted murder. Garcia took two shots at a woman there, one of the bullets taking effect in the face, the other in the small of the back. Justice Silva bound him over to await the action of the grand jury.

Rio Grande *Republican*, August 14, 1896

A Bloody Record

Jesus Garcia, who was bought to the county jail from Colorado a couple of weeks ago, on the charge of attempted murder, will he held for murder, as the woman he shot has since died. It is reported that this is Garcia's third victim. The first victim was his wife, who he killed in Mexico, the second killing was in Arizona where he disemboweled another woman, while the latest act was committed with a gun, taking four shots at her while she was getting mesquite beans.

Rio Grande *Republican*, October 9, 1896

"Jesus Garcia was this week convicted and sentenced to hang on November 6th, for the murder July 26th, of Isabel Montoya, up in Loma Parda, this county".

Rio Grande *Republican*, November 6, 1896

Jesus Garcia Hanged

The murderer of Isabella Montoya
Publicly Executed Today.

At 1: o'clock today the execution of Jesus Garcia, convicted of the murder of Isabella Montoya of Loma Parda July 26th last, took place in public in the court house yard. The prisoner for the past few days had been very nervous and had eaten little for two days, nor had he slept but little for several nights.

Quite a large crowd, numbering several hundred, about one fifth being women, were present. Sheriff Pat Garrett and Deputies Brent and Rudesill escorted to the scaffold the prisoner, who was supported by Father Lasesigne, who remained with him to the last. After arriving at the scaffold, the prisoner's legs were pinioned by Deputy Brent, the black cap was drawn over the face, the rope adjusted by Sheriff Garrett and at a given signal the trap was sprung and the body shot through the trap door, falling a distance of six feet, breaking the neck. No convulsive movements followed. After hanging seventeen minutes, Dr. E. V. Cowan pronounced him dead, and three minutes later the body was lowered into the coffin and turned over to his friends. It was taken to the Catholic Church, and thence to the cemetery. There was no hitch in the arrangements. One spectator, an old man, fainted.

Sheriff Patrick Floyd Garrett of Doña Ana County, New Mexico. Courtesy Museum of Lawmen Photo Collection, Doña Ana Co. Sheriff's Dept. Garrett executed Jesus Garcia on July 26, 1896 for the murder of a woman.

Sources:

Rio Grande *Republican,* July 31, August 14, October 3, November 6, 1896

Toribio Huerta

Toribio Huerta was a 31-year-old man from Northern Zacatecas, Mexico. There he worked in the fields and occasionally on the railroad to support his wife and three children. One night he went into town and saw a well dressed man. Toribio learned that the man had just returned from working in the fields in Colorado, where a man could make his fortune. Toribio decided he would leave for Colorado and make a fortune to support his family. He left on foot with 5 pesos, tortillas, frijoles, and an old revolver that belonged to his father.

He made his way to Cuidad Juarez, Mexico and crossed over into New Mexico. Toribio crossed at a Southern Pacific Railroad bridge across from the Asarco Smelter. Toribio followed the railroad tracks through Anapra, Strauss, Aften, Lanark, and Aden. On February 21, 1901, after three days of walking, he stopped to rest at the Chappel switch station located between Aden and Cambray. A wooden bridge crossed over a culvert at this location. While resting he saw a stranger walking toward him. The stranger was 19 year old Pablo Rivas. Toribio offered him some of his dinner, which consisted of sardines, bread, and coffee. During dinner, Toribio learned Pablo was an orphan. Pablo told his new friend he was returning from Colorado. He eagerly showed Toribio his pay, which was either $40 or $60 according to different accounts.

The next morning after breakfast Pablo showed an interest in Toribio's old pistol. Toribio placed a rock as a target for Pablo to shoot at. Pablo missed the target two times. Toribio told Pablo, "Throw up your hat in the air and I will shoot it." Pablo threw his hat in the air, but Toribio leveled the pistol at Pablo. Toribio fired one time, striking and killing Pablo instantly.

Toribio removed Pablo's money from his pocket, and dragged his body under the bridge. He then placed dead weeds on the body and set fire to both the clothing and weeds. Toribio left and continued on his way as if nothing had happened. He didn't give any thought to the train that passed by him on his way to Cambray. When the train approached the bridge the conductor, seeing the smoke, stopped the train believing the bridge was on fire.

When the conductor kicked dirt on the fire, he discovered Pablo's body. E.H. Mead, the section foreman at Aden, sent a telegram to the El Paso station requesting the Sheriff and the Coroner. He also provided descriptions of three Mexican men he had seen walking along the railroad tracks. El Paso Police Chief Lockhart jailed the three men in the El Paso Jail. Doña Ana County Sheriff Jose Lucero investigated the murder and sent another Deputy to escort the three suspects back to the Las Cruces jail. The Doña Ana County *Republican* dated February 23, 1901, listed the three suspects of the murder as Toribio Huerta, Cruz Vigil, and Jose Garcia. The paper said, "The evidence is over whelming and Garcia knows something of the affair."

On March 2, 1901, a hearing was set before Judge Parker. Cruz Vigil turned states evidence against Huerta. Vigil claimed he was an unwilling witness to the affair through intimidation. Sheriff Lucero learned that the motive was the robbery of $60 dollars. Pablo died instantly from one bullet wound to the back. The paper wrote, "Murder will out, for within six hours of the crime they were behind bars." The newspaper failed to list the victim's name, but other sources did identify him as Pablo Rivas.

On March 16th, 1901, both Toribio Huerta, and Jose Garcia were indicted for murder. On March 30, 1901, Toribio was found guilty of murder in the first degree. Judge Parker sentenced Toribio to hang by the neck until dead at the jail yard adjacent to the courthouse. The execution was to take place on April 26, 1901, between the hours of 10:00 am and 4:00 p.m.

Toribio told Judge Parker that his intentions were only to shoot through the victim's hat, and to rob him. He said that the gun exploded prematurely and shot the victim in the back. He then shot him again to kill him. The newspaper does not indicate what happened to Vigil or Garcia, nor why they were arrested.

On April 20th, 1901, Sheriff Lucero began issuing admission cards to the execution. On April 26, 1901, Toribio walked up the stairs to the scaffold platform. Toribio made a 35-minute speech to the five or six hundred spectators present to watch the execution. After the speech, he announced that he was ready and bade goodbye to all. He requested that he be allowed to give the word when the trap door should to be sprung. At exactly 10:45 a.m., Deputy Sheriff Bob Burch sprung the trap door, dropping Huerta to his death.

The following is the headlines and short story as printed in *The New Mexican.*

TORIBIO HUERTA IS HANGED

He acted the Bravado and kept his nerve
To the last minute answering the
Sheriff's last minute query with a
Strong voice.

A very large crowd was present

Special to the *New Mexican*:

Las Cruces, N.M., April 26 – Toribio Huerta was hanged here this morning in the presence of a large crowd. Just before the final act the deceased made a long rambling address of little importance. He admitted the crime, but considered his fate as his misfortune. There was hardly any sign of nervousness.

Indeed the predominant thought seemed to be that it was his duty to show he had no fear, and his appearance was almost that of bravado.

Toribio Huerta, left, and Sheriff Jose Lucero, on the day of Huerta's execution. Courtesy, Rio Grande Historical Collections, NMSU, Las Cruces, NM.

He had asked and was granted permission to give the signal for the drop after the black cap had been adjusted. He was asked, "Are you ready, Toribio?" When the question had been propounded three times, the answer came in a strong voice: "I am ready". The fall broke the neck and death came in fourteen minutes.

Sources:

Doña Ana County *Republican*, February 23, 1901
Mesilla *Democrat*, April 26, 1901
Santa Fe *New Mexican*, April 26, 1901
San Francisco *Chronicle*, April 26, 1901

Chapter 5

Eddy County

James Barrett   September 14, 1894

James Barrett

James Barrett was the only man ever executed in Eddy County, New Mexico. He arrived in the Pecos Valley, in 1892, after committing several crimes in Texas. At Seven Rivers, he gained employment as a laborer at a grading camp. There he tried to establish a reputation as a dangerous man among the other workers.

On July 23, 1893, James Barrett was involved in an altercation with John Holehan and James Barnes. After the fight, Barrett stayed up late into the early morning hours getting drunk from whiskey. Once drunk and full of courage from the liquor, Barrett armed himself with a shotgun. He then approached the night watchman and demanded he show him the tent where the two men sleep. As the watchman held the lantern up in the tent for light, Barrett shot and killed both men as they slept. In retreating back out of the tent, Barrett threatened everyone and said he would kill anyone who tried to stop him. Sheriff Kemp captured Barrett the next day on a charge of murder.

The murder trial was held at Lincoln County on a change of venue. There James Barrett made a plea of "temporary insanity." This plea was given no weight in his defense and he was convicted of two counts of murder in the first degree. An appeal was made to the Territory Supreme Court and the judgment of the lower court was sustained. The *Weekly Eddy Argus* wrote, "There is a salutary lesson taught to revengeful, murderous men, and the dignity of the law sustained."

The Santa Fe *Daily New Mexican* had the following story of the execution.

Eddy Execution.

James Barrett, the double murderer, was executed at Eddy last Friday at 2:05 p.m. in the presence of about 1,000 people. The Eddy *Current* has an excellent report of the affair.

At 1:15 o'clock he was taken from the jail just after eating a hearty meal and carried to the place of execution. He showed no signs of excitement and to the last was as cool as if he were going about the most ordinary detail of business. The drop fell at the hour above named and in ten minutes he was dead. His last request was that his boots be taken off, saying: "I have been told I would die with my boots on. I'll just fool you a trip, so here goes my boots." Sheriff Kemp assisted by Deputy Sheriff Bush officiated.

Barrett killed two men, John Holehan and James Barnes, on July 23, 1893, in a Seven Rivers grading camp. He was arrested July 24 and a change of venue was granted him to Lincoln County. He was tried there March 26, '94. His case was appealed, the judgment affirmed and a commutation of sentences refused him by Gov. Thornton. His hanging was the first legal execution in Eddy County.

Sources:

Santa Fe *Daily New Mexican*, September 20, 1894
The Weekly Eddy *Argus*, September 14, 1894

Chapter 6

Grant County

Charles Williams	August 21, 1880
Louis A. Gaines	August 21, 1880
Richard Remine	March 14, 1881
William Young	March 25, 1881
Pilar Perez	July 6, 1888
Jose Sanchez	July 5, 1901
Lucius C. Hightower	November 10, 1916
Pedro Montes	July 27, 1917
Eleuterio Corral	January 20, 1922
Rumaldo Lozano	January 20, 1922

Louis A. Gaines & Charles Williams

Louis Gaines was a black man who was found guilty of murder in the first degree. Judge Warren Bristol sentenced Gaines to death for the murder of a soldier. Gaines, on the day of the murder, got drunk with a soldier from the ninth cavalry by the name of Johnston. On the road between Silver City and Fort Bayard, the men's conversation had turned into an argument. Gaines mortally wounded Johnson with a knife. The soldier was able to make it back to Fort Bayard, but died after arriving. Sheriff Harvey H. Whitehill had the scaffold built beyond Silver City, in a little draw alongside the road leading to Pinos Altos and Central. Once Louis Gaines stood on the scaffold, he thanked the Sheriff for his kindness and made a political speech on the Sheriff's behalf for re-election.

Executed at the same time was Charles Williams who had been found guilty of murder before Judge Warren Bristol. He had killed a Mexican musician in Georgetown for no reason. When first being lead out of the cell, Williams fought the guards off. It took several men to subdue him. Once the men were able to control Williams, he displayed no further violence towards the guards. Several guards were present to insure Williams did not escape for it had been rumored there would be an attempt to rescue him.

SOME SWINGING.

———

The Knot and the Noose do
Good Work at Silver City

———

How two Murderers Met Death
Without Fear or Pity.

———

Each Man Makes a Speech, but
Neither One Entreats to be
Forgiven.

———

They cease from Earthy Toll,
Shuffle off the Coll,
And go to Heaven.

———

Special Dispatch to the *New Mexican.*
Silver City, August 21. – At length the law in regard to murder has been vindicated in Silver City, by the legal execution of two men, each of whom

had been found, by the regular course and after a fair trial, guilty of that highest offense against society, the unjustifiable taking of a human life. Charles Williams and Louis A. Gaines, two noted criminals, were yesterday taken from the jail in which they had been confined for months, and suffered the penalty of death at the hands of the officers of the law and in accordance with the sentence of the court.

Grant County Sheriff Harvey H. Whitehill, executed Louis A. Gaines and Charles Williams minutes apart on a hot summer day. Photo courtesy Silver City Museum.

Each man had committed his murder depending for escape upon the lax way in which the perpetrators of such offenses have heretofore been dealt with in Grant County, or upon some technicality or accident occurring by which they might do as too many others have done and get off with a trifling punishment. Their crimes were uncalled for and cold blooded, and the people,

TIRED OF SUCH OUTRAGES,

Determined to make examples of them for others of the same ilk and for the benefit of the community. At the last term of court in Grant County the two men were tried and found guilty of the offenses with which they were charged, the details of which have been published. The sentences were passed and application for a warrant of execution sent in to Governor Wallace at Santa Fe. The paper was sent here promptly and the execution took place yesterday afternoon on the flat to the northeast of the city. There was an immense crowd present, and the usual scenes incidental to such occurrences were enacted.

The prisoners were taken from the jail at 2:30 o'clock. They were guarded by sixty armed men, summoned by the sheriff to prevent their escape and to prevent any attempt at rescue which might be made from being successful.

Before leaving the jail, Gaines called up a fellow prisoner and in a somewhat tremulous voice bade him farewell telling him never to kill a fellow creature. Afterwards, however, and before leaving the jail he assumed a careless manner and laughed and joked with the men about him.

ON THE WAY TO THE GALLOWS,

Neither of the men showed any signs of fear of the death that awaited them. Williams was quiet and composed. Arriving on the ground, however, he made a speech in which he said that his identity would ever remain a secret, as Williams was not his real name, but only one of his many aliases.

Gaines also made a rambling speech in which he declared that he had never killed a fellow creature in cold blood. His life had been a very wild one, but he had never been guilty of this crime. On the scaffold were the sheriff, Rev. E. H. Brooks, Father Stagbud, the deputy sheriff (Dan Tucker) and the counsel for the prisoners. The noose was adjusted at twenty-five minutes before four o'clock, both men being perfectly calm, and at exactly twenty minutes to four the drop fell with a dull thud, and Charles Williams and Louie A. Gaines were

USHERED INTO ETERNITY.

Every arrangement was perfect and the men died almost without a struggle, the necks of both being broken immediately. After hanging fourteen minutes Gaines was pronounced dead by the attending physicians, and a minute or so later Williams' heart ceased to beat. The remains were then cut down and taken to the place of burial in the valley east of the scaffold.

About 4,000 people attended the execution, a fair proportion of these being women and children, a good many persons being from adjoining towns and various portions of the Territory. After the execution the crowd dispersed quietly and without excitement. The impression here is that the hanging will have a most salutary effect.

The hanging of Louis A. Gaines and Charles Williams, near Silver City in 1880. Photo courtesy Silver City Museum.

Sources:

Weekly New Mexican, August 23, 1880
Silver City *Independent*, July 9, 1901

Richard Remine

Richard Remine was executed in Silver City on March 14, 1881, for the murder of Patrick Rafferty. Both men were partners in a mining operation near Georgetown. As partners, the two men shared a small, one-room cabin and slept together in the only bed.

In the early morning hours of March 16, 1877, Richard Remine returned to the cabin drunk and found Patrick Rafferty sleeping diagonally across the bed. Remine, angered by the inconsideration of Mr. Rafferty, picked up a single-jack (a type of sledge-hammer used in mining that can be swung by a strong man with one hand) and began striking the victim in the head, face, and chest with the tool. Afterwards he dismembered the body with an axe. The next morning, neighbors found Remine lying passed out asleep in the same bed in which he had killed Rafferty.

Richard Remine was found guilty of first degree murder and sentenced to hang by Judge Warren Bristol. The execution for the murder of March 16, 1877, was delayed over the next four years while the case was reviewed by Governor Wallace and by the New Mexico Territorial Supreme Court. It was the strong opinion of the people of Silver City that Richard Remine would escape the death penalty. Sheriff Whitehill believed the same and employed Remine as a trusty of the jail. Each morning Remine was released from his cell. During the day, Remine would clean the jail and retrieve the meals for the other prisoners. In the evening Richard Remine would gamble and drink in the local Saloons giving little thought of leaving Silver City, or of his murder case being reviewed. Sheriff Whitehill was so relaxed with Richard Remine that on one occasion he verbally reprimanded Remine for returning to the jail after 11:00 p.m. Sheriff Whitehill told Remine that the next time he would be locked out of the jail for it was too much trouble to open the jail at that late of an hour.

It was later rumored why Remine did not flee the area. A woman named Dora Dwenger was held in the jail for her part in the murder of her husband Henry F. Dwenger. Remine supposedly had romantic feeling for Mrs. Dwenger and believed if he waited for her, she would be freed. About a week prior to the execution, Sheriff Whitehill received a telegram from Santa Fe. The message instructed the Sheriff to proceed with the execution of Richard Remine the following Friday for all appeals had been exhausted. When Remine returned from gambling, Sheriff Whitehill locked Remine in his cell and told him of the hour and day of his execution.

Richard Remine remained in his cell until the Sheriff led him to the scaffold. While leading Remine to the scaffold, the Sheriff carried a box of cigars. The Grant County *Herald* dated March 18, 1881, described Richard Remine's demeanor: "The doomed man was remarkably cool, and except for an occasional nervous twitching of the fingers, gave no outward sign of emotion. He was smoking a cigar as he ascended the scaffold, and this he retained in his possession until Father Stagnon was prepared to administer the last rites of the church." Richard Remine told the spectators he hoped that those before him would live a better life than he had. He told the public he had been kindly treated by Sheriff Whitehill and his deputies over the past four years. The Santa Fe *New Mexican* had the following headlines and article.

Richard Remine Hangs at
Silver City for Murder.

BROKE HIS NECK
- - - - - - - -
By a Fall from a Scaffold; which was
The Unhappy Fate of Richard Remine
Yesterday.
- - - - - - - -

Special Dispatch to the *New Mexican.*
Silver City, March 14, 1881.

A large crowd from Silver City and the mining camp and settlements in the neighborhood witnessed the execution of Richard Remine, sentenced to death for murder, this afternoon. This is the third execution by due process of law which has taken place in this town within the last few months, and for some time past it has been a matter of much doubt with the people here whether or not the sentence of the court would be carried out but, as the strongest efforts were made by the doomed man's attorneys to save him.

The Crime.

The crime for which Richard Remine suffered was the murder of an old Irishman, Patrick Rafferty, well known here, and wherever he has lived as being one of the survivors of the Light brigade of the Six Hundred who charged at Balaklava. He was a harmless, inoffensive old man, and very generally liked, consequently when he was murdered at Georgetown, four years ago, the indignation of the people was intense, and the strongest efforts were made to bring his murderer to justice, which were at last successful.

A HARD FOUGHT CASE.

Remine stoutly denied that he had killed Rafferty, and accused one Winterburn of the deed. There can be no doubt, however, that the old man was murdered by Remine in a fit of passion when inflamed by liquor; indeed this was very clearly brought out in the evidence produced at various trials of the case, as well as the fact that Winterburn was not connected with the matter. Still the case was fought to the last. Remine had friends and employed by their assistance the best legal talent in the Territory. The trial of the case has lasted over three years, but it was finally settled at the last term of the Supreme Court in Santa Fe, and an effort by Remine's counsel to take the case up to the United States Supreme Court failed. He made up his mind to die.

TAKING IT COOLLY.

The order for Remine's execution was received by Sheriff Whitehill a few days ago and the prisoner was informed of the day and hour at which he would be able to rank one of the wisest men in this world in a knowledge of the mysteries of the other. He took the matter very coolly, ate with a good appetite and slept soundly every night, employing himself as usual during the day and in general deporting himself about as usual, without exhibiting a trace of fear or nervousness. Once in speaking to an acquaintance who asked him how he felt, he remarked, "Well, its pretty damned rough to have to croak so soon, but a good many better men than I have gone the same road and I guess I can stand it." At another time also he said that he didn't mind dying so much but, "I hate like hell to die letting everybody believe I am a murderer."

THE DROP.

This morning the preparations which had been going on for the hanging were completed and at an early hour in the afternoon the crowd began to gather around the scaffold. Remine was brought out of the jail by the sheriff and conducted to the scaffold which he ascended at 2:40. He displayed great calmness to the last, walking to and upon the scaffold with a firm step and no appearance of trepidation or a tremor. He made no remarks with the exception of a brief statement, which was listened to with the closest attention by those present, to the effect that he had left a letter which would be published in one of the local papers. In this he had asserted his innocence and had ascribed the crime to Winterburn, now dead. His arms were then pinioned by an assistant of the sheriff, the black cap was drawn over his face, and at 2:45 the lever was pulled and the drop fell. The fall broke Remine's neck and he died quietly save a few twitches of the arms and legs, and an involuntary movement of the hands. At 2:55 he was pronounced dead and at 3, the body was cut down and consigned to the grave awaiting it. The whole execution passed off without a bungle, every detail being attended to carefully and skillfully.

Sources:

Grant County *Herald,* March 18, 1881
Daily New Mexican, March 15, 1881

William Young

Henry F. Dwinger was a man whom many believed to have a considerable amount of money, property, and a prosperous mining claim. Dora Dwinger was a young woman who Henry Dwinger married. Many people believed Dora Dwinger had married "Old Man" Dwinger simply for his money. Wanting everything for herself, Dora conspired with William Young and William H. Dwinger, Henry's own son, to murder her husband.

William Young was also known as Parson Young and "Silver Plate Dick." Young had convinced people he had a silver plate covering a fracture in his skull. For his part in the murder, Dora promised him a portion of the property. In July of 1879, William Young asked for Henry Dwinger to accompany him to a prospect hole to inspect some mineral near Santa Rita, New Mexico. Once the two men arrived, William Young directed Henry Dwinger to the hole. While the old man was bent over looking down the prospect hole, his son William came up from behind him and shot his father in the back of the head. Dora Dwinger and the two men then buried the body in a shallow mountain grave.

Several months went by before anyone's suspicion was aroused by the absence of "old man Dwinger." Sheriff Whitehill soon thereafter began investigating the disappearance of Henry Dwinger and picked up Dora and William Dwinger. During questioning neither person could keep to their story and confessed to the murder. The three were lodged in the Grant County jail for trial. The case was tried in Mesilla, Doña Ana County, on a change of venue.

Dora Dwinger was tried in March of 1880. She was found guilty of fifth degree murder and sentenced to ten years in the penitentiary. New Mexico did not have a penitentiary at the time, and therefore she was transported to the Kansas State Prison in Lasing, Kansas. Governor Edmund G. Ross suspended the remainder of her sentence on February 7, 1886 on the condition she did not return to New Mexico until the remainder of her sentenced had expired.

William H. Dwinger went to trial on April 12, 1880. After a three day trial, the jury returned a verdict of guilty of murder in the second degree. Judge Bristol sentenced William Dwinger to life in prison. Like Dora, the Governor suspended the remainder of Williams sentenced on December 18, 1886. William Young next went to trial and was found guilty of murder in the first degree. Judge Bristol selected February 23, 1881, as his execution date. The scheduled day was postponed on a question of William Young's sanity. Young's attorney's never made a motion, or a defense of insanity in District Court. It was further believe the insanity plea for Young was a last resort by the defense to the Governor because the insanity claim was not mentioned in the appeal to the Supreme Court.

Governor Lew Wallace felt the murder was a "deliberately planned and a coolly executed crime, and in the absence of any sufficient evidence showing the insanity of the prisoner," Governor Wallace ordered Sheriff Whitehill, "to take charge of William Young and on March 25, 1881, between 10 a.m. and 3 p.m. hang him by the neck until he is dead." The Santa Fe *Daily New Mexican* had the following headlines and story.

YOUNG'S YOKE

_____

Which Happened to be Made of Hemp,
Strangled Him.

_____

Special Dispatch to the *New Mexican*.

Silver City, March 25. The hanging of William Young for the murder of H. F. Dwinger, took place in the jail yard this morning. The doomed man was quite cool when he ascended the scaffold, but displayed some emotion just before the hanging took place, requesting the sheriff to

LET HIM DOWN EASY,

And not drop him "like a beef steer." The execution was unmarked by any unusual incident. A large crowd was in attendance, and the best order prevailed. The drop fell a few minutes before two o'clock, and Young's death must have been almost instantaneous, as his neck was broken by the fall.

THE BODY REMAINED HANGING

About fifteen minutes when it was cut down and a post mortem examination had by Dr. Wood. The skull was found to be of unusual thickness, but there was no silver plate, such as Young claimed had at one time been inserted, found. This is the fourth legal execution that has taken place in Silver City within the past ten months.

Sources:

Grant County *Herald*, March 19,1881
Santa Fe *Daily New Mexican*, March 26, 1881
Silver City *Independent*, July 9, 1901

Pilar Perez

Thomas Hall was a Deputy Sheriff for Grant County and commissioned as a Deputy U.S. Marshal for the territory. Deputy Hall was married, father of five children and lived in the small village of Pinos Altos.

On Tuesday, March 16, 1886, Deputy Hall had been notified to look for a group of Mexicans who had shot and killed Aguilar Santiago, who had attempted to stop the abduction of a fifteen year old girl, Reyes Alverez, the previous week. When not finding the party, Deputy Hall decided to return to Silver City. A short distance from Silver City on the Pinos Altos road, Deputy Hall rode up onto the party of Mexicans with the abducted girl. Not wanting to alert the group he was a law officer or suspecting them as the wanted party, Deputy Hall engaged in small talk. One of the Mexicans, Pilar Perez pulled back from the group. While Deputy Hall was in front, Perez shot him in the back and right arm.

A passing team found Deputy Hall weak but still alive at 10:00 o'clock that night and carried him into town. Sheriff Woods and Doctor Slough urged Deputy Hall to tell them who had shot him for he was bound to die. All Deputy Hall could tell them was that he had been shot by a Mexican, but he could not provide his name. Deputy Hall did expire at 2:00 o'clock on the morning of March 17, 1888. His horse arrived later in town still saddled and bridled. The paper described Deputy Hall as a brave and valiant officer.

The Las Vegas *Daily Optic* told the entire story, including the capture and execution of Pilar Perez.

Las Vegas *Daily Optic*, Monday, July 9, 1888

PILAR PEREZ PAYS THE PENALTY

The Murderer of Thomas Hall Expiates
His Crime on the Scaffold
Last Friday.

The condemned man passed his last night as though he had a long life still before him. He slept well, ate a hearty breakfast, and when asked by Sheriff Laird at 9 o'clock whether there was anything he wanted, replied, "No, I have had plenty." He confessed to Father Girard on Wednesday and on Thursday received the sacrament.

He seemed to have lost none of his bravado style notwithstanding his religious professions. The evening previous a woman peddling candy and fruits called at his cell and inquired as to whether he wanted any fruits or candy. He replied that if she would call for her money to-day after four o'clock that he would make some purchases merely to patronize her.

He seemed the least concerned of any person about the jail, except, possibly, the darky Wilson, who pulled the rope that let the fatal drop fall. Wilson felt honored to be allowed to pull the rope and would not have missed the opportunity to thus distinguish himself for many dollars.

Sheriff Laird gave the signal by dropping a handkerchief at 9:58, and Wilson, who was enclosed in a box out of sight of the spectators, pulled the rope. The drop was nearly seven feet. Pilar's neck was broken in the fall. Thus the law is vindicated and the death of Thomas Hall is avenged by the hanging of one of the most desperate young murderers ever known in the southwest. There was one thing remarkable about the spectators present, not a single expression of sympathy was manifest for the condemned man during the breathless moments preceding the hanging. It was evident that the murderer had no real friends among the spectators.

Grant County Sheriff Andrew Laird executed Pilar Perez for the murder of Deputy Sheriff and Deputy U.S. Marshal Thomas Hall.

The detailed history of the murder of Deputy Sheriff Hall two years ago by Pilar Perez, has been published so often of late in connection with the trial and sentence, that no extensive account will be given here.

Pilar and his sweetheart were coming to Silver City, on the Pinos Altos road, when they were overtaken by Hall. Pilar and other Mexicans had engaged in a fatal shooting affray on the Mimbres River because of the abduction or elopement of the girl. The officer had been notified and had gone on a trip to intercept the shooting party. Not finding them he was returning to Silver City, and was just above town when he encountered Pilar and the girl and rode along with them a short distance. He was probably recognized by the fugitive, but did not know Pilar, who watched for an opportunity and shot the officer in the back, fatally. The murderer fled to Socorro, then to Albuquerque, next to Arizona. The girl, who came to the city, had promptly told who did the killing. For nearly two years Pilar was at large. Sheriff Laird had been given a pointer and employed a colored acquaintance of the murderer to shadow the fugitive. When Pilar went into Flagstaff one day from a sheep ranch where he was employed he met the colored man and recognized him. The frightened fellow had saved $100 and concluded to use it in fleeing to California. However, the colored man gave a deputy sheriff proper information. It was arranged to invite Pilar to a baile and while he was there his capture was easily effected. While in jail at Flagstaff, he acknowledged the killing, saying that Hall shot twice at him. This was easily disproved by the condition of Hall's revolver when found and the testimony of the Mexican maiden. However, the accused has stuck to his story and accused the girl of falsehood. At the last term of court the trial took place, there was practically no defense, and in a few minutes a verdict was given that sealed his doom.

He claimed that instead of abducting the girl he had won her away by love. Pilar was only about twenty-seven years of age, rather short of stature, but fairly good looking and by no means stupid. He joked with the other prisoners, said he would return in spirit to see them hung, and remarked that as a man was not born to live always he had as well die one day as another. He jocularly said he wanted to go to hell on a black horse.

Several days ago carpenters erected a scaffold on the north side of the court house and built around it a high board fence reaching such a height that people on the hill tops and neighboring houses could not see anyone upon the scaffold. About 60 tickets of admission to the enclosure or the offices commanding a view were issued.

Sources:

Santa Fe *Daily New Mexican*, March 18, 1886
Las Vegas *Daily Optic*, July 9, 1888
Silver City *Enterprise*, July 6, 1888

Jose Sanchez

Jose Sanchez was from Parrel, Mexico, un-married and 28 years old when executed on the Courthouse grounds in Silver City on July 5th, 1901. He was convicted in Judge F. W. Parker's court, of shooting Catrino Alemandarez, (also spelled Alamandarez) three times. Alemandarez identified Jose Sanchez and made a dying declaration to that affect before he passed away. Jose Sanchez had been seen in the area of the shooting and admitted he had been in the area a mile or so beyond Santa Rita on the Georgetown road looking for items stolen form his camp. The day of the theft, Sanchez had argued with and accused Alemandarez of stealing his blankets.

Although he had testified in his own defense, the jury was not swayed by Sanchez's testimony. They returned a verdict of guilty of murder in the first degree in less than thirty minutes. After the verdict, Jose laughed and joked with the officers. The paper described Jose Sanchez as, "evidently of a low type of intelligence and has but small appreciation of the enormity of his crime or the doom which awaits him." Judge Parker had sentenced Jose Sanchez to die on the gallows on June 7th along with 17-year-old Andres Calles, but he was given a temporary reprieve so physicians could examine his sanity. People who knew Jose Sanchez called him "Loco Joe" and he was described as having, "a fierce and violent temper and would break upon the slightest provocation."

Judge Parker passed the following sentence upon Jose Sanchez.

Judge Parker: "You have been tried and convicted of murder in the first degree; have you anything to say to the court why judgment and sentence of the court should not be passed upon you?"

Sanchez: "All I have got to say is that crime which has been raised against me is unjust, and I can swear that nobody saw me and I did not do it. They can do all they please with me."

Judge Parker: "You have also been convicted of the highest crime known to the law; what I said to Andres Calles applies to yourself. I have taken some pains to inquire into your history as much as I could. You have been what is known as a tramp; you have wondered about place to place, stealing everything that you could get your hands upon, so I am informed. It is the same story, beginning with small crimes, people end with large ones, and you find when the end comes people are either imprisoned for life or hanged.

"It is a sad duty which the court is compelled to perform in being the instrument whereby the life of a human being is taken. It seems, however, to be necessary in your case. This penalty is not entirely by way of punishment to you. In the wisdom of the legislative department of the government they have provided this punishment as a solemn warning to others who are inclined to commit this kind of a crime.

"If you are of a religious faith it would be well for you to atone as much as possible by repentance and confession to your spiritual advisor, and thus prepare yourself for the end as well as you can, if at all, as much as the limited time will permit."

Drawing of Jose Sanchez that was published in the Silver City Independent *on July 9th, 1901.*

"The judgment and sentence of the court is that you be remanded to the custody of the sheriff of this county, and be confined by him safely in the common jail of this county until the 7th day of June, 1901; that on said day, between the hours of 10 o'clock in the forenoon and 4 o'clock in the afternoon on said day, in an enclosure to be erected by the sheriff on the court house grounds in the town of Silver City, Grant County, New Mexico, you be then and there by said sheriff hanged by the neck until you are dead, and may God have mercy upon your soul."

The Silver City *Independent* had the following headlines and story.

Silver City *Independent,* July 9th, 1901

Sanchez Dropped
Into Eternity

———

A Successful Execution by Sheriff Goodell – The Condemned
Man Made No Statement – Died Repeating a Prayer –
The Story of the Crime and Conviction.

———

The first legal execution in Grant county in fifteen years to a month took place Friday in the court house yard in this city.

The man who thus suffered the severest penalty which the law could inflict was Jose Sanchez, a Mexican who on the 26th day of December, 1900, shot and killed a fellow Mexican named Catarino Alemandarez near the mining camp of Santa Rita in this county.

He met death calmly and was probably the most unconcerned man present. The drop fell at exactly 12:08. His neck was broken by the fall. At 11:45 Sheriff Goodell read the death warrant to the condemned. It was interpreted by officer Perfecto Rodriguez to Sanchez, who received it in a stolid manner.

It was 11:58 o'clock when the prisoner was taken from his cell and the solemn march to the gallows commenced. He was accompanied by his spiritual adviser, Father Morin, who walked alongside whispering word of comfort, and Sheriff Goodell and deputies. It was only a few feet to the gallows, which Sanchez mounted firmly. He made no statement. Immediately after he had reached the platform and stepped upon the trap, his legs and arms were firmly pinioned by the officers and the black cap adjusted. A moment more and the signal was given which sprung the trap.

Sanchez dropped suddenly down into space to the length of the five and one half foot rope. There were a few convulsive movements of the body and limbs and all was over. He was left hanging until life was pronounced extinct by the county physician. The body was cut down at 12:15. As soon as the remains were cut down they were taken in charge by W. S. Cox for interment in the county plot.

Sanchez laid down on his hard bunk in his steel cell about nine o'clock Thursday evening, but for the first time since he has been an inmate of the county jail, did not rest well. He tossed about and exhibited other symptoms of nervousness until about two o'clock this morning, after which hour he became more quite, but continued to wake at frequent intervals until daylight, when he arose and put on his clothes.

He breakfasted at eight o'clock Friday morning and his impending death did not in the least interfere with his desire for good things to eat. He gave the subject of his last meal on earth considerable thought, and when Sheriff Goodell sent for his order he asked for beefsteak smothered in onions, ham and eggs, potatoes and several other articles of diet. These were all furnished and after they had been handed into his cell, Sanchez partook heartily and seemed to thoroughly enjoy the meal.

An Independent reporter went in to give Sanchez goodbye, while he was breakfasting. He was cheerful in his greeting, but was nervous. He asked concerning his attorney and said that he had done everything that he could to help him out of his trouble and was sorry that he had not succeeded in saving him. He also expressed a request to see Ex-county School Superintendent, B. T. Link, of whom he seemed to be attached, but when told that Mr. Link was out in the country and would probably not be able to be present, was perfectly satisfied.

At ten o'clock Sanchez dressed himself for the grave. He was furnished a neat black suit by Sheriff Goodell, with all the necessary adjuncts and these clothes he put on with considerable pride. The shirt worn was negligee in order that the collar would not interfere with the proper working of the knot.

It was not until Wednesday afternoon that Sanchez was informed that all hope was gone. The unpleasant duty of telling the condemned man that his doom was only a comparatively few hours distant devolved upon Father Morin of the Catholic church; and that kind hearted priest broke the news and gently as possible. Sanchez, however, manifested no emotion and his spirit did not appear to be in the least depressed. He talked and chatted with the priest upon subjects foreign to himself in the most complacent manner possible and among other things mentioned the fact that the next day would be the fourth of July; that it was not likely that he would be allowed to leave his cell on that day. Up to the morning of his death he continued to sleep soundly and eat heartily and exhibited no evidence of fear. He was a good deal of a gormandizer and greatly appreciated the delicacies which Sheriff Goodell kindly furnished him.

He did not for an instant appear to appreciate the fate which awaited him, or if he did he certainly gave no manifestation of his feeling. He at one time expressed a wish to have the hanging over with in order that he might "get out into the country." Whether this was intended as an effort to demonstrate his insanity, or whether it was an utter ignorance of what hanging meant will never be known. From his conversation at times, it would almost seem that he did not know what death was.

The Story of the Crime

The crime for which Jose Sanchez paid the penalty with his life was the murder of Catarino Alamendarez on the Georgetown road near Santa Rita;

this county, on the 26th day of December, 1900. The testimony produced by the territory at the trial of Sanchez at the April term of the Grant County District Court was so clear and convincing that the jury lost no time in returning a verdict of murder in the first degree.

The evidence was to the affect that the camp of Sanchez had been robbed the night before of a small quantity of provisions and some articles of wearing apparel. Sanchez was in a very bad humor over the affair and appealed to the precinct officer to aid him in finding the guilty party. A search warrant was issued by the justice of the peace, and careful investigation made, but no trace of the missing articles could be found. Sanchez then started out on his own account. He overtook Alamendarez on the morning of the 26th of December, and whether suspecting him of the robbery or not, shot him down in cold blood.

A short time after the shooting, parties driving along the road found Alamendarez in a dying condition and went to Santa Rita to notify the authorities. When found Alamandarez had described his assailant and Sanchez had also been seen in the immediate vicinity. Deputy Sheriff Edwards, from the description obtained from Alemandarez, arrested Sanchez and locked him up. Later in the day Sanchez was taken before the dying man and positively identified as the guilty one, the statement of Alemandarez being placed in the form of a dying declaration; and it was largely upon this, his positive statement and identification, as admitted in evidence at the trial, that Sanchez was convicted.

Sources:

Silver City *Independent,* July 9, 1901
Santa Fe *New Mexican,* July 5, 1901
Albuquerque *Daily Citizen*, May 1, 11 and 24, 1901

Lucius C. Hightower

Lucius and Hallie Hightower along with two of their children left Colorado City, Texas for New Mexico. Lucius Hightower settled in the Mining community of Tyrone, 14 miles southwest of Silver City, after gaining employment as a teamster. Fifty-year-old Lucius Hightower was described as a tall man, 200 pounds, with iron gray hair, beard, mustache, blue eyes, and a sharp pointed nose. Over the previous twenty-four years he had been married to Hallie Hightower, and five children were born into the family. Their marriage was not always a happy one because Lucius drank alcohol to excess, which was the case on September 30, 1915.

On that night, Mrs. William Bailey was cooking dinner on a stove outside in the yard, when she observed Lucius approaching his home drunk. Seeing his angry demeanor, she left the outside stove and returned to her tent home. Once Lucius entered his home, words were immediately exchanged between Hallie and Lucius. After supper, Lucius asked Hallie to join him in their bed, but she quickly refused. Lucius made the comment to Hallie that if they kept fighting he would kill himself. Hallie responded back by telling Lucius, "I'll go get Bailey's Winchester and kill you, saving you the trouble of doing it." Hallie then turned as if to walk toward the front door. Lucius yelled for her to stop and upon her refusing to do so, Lucius jumped up out of bed, grabbed his shotgun from the bedroom and went after her.

Hallie ran twenty yards to the Bailey tent, entering it and crying out "save me, oh save me." At this same moment, Lucius entered the tent home with the shotgun raised. Mrs. Bailey attempted to shield Hallie from her husband by pushing her to the side of a bed. One of the Hightower children had followed their mother into the tent. Mrs. Bailey picked up the child and ran out of the room into another portion of the tent. Lucius Hightower fired the weapon striking Hallie in the left side with the full charge of the shotgun (the child was not hit). Lucius said outloud, "I now kill myself" and walked out of the tent. A second shotgun blast followed seconds later and all believed Lucius had commented suicide. He had not. A few minutes later, Lucius returned to his wife and the couple kissed. Lucius then left his wife and fled into the hills with the shotgun.

Officers from Tyrone telephoned the Grant County Sheriff about the shooting. Hallie Hightower was removed to the mining camp hospital and died two hours later. Officers, not finding Lucius, guarded the house and corral where his horses were. Three hours later, officers saw Lucius approaching his home carrying the shotgun. Sheriff's deputies ordered him to throw up his hands and drop the shotgun. Lucius told the officers after his arrest that if he had additional shotgun shells they would not have taken him without a fight. When asked about the second shot fired after he left his wife, Lucius said he fired the shotgun at himself but missed. Lucius Hightower was taken before Justice of the Peace, Judge George Lawson. He was arraigned on the charge of the murder. In answering to the charge, Lucius said, "I'm guilty." Judge Lawson ordered him held in the Grant County jail without bond to await action by the Grand Jury.

The Grand Jury indicted Lucius Hightower for murder in the first degree, and trial was scheduled for Monday, March 20, 1916. Judge Colin Neblett presided over the trial. During the trial, Lucius was the only witness in his defense. On the stand, Lucius denied that he had been drunk when he shot his wife. He told the jury the shooting was accidental for he believed the shotgun was unloaded. On the night of March 21st at 9:30 the jury retired for deliberation. Twenty-two minutes later the jury returned with a verdict of guilty of murder in the first degree.

On April 6th, Lucius Hightower was brought before Judge Neblett for sentencing. The judge asked Lucius if he had anything to say before sentence was passed. Lucius stood and said, "I've got something to say, but I don't know as I ought to say it at this time. Well, all I've got to say is that I'm not guilty of the crime as charged." Judge Neblett responded by telling Lucius, "You have been tried in a fair and impartial manner and found guilty by a jury of your fellow man and it becomes the painful duty of the court to carry out the sentence imposed by the decree of the jury. The judgment and sentence of the court is that you be remanded to the custody of the sheriff of Grant county, New Mexico, and that you be by him safely kept in the common jail of said county of Grant until Friday, the 5th day of May, 1916; that on said day, between the hours of 6 o'clock in the forenoon and 6 o'clock in the afternoon of said day, in an enclosure to be erected by said sheriff on the court house grounds in the town of Silver City, the county seat of said Grant County and state of New Mexico, you be then and there by said sheriff of said county of Grant, hanged by the neck until you are dead and may God have mercy on your soul."

Sheriff McGrath immediately started construction of the gallows for the double hanging of Lucius Hightower and Pedro Montez, also sentenced to hang for murder. Sheriff McGrath built the gallows between the mess hall and the courthouse off the north door of the jail. The county still possessed the trap used for the execution of Pedro Sanchez on July 5, 1901. The Sheriff said he intended to test the trap and if it was still in working order he would reuse the old trap for the double execution. Two days before the execution, an appeal was made to the Supreme Court which acted as a stay for 120 days. The Supreme Court affirmed the sentence and rescheduled the execution to take place on May 10th.

On the morning of May 10th, Lucius Hightower was awakened at 6 o'clock in the morning for breakfast. According to one account, he ate a large breakfast and took his time smoking a fine cigar. At 6:59, Sheriff McGrath told Lucius his time had come. Lucius shook hands with the sheriff and deputies. He then handed Sheriff McGrath letters he had hand written for his children. Lucius asked the sheriff to deliver the letters to his children who were living with Hallie's parents. Deputies then bound his arms and escorted him out of the cell and into the courtyard. Rev. Henry Heitz of the Catholic Church followed Lucius to the gallows as his spiritual advisor. Without any signs of nervousness, Lucius mounted the steps and was placed over the trap. While his legs were being bound, Sheriff McGrath asked Lucius if he had any final words. Lucius told the twenty witnesses he forgave all who had convicted him and were responsible for his hanging. At the conclusion of his statement, the noose was placed around the neck. After the black cap was in place, the trap was released at 7:15. The Silver City *Enterprise* headlines described what happened next.

HIGHTOWER HUNG
THIS MORNING

HEAD COMPLETELY SEVERED
FROM BODY.

By Force of Fall – gruesome Sight
Witnessed By Dozen Spectators

With the head completely severed from the body, by the force of the drop, Lucius C. Hightower this morning at 6:59 paid the penalty for the murder of his wife, by his own life when he was legally executed in the jail yard at the Grant County court house. Sheriff H. J. McGrath sprung the trap promptly at one minute before seven o'clock. The body shot downward with such great force, that the body was completely severed and the headless trunk fell to the ground below.

The sight was a horrible one and sickened those who were witnesses of the execution. No medical examination was necessary and the two physicians present left the scaffold enclosure with the other witnesses after the body had been stretched and covered over.

Hightower spent a restless night and although a nice breakfast had been prepared for him at the jail kitchen he did not eat anything, but drank a cup of coffee. The march to the scaffold began a few minutes before 7 o'clock. Hightower was dressed in a brown coat and overalls. A small flower adorned the buttonhole of his coat. The little procession was headed by Father Heitz of the Church of St. Vincent de Paul. Behind him walked Hightower flanked on either side by a deputy sheriff. Behind walked Sheriff McGrath. Hightower's hands were tied to his sides.

As he passed out of the jail door, Hightower spoke to some of the jail attendants, saying, "Good-bye, boys." They repeated "good-bye." After ascending the scaffold no time was lost in tying the knees and feet of Hightower. Sheriff McGrath then asked the condemned man if he had anything to say. Hightower answered in a strained voice: "Nothing, except that I want you all to know that I forgive you all. I have made peace with my maker and have no fear of the hereafter. And I want to tell you all that if you want to be happy in this world you must stay clear of all evil and live a Christian life. That's all."

The sheriff then placed the noose over the doomed man's head, while Chief Deputy Stancel adjusted the black cap. Immediately after the sheriff pulled the trigger that controlled the trap. There was no noise and all was over before the spectators had realized it. The body shot downward like a bullet and the rope seemed hardly to tighten. This was due to the severing of the head from the body. The remains were turned over to Cox undertaking establishment for burial.

An interesting feature of the execution was the presence among the spectators of the condemned man's father-in-law, J. D. Aiken, of Cliff, who came in to witness the execution of his daughter's murderer. After the trap had been sprung, and the witnesses stood about the body, Mr. Aiker turned to an Enterprise representative and said: "That is just as I would have it. This act of the law has relieved me of a cloud of responsibility which seemed to demand that I avenge my daughter's death."

The remains were buried in a potter's field in Silver City after no one claimed the corpse.

Sources:

Silver City *Enterprise*, March 24, 28; April 14; November 10, 1916
Albuquerque *Morning Journal*, November 12, 1916
Santa Fe *New Mexican*, November 13, 1916

Pedro Montes

Pedro Montes was a twenty-two-year old man who fell in love with sixteen-year-old Rufina Villaneuva. Pedro asked Rufina to marry him, but Rufina's family objected to her accepting the proposal. They believed Pedro did not have the means to support her and that she could find a better suitor.

On the evening of January 7, 1916, Rufina Villaneuva was walking along Pinos Altos Street in Silver City with her friend Josefa McKin. At 5:00 p.m., the two girls were walking past the home of Mrs. Lettie B. Morrill at 209 Pinos Altos when Pedro Montes arrived on horseback. Without warning, Pedro drew a .32 caliber pistol and fired the weapon at Rufina. The bullet struck the top of the right side of her head. Rufina fell to her knees and clasped her hands together as if she was praying. While in this position, Pedro fired a second bullet. The bullet severed the fingers of her right hand and the projectile struck her in the head near the first wound.

Pedro turned his horse and gallop towards the courthouse and surrendered to jailer Ventura Bencoma, saying he just shot a girl. Rufina was rushed to the hospital but died two days later. Charged with murder, the case was called before Judge Neblett on March 22. District Attorney James S. Vaught began the prosecution at 3:00 p.m. after the jury had been selected. Pedro did not testify in his own defense and his attorney, Mr. R. R. Ryan did not call any witnesses. At the conclusion of closing remarks the jury went into deliberation at 8:40 p.m. They rendered the verdict of guilty of Murder in the first degree 10 minutes later.

Pedro Montes was executed for the murder of a 16 year old girl whose family objected to his marriage proposal to her. Photo courtesy of the New Mexico State Records and Archives, Neg. 627 USJ.

On April 6th, Judge Neblett called for the Sheriff to bring both Lucius Hightower, who was awaiting sentencing, and Pedro Montes before him to be sentenced. Judge Neblett sentenced both men to hang by the neck until dead on Friday, May 5th, 1916. Two days prior to the execution, an appeal was made on behalf of both men to the Supreme Court. The Supreme Court affirmed the lower courts decision and reset the execution to take place on July 27, 1917.

Four days prior to the execution, Sheriff McGrath returned Pedro Montes to Silver City from the Penitentiary in Santa Fe. While awaiting his execution in the death cell, Pedro was visited by family and friends. A friend asked Pedro if "he was ready?" Pedro answered, "Yes, I am ready and am not afraid. I am no coward. I know when I am going to die and you don't." On July 27th, Pedro Montes was awakened at 5 o'clock in the morning for breakfast. Pedro refused to eat his last meal and asked only for coffee. His spiritual adviser, Rev. Father Henry Heitz remained with the condemned man up until the execution.

The same scaffold and trap were used to execute both Lucius Hightower and Pedro Montes. The rope used to execute Montes was the same rope that had decapitated Hightower, and had been used for six executions in Deming, New Mexico, earlier that month. At 5: 40 in the morning the trap was sprung dropping the body six feet through the opening and breaking the neck. After hanging for fifteen minutes, County Physician E. W. Hooper pronounced the body dead. The Silver City *Enterprise* printed the following story and headlines.

MONTES IS HANGED
FOR GIRL'S MURDER

———

Answers for Killing of His Sweetheart in January

———

Walks Calmly to Fate

———

Trap is Sprung at 5:40 and Death was
Instantaneous According to Physi-
Cians – Body Cut Down Fif-
Teen Minutes Later and
Given to Friends for
Burial – Story of
Crime

——

Pedro Montes was hanged at 5:40 this morning. Convicted before a jury of his peers of the killing of Rufina Villanueva, the evidence reviewed and the sentence of the lower court affirmed by the Supreme Court of the state, examined by physicians and declared sane, Pedro Montes expiated his crime by death upon the scaffold.

An awesome silence was the most significant feature of the execution. Silence hung over the court house and the jail like a cloud. The guards and officers scarcely spoke and then in whispers. The witnesses and representatives of the press were silent. The heat was oppressive. The silence was finally broken by the sheriff reading the condemned man the executive order for his execution. Montes seemed unconcerned, the sobs could be heard from near relatives who had spent the last hours in silence with him.

The procession to the scaffold began at 5;30. Sheriff McGrath led the way followed by the prisoner. Then came Father Henry Heitz, his spiritual adviser, and several deputy sheriffs. In silence they passed through the corridors of the jail and out the north door of the building where the scaffold had been erected. It was enclosed by a high board fence. Members of the jury and spectators occupied the space between the scaffold and the jail building. The clatter of footsteps on the bare planks of the stairway leading up to the scaffold was the only sound. Montes walked as steadily and firmly as any one in the group. His head was held erect. Reaching the top the doomed man was guided by a touch of the sheriff's hand to the exact center of the trap door. His legs were tied together and his hands tied firmly to his sides. Montes watched this silent operation with apparent interest. The blindfolding came next and without a sound Montes took his last glimpse of the sun which was flooding the entire scene with golden light. The noose was carefully adjusted with the peculiar tie which is known as the hangman's knot squarely under the ear. The black cap was firmly pulled over the condemned man's head and almost instantly and without any warning sound the lever was pulled and Pedro Montes shot into eternity.

Pedro Montes had paid with his life the penalty of the law for the crime he had committed. There were a few convulsive movements of the body as it whirled round and round. The spectators moved silently but quickly out of the enclosure.

THE SCAFFOLD

The scaffold used for the execution was the same as that upon which Hightower paid the penalty. It consists of a platform containing the trap, with an enclosed space below and above a solid piece of timber to which the rope is affixed. The trap door is about 3 by 4 feet in size and is placed so that it reaches from the edge to a point well past the center of the platform. The mechanism by which its easy and sure operation is secured is simple. The trap door is held in place by a piece of timber set at an angel after the fashion of a brace. This piece of timber id hinged in the center. A sudden pressure on the joint thus formed, which is given by means of a stout wire running around the pulley and up to the platform above, breaks the joint and the weight of the person above only accelerates the opening of the door. Its action is positive.

The rope used is a very strong one made of the purest manilla. It is so tied that the jerk is not a direct one but is combined with a side thrust due to the pressure of the large knot upon the victim's jaw. This twist dislocates the spinal vertebra and causes instant death, painless death.

Brought Here Tuesday

Montes was brought from the penitentiary at Santa Fe on Tuesday and lodged in the county jail. Owing to the fact that there had been rumors of various kinds floating around every precaution was taken to guard the condemned man from any attempt at a rescue. His food was carefully supervised and all visitors kept at a distance of several feet. Five men were used in relays as the guard was maintained day and night.

Montes had very little to say to his guards or to relatives who visited him. From the time of his return to Silver City he seemed to have given up all hope of a reprieve or a commutation of the death sentence. He slept very little and ate very sparingly of the generous meals provided by the sheriff.

Rev. Father Heitz, his spiritual advisor, spent a considerable amount of time with him in his cell every day since his return from Santa Fe. The ministrations of the parish priest had more effect than anything else upon the boy and were evidently appreciated by him.

The Crime

The crime for which Montes paid the extreme penalty was the killing of his sweetheart, Rufina Villanueva, who was only sixteen years old. The tragedy took place near the corner of Broadway and Pinos Altos streets on Friday, January 7, 1916. The lovers met at that point. Montes was riding a horse, the girl was on foot. What happened was never made clear but Montes drew a .32 caliber revolver and fired twice, both bullets taking effect on the side of the girl's head. She fell and he rode directly to the court house where he surrendered to the officers saying that he "had just shot a girl." He was placed in a cell and in the meantime officers and others who heard the shots rushed to the scene and had the wounded girl taken to the home of her sister, Mrs. Eduardo Montes. She lingered until Sunday night at midnight although no hopes were entertained of her recovery.

Reports circulated at the time of the crime were to the effect that the girl had rejected the attention of the young man because of the opposition of relatives and another report was to the effect that Montes was not considered eligible because of his lack of means. Color was lent to this fact that one of the two horses which Montes owned and upon which he partially relied for a livelihood had died, leaving him but one horse. In any event the attention of the suitor had become so distasteful that the girl was about to go to the country in a visit to friends to avoid him, when the tragedy occurred.

Montes came to trial before the District Court and was convicted of murder in the first degree. He was sentenced to hang but an appeal to the Supreme Court acted as a stay of execution until the case could be heard. The Supreme Court after reviewing the evidence affirmed the sentence of the lower court and June 29 was set as the date upon which the death sentence should be carried out. Sheriff McGrath had gone to Santa Fe to bring Montes back to Silver City when Governor Lindsay issued an order postponing the execution for 30 days in order that the condemned man's sanity might be passed upon by experts. This was the first time that any question of the sanity of the man had been raised. The report of the physicians was to the effect that Montes was sane and responsible for his actions.

New Mexico State Penitentiary.

DESCRIPTION OF CONVICT.

No. CJ 627   Name Pedro Montes

County received from Grant   Date of receipt April 10th 1917

Sentence Safekeeping   Date of Sentence

Crime Murder 1st Degree   Plea at trial

Sex *Male*   Age *20*   Build *Slender*,

Nationality *Mexican*   Where born *Silver City N. M.*

In New Mexico *20* years.   In United States *20* years.

Previous convictions *No*

In other prisons *No*

Trade or occupation *Laborer*   Religious instruction *Catholic*

Habits   Read *Yes*   Write *Yes*   Education *16-1*

Smoke *Yes*   Chew *Yes*   Liquor *Yes*   Drugs *No*

Married or single   Children

Parents *mother*   Conjugal

Father born in *Mexico*   Mother born in *Mexico*

Relatives *Mrs Felicita Leyba, Silver City N. M. brother*

Height 5 ft. 4½   Weight 108   Hair Black   Eyes Brown

Complexion Dark   Bust 34-   Waist 31   Thigh 16

Neck 13½   Hat 6¾   Shoes 6   Teeth Good

Marks on body

Cut so center forehead - Vac so lt upper arm outer - Cut on rt leg front - Third finger rt hand stiff at 1st joint.

From the State Penitentiary files, description of Pedro Montes at the time of his hanging. Note "Nationality: Mexican", "Where born: Silver City, N.M."

Sources:

Silver City *Enterprise*, March 24, 28; April 14, 1916; July 27, 31, 1917

Rumaldo Lozano & Eleuterio Corral

Eleuterio Corral and Rumaldo Lozano were confined together in a cell at the Grant County jail in Silver City, New Mexico.

Eleuterio's parents had recently moved to Santa Rita from the mining town of Mogollon. Listed as being 16 years old, he had been sentenced to a reform school for robbery of an elderly Mexican man.

Rumaldo Lozano was originally from Mexico and had arrived at Santa Rita a few months earlier. Rumaldo was said by relatives to be 17 years old. After finding work as a dishwasher in Santa Rita, he was arrested for attempted larceny. Found guilty of the attempted larceny, he was ordered to serve a 30 day jail sentence. By April 2, 1921, Rumaldo had served half of his sentence.

Sixty-year-old Ventura Bencoma had been a jailer for the Sheriff's office for twelve years. For over a week, Jailer Bencoma had been sick with the flu. In the early morning hours of April 2nd, he went to lie down on his cot in the jail to get some sleep. While asleep, Eleuterio and Rumaldo were able to escape from their cell and into the corridor. An empty cell had been used to store both wood and coal. Inside the cell was an axe for splitting the wood. The young men retrieved the axe and quietly snuck up on the sleeping jailer. Without warning, the jailer was struck with a full blow to the head with the axe head. The jailer's keys, cartridges and pistol were removed from the dying man.

The other prisoners were threatened with the pistol to remain quiet or they would be shot. With the keys taken from the jailer, the young men attempted for several minutes, without success, to unlock Jesus Rocha's cell door. The attempt was given up, and both men escaped into the darkness after unlocking the back door of the jail.

Once the prisoners escaped into the darkness, a female inmate named Ruby Bradshaw screamed out for help for the Sheriff who was asleep in his quarters on the second floor. Sheriff Casey rushed downstairs to investigate the disturbance and found his jailer's head split open, and that two prisoners gone. While Jailer Bencoma was being transported to the hospital, the Sheriff organized a posse of men. At 5 o'clock in the morning, the manhunt changed from capturing two jail escapees to capturing two murderers, when Jailer Bencoma died of his wound.

The Sheriff's efforts in finding the two young murderers failed for the first three days. Then on April 4th, a transient reported to the Sheriff that he had seen both men and described the clothing they were wearing. On the morning of April 5th, a boy walking along the railroad tracks told the Sheriff, a person matching Eleuterio Corral had asked him some questions. Officers soon turned their efforts to searching the numerous mineshafts, prospect holes and tunnels in the nearby hills of Fierro, located about two miles from

Hanover. In a mining tunnel, Rumaldo Lazano was discovered and captured unarmed. The other posse members moved in closer to the other shafts in search for Eleuterio Corral.

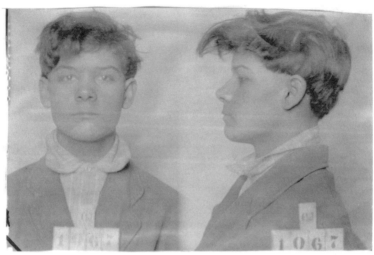

Three physicians told Governor Mechum that Eleuterio Corral had passed his 19th birthday. Family members and prison records list his age as 16. Photo courtesy of the New Mexico State Records and Archives, Neg. 1067 CJ.

Rumaldo Lozano claimed to be 17 years old. He was executed on January 20, 1922, just minutes after Eleuterio Corral. Courtesy of the New Mexico State Records and Arhcives, Neg. 1068 CJ.

Deputy John Parrot was approaching a mineshaft when several bullets were fired at him. The deputy returned fire, using his Winchester rifle, at Eleuterio who was shooting the pistol from within the edge of the opening. The rifle shots attracted the other posse members who centered on the shaft. Eleuterio ran from the hole to a shack and closed the door. The posse quickly surrounded the shack. After Eleuterio refused to come out and surrender, Sheriff Casey kicked the door open and captured him without any further resistance. Eleuterio told the sheriff he was not afraid of death or any man.

Both Eleuterio and Rumaldo bragged outloud of their escape and short freedom. Both men told Sheriff Casey it was Jesus Rocha who planned the escape and was to have joined them. Sheriff Casey learned from the two that after Jailer Bencoma's keys and pistol were removed, they were to unlock the steel cell door to Jesus Rocha. Once he was released, the three were to go up to the second floor where Sheriff Casey's quarters were and call him to the door. Once the Sheriff opened the door, he would be shot and killed with the jailer's pistol. The three would then arm themselves with the Sheriff's rifles and ammunition. They planned to saddle the horses in the Sheriff's corral and flee to Mexico. The plan began to fall apart after both failed to unlock the cell door to Jesus Rocha.

Jesus Rocha was charged along with Eleuterio and Rumaldo with murder in the first degree. The trial was held during the May term of District Court. On the stand Eleuterio told the jury he was the person who had the axe. Both Eleuterio and Rumaldo denied their earlier statements implicating Jesus Rocha as the leader and organizer of the murder and escape. All three were found guilty of murder in the first degree. Judge R. R. Ryan sentenced the three to death by hanging on Friday, June 13, 1921. An appeal to the Supreme Court acted as a stay. The Supreme Court reversed the conviction on Jesus Rocha based on the testimony of both Eleuterio and Rumaldo. The Supreme Court did affirm the conviction and sentence of the other two defendants and reset the execution for January 20, 1922.

Relatives of both defendants, along with the Mexican Consulate General, petitioned for Governor Merritt C. Mechum to commute the sentence. Family members claimed both were less than 19 years of age. Governor Mechum requested three physicians to examine the two at the penitentiary in Santa Fe. The three physicians reported to the Governor that Eleuterio had passed 19 years of age and Rumaldo was past 20 years old. Based on the Doctors examination, Governor Mechum twice refused any interference.

On January 17th, Sheriff Casey had traveled to Santa Fe to pick up the two killers. Sheriff Casey asked Governor Mechum if he contemplated taking any action. Governor Mechum replied, "No, every guard's life out there would be in danger with those two in the penitentiary." Prior to Sheriff Casey's arrival, Deputy Warden P. J. Dugan conducted a surprise cell inspection. In both Eleuterio's and Rumaldo's mattresses, he found prison-made knives and a hacksaw. The two planned to cut themselves out of the cell and then stab and slash their way to freedom.

The New Mexico State Penitentiary.

DESCRIPTION OF CONVICT.

No. __1067__   Name __Eleuterio Corral__   ~~Age~~ / T / Ta   9

County received from ____Grant____   Date of receipt ____May 22, 1921____

Sentence ____Safekeeping____   Date of Sentence _____

Crime _____   Plea at trial _____

Sex ____Male____   Age __18__   Build ____Small____

Nationality ____Mexican____   Where born ____Tepeguane State of Durango____   Mexico

In New Mexico ____two____ years.   In United States ____2____ years.

Previous convictions ____None____

In other prisons ____None____

Trade or occupation ____Laborer____   Religious instruction ____Catholic____

Habits _____   Read ____Yes____   Write ____Yes____   Education __C/ S.__

Smoke ____Yes____   Chew ____No____   Liquor ____No____   Drugs __No__

~~Married or~~ single _____   Children _____

Relatives ____Marcelina Corral Santa Clara N.Mex.____   __Mother__

____Mercedes Saucedo____ "   "   "   ____Grandmother____

Height __5__ ft. __5__   Weight __121½__   Hair ____Dark Brown____   Eyes ____Brown____

Complexion ____Dark____   Bust ____31____   Waist ____29____   Thigh ____19____

Neck __14__   Hat ____7____   Shoes ____7____   Teeth ____Good____

Marks on body __L cut scr left side of head; mole left cheek; cut scr left__
__jaw; 2 vac scrs left arm muscle; ab scr left neck back; white spots__
__left shoulder blade; ab scr right arm muscle back.__

The Description of Convict form for Eleuterio Corral from the New Mexico State Penitentiary.

On the morning of the execution, Sheriff Casey selected Eleuterio Corral to be hanged first. Sheriff Casey read the death warrant outloud in Spanish to Eleuterio. After the reading, Father Carnet of the Catholic Church walked beside Eleuterio to the gallows. On the gallows the legs were bound, and Sheriff Casey asked Eleuterio if he had anything to say. Eleuterio said a brief prayer and told the 20 witnesses he was sorry for his crime and asked forgiveness. Eleuterio murmured, "May God almighty have mercy on my soul." The words had barely left his lips when the lever was pulled and Eleuterio dropped to this death. The rope broke the neck from the fall. After hanging for thirteen minutes, the doctor pronounced Eleuterio dead and the body was cut down.

As Eleuterio body was being removed, Sheriff Casey returned to the jail to lead Rumaldo Lozano to the gallows. Once Rumaldo was on the scaffold, and was placed over the trap, the death warrant was read as the noose was being placed over the neck. Immediately after Rumaldo finished his prayer, the trap was released breaking the neck. Doctors pronounced life extinct sixteen minutes later. No relatives were present to claim either body. Both bodies were released to Undertaker W. S. Cox for burial. The following day, both remains were buried at the city cemetery after a funeral was held at the Catholic Church. The Silver City *Enterprise* had the following headlines and story.

HANGING PASSES
WITHOUT HITCH

YOUTHS FACE DEATH WITH A
SMILE AND WITH GREAT
CALMNESS

They Ask Forgiveness

Eleuterio Corral and Rumaldo Losano
Pay Penalty for the Murder of
Jailer Bencoma on scaffold

Rumaldo Losano and Eleuterio Corral were hanged at the Grant County jail this morning. Corral was led to the scaffold first. The trap was sprung at 7:05. He was pronounced dead thirteen minutes later. As soon as the body could be taken down Losano was brought out. He was pronounced dead 10 minutes after the trap had been sprung.

Losano, who yesterday showed signs that his nerve was weakening, had completely regained his composure and walked to the scaffold with a firm step. He was cooler than Corral when the final moments came. Both men made a short statement asking the people and God Almighty to forgive them for what they had done.

The condemned men were brought from Santa Fe Tuesday and were carefully guarded day and night from that time on. They seemed to enjoy the trip and took a keen interest in what was to be seen. During Thursday they spent a good deal of time singing. Later they wept and sobbed for several hours. They spent a restless night, though both slept for short periods. They were given a good breakfast early this morning but neither ate much.

The order for the execution of the men was read to them by Sheriff Casey and shortly the procession to the scaffold, which had been erected just at the south side of the jail, began.

Corral was selected to go first. He looked like a small boy beside the towering deputies, and presented a pathetic figure. He was dirty and wore a shirt which he might easily have worn since his arrest. His toes were sticking out of one of the shoes. He was a little shaky but managed to walk up the ten or twelve steps to the scaffold without help. He seemed to take comfort from the close proximity of Father Gerey. After the brief statement that he hoped for forgiveness he was placed on the trap door. The rope was adjusted about his neck by former Sheriff McGrath, while Deputy Grayson placed the black cap over his face. Sheriff Casey sprung the trap almost immediately after arrangements were complete. Drs. Westlake and Tabor were there in official capacity and after 13 minutes declared Corral dead.

The New Mexico State Penitentiary.

DESCRIPTION OF CONVICT.

No. 1068   Name Romaldo Rosano

County received from Grant   Date of receipt May 22, 1921

Sentence Safekeeping   Date of Sentence

Crime   Plea at trial

Sex Male   Age 17   Build Small

Nationality Mexican   Where born Casas Grandes State of Chiu,

In New Mexico Two years.   In United States Two years.

Previous convictions None

In other prisons None

Trade or occupation Laborer   Religious instruction None

Habits   Read No   Write No   Education None

Smoke Yes   Chew No   Liquor No   Drugs No

Married or single   Children

Parents Father   Conjugal

Father born in Santa Rosalia Camargo Mexico Mother born in Do Not Know

Height 5 ft. 2½   Weight 117½   Hair Brown Curly   Eyes Green

Complexion Fair   Bust 32   Waist 31   Thigh 18

Neck 15   Hat 7   Shoes 5   Teeth Good

Marks on body Hole left side of neck; cut scr right ribs; cut scr left ribs; cut scr right taigh; ab scr right knee cap; cut scr left shinn; cir cut scr base of thumb on left hand; ab scrs right neck back; cut scr right shoulder blade; ab scr right muscle arm outer; ab scr left forearm outer; cut scr back of right hand; cut scr first finger of right hand.

The Description of Convict form for Romaldo Lozano from the New Mexico State Penitentiary.

The proceeding in the case of Losano were almost precisely similar. His attitude was largely of curious indifference and he looked up at the rope and scaffolding and around at the spectators. Losano was declared dead ten minutes later.

Sheriff John A. Casey, Grant County Sheriff, was summoned by another inmate after the two murderers escaped the jailhouse.

About the Crime

The crime for which these two paid the extreme penalty of the law was committed within fifty feet of where they were hanged. The two were confined in the county jail. Corral was suspected of stealing. Losano would have been released within a few days.

They loosened some bricks in the wall of their cell and climbed through a fan light into the corridor and one of the two struck jailer Ventura Bencoma, who was asleep, with an axe, almost cutting his head into two parts. They then made an effort to release another prisoner, Jesus Rocha, who was locked in a cell, and failing in this unlocked the outside door and made their escape. Bencoma died a few hours later. The alarm was given by a woman prisoner and soon the officers were in pursuit. The two were captured near Fierro several days later.

It was the theory of the officers that Rocha had been the ringleader and instigator of the crime. He was tried jointly with the two boys and all three were convicted of murder in the first degree. The Supreme Court reversed the finding of the District Court in the case of Rocha but confirmed it as to the other two. It was believed that Corral, the younger of the two, struck the blow that killed the jailer. Losano was probably present but being ignorant, probably did not realize that as an accessory he would be held equally guilty.

Sources:

Silver City *Enterprise*, April 8, 1921; January 20, 1922
Santa Fe *New Mexican*, April 5, 1921; January 20, 1922
Albuquerque *Morning Journal*, January 21, April 3, 1921
Silver City *Independent*, January 24, 1922

Chapter 7

Lincoln County

William Wilson   December 10, 1875

William Wilson

After purchasing a ranch on the Rio Hondo between Lincoln and Roswell, Robert Casey and his wife moved from Texas to New Mexico. After opening a mill, Mr. Casey hired William Wilson to help out on the ranch.

On August 1, 1875, Mr. Casey attended a county political convention to select candidates for the up-coming election. During the selection of candidates, Robert Casey rallied against nominations supported by Lawrence Murphy and James Dolan who were partners in a mercantile enterprise. At noon the convention adjourned for lunch, and Mr. Casey and Edmond Welch started out for the Worthy Hotel. While walking to the hotel, Mr. Casey invited William Wilson to join them. At 2:00 o'clock, Mr. Casey paid the bill and began walking up the street.

It is believed Lawrence Murphy and James, angered by the opposition of Mr. Casey, approached William Wilson to kill his employer. In return they would pay him $500.00 dollars, and assured him they would take care of his legal problems for they had friends in high places who could use their political influence with the Governor. In accepting the offer, Mr. Wilson was provided with a Winchester rifle, ammunition and told a fast horse would be waiting.

Mr. Wilson took a position on the side of a building and waited. Once Mr. Casey was within 15 to 20 paces of him, William Wilson step out from behind the building. He then raised the Winchester and fired. When the bullet struck Robert Casey in the hip, he ran behind a vacant building for cover. Mr. Wilson ran to the opposite side and shot Robert Casey through the mouth at close range. William Wilson put his back up against the wall as the crowd arrived, but surrendered to Sheriff Saturnino Baca. Mr. Wilson was then transported to Fort Stanton and jailed within the guard shack. The post surgeon, recognizing there was no chance for recovery, did what he could to make Robert Casey comfortable. Robert Casey died the following day.

On October 11th, both William Wilson and Charles Myrick were indicted. It had been learned that Charles Myrick was to have been holding the reins to a saddled horse which Wilson was to use to escape with after killing Casey. When the shooting started, Mr. Myrick lost his nerve and rode off on the escape horse, leaving the county forever. On October 15, 1875, Judge Bristol Warren presided over the trial. Two well known lawyers, William Rynerson and S. B Newcomb, represented the defendant. District Attorney John D. Bail and Col. Albert Jennings Fountain represented the Territory. During the trial, William Wilson claimed he shot and killed Robert Casey over an eight dollar debt owned him for labor. At the end of the three day trial, the jury deliberated only fifteen minutes before returning a verdict of guilty of murder in the first degree. Judge Bristol set the execution date for November 11th. Governor Samuel Axtell granted an immediate 30-day stay.

Possibly fearing Lawrence Murphy was not keeping his word to secure his release, Wilson made a desperate attempt to escape on October 19th. In his escape attempt, Wilson was seriously wounded by the guards and captured. In the early morning hours of December 10th, carpenters worked throughout the early morning hours erecting the gallows in front of the Lincoln County Courthouse. At 11:00 O'clock, William Wilson was transported to Lincoln by ambulance, escorted by the 8th cavalry. On the way, the escort temporarily stopped at the Sheriff's home to allow the condemned man the opportunity to change into the funeral clothes purchased for him by Lawrence Murphy. Afterwards, the escort continued to the gallows, where Wilson shook hands with friends and then mounted the steps to the platform. There waiting for him was his spiritual advisor, Father Lamy, Sheriff Baca and Lawrence Murphy. The warrant was read in English then Spanish. After the reading of the warrant the Sheriff announced the execution would be delayed for a half hour. After an angry protest by the town leaders, the Sheriff resumed with the execution without any more delays. When the Sheriff asked Wilson the customary question if he would like to make a final statement, William Wilson turned to Lawrence Murphy and said: "Major, you know you are the cause of this. You promised to save me, but ….." Before Wilson was allowed to finish his statement, Lawrence Murphy kicked the lever, releasing the trap door.

The body hanged for 9 ½ minutes before being cut down and placed within the coffin. As the body lay in the coffin, a curious Mexican woman approached to view the body. The woman screamed out, "For God's sake, the dead has come to life." Although unconscious, it was discovered the body had resumed breathing. Men quickly placed a noose around Wilson's neck and the other end of the rope was again thrown over the top of the upright post of the scaffold. Towns people pulled on the other end of the rope and jerked the body out of the coffin where it was suspended for twenty more minutes. After being cut down, the body was returned to the coffin and buried. The *Daily New Mexican* had the following headlines and story.

The Execution of Wilson.
Lincoln, Lincoln County,
December 15, 1875.

Editors *New Mexican*:

As I informed you in my last, Wm. Wilson, convicted of the murder of Robert Casey and sentenced to death, was to be have the penalty of the law executed on him last Friday. On the day appointed before day-break the carpenter's were at work erecting the gallows and even at that early hour strangers, men, women and even children were pouring in from adjacent country.

At eleven o'clock the prisoner in an ambulance, accompanied by Capt. Stewart, commander of the post, Dr. Carballo, Medical Director and Rev. Lamy of Manzano, preceded by company G. 8th U. S. Cavalry, under command of Lt. Gilmore arrived at this town and proceeded to the residence of the sheriff. The prisoner then arrayed himself in his funeral clothes and the procession moved to the gallows. Before mounting the platform, Wilson shook hands with several he recognized, and mounted the scaffold calm and collected. The escort was drawn up a line fronting the gallows, whilst four men dismounted and kept back the crowd which by this time had increased considerable.

Whilst on the scaffold the death warrant was read first in English and then in Spanish, after which the dying declaration written and signed by Wilson was read and translated; he then received the extreme unction and the *merciful* sheriff declared that the execution would be stayed for half an hour.

However, the leading men of the town actuated by pity for the poor unfortunate entered such a vigorous protest against such barbarous proceedings that the sheriff proceeded with the execution. The priest descended from the scaffold, the black cap was adjusted and the prisoner, with his hands tied behind and the noose around his neck awaited his doom. The sheriff descended from the scaffold and in an instant justice so long outranged was avenged, and the perpetrator of one of the foulest murders which has ever disgraced a civilized community was no more. After hanging 9 ½ minutes the body was cut down and placed in the coffin, when it was discovered that life was not yet extinct. A rope was then fastened round his neck and the crowd drew the inanimate body from the coffin and suspended it from the gallows where it hung for twenty minutes longer; it was then cut down and placed in the coffin and buried.

Sources:

The *Daily New Mexican*, September 3, October 21, November 3, December 21, 1875

Weekly New Mexican, December 28, 1875

Chapter 8

Luna County

Martin Amador	January 13, 1908
Franciso Alvarez	June 9, 1916
Juan Sanchez	June 9, 1916
Eusevio Renteria	June 30, 1916
Taurino Garcia	June 30, 1916
Juan Castillo	June 30, 1916
Jose Rangel	June 30, 1916

Martin Amador

Martin Amador had affectionate desires for a Ms. Cepcion Mendosa who continued to turn down his advances. Angered by her refusal, he yelled threatening remarks to her. Frightened by what Martin had said to her, Ms. Mendosa went to a nearby friend's home until she felt it was safe to return home. As she walked home late into the night, Martin Amador, waiting in hiding for her to return, shot and killed her. The Deming *Headlight* had the following headlines and stories.

Deming *Headlight*, Deming, Luna County, Thursday, July 25, 1907.

A Fiendish Murder
———

Mexican kills a native woman
At Victoria
———

Because she refused to live with him or have anything to do with him Martine Amador a miner in the Bradley Camp, at Victorio, twenty miles west of this city, waylaid, shot and killed a Mexican woman named Cepcion Mendosa last Friday night about 11:30.

Mr. Frank Wyman who was on the ground at the time states the case as follows:

Martine Amador, the man who done the killing, has for sometime past been pestering the woman to get her to live with him, but she had persistently refused to have anything to do with him and was keeping a miners boarding house for the unmarried men who worked in the camps of Mr. Wyman and also for the men of the Bradley camp. The woman is spoken of by Mr. Wyman and others as a hard working and industrious person and one who attended strictly to her own affairs. Last Friday in the early part of the evening, Martin Amador went over to the house of Cepcion Mendosa and began to talk and raise a fuss so that the woman became afraid of him and left her house, going to the house of a neighbor where she spent the evening. About half past eleven in the night she started to go home, supposing that Martin had gone to his own camp by that time, but when near her house she was shot by the villain who had remained secreted awaiting her return. The weapon used was a twenty-two rifle and the bullet entered the heart, the woman dying in a few minutes after being shot. The alarm was at once given and men scattered in all directions to try to capture the murderer before he could escape into Mexico.

Mr. Wyman at once preceded to the station of Gage about four miles from the camp and wired to the authorities in this city. Sheriff Johnson was absent at the time in Arizona on official business but deputy J. A. Baker at once proceeded to the scene of the crime and took the trail which led to the railroad where Martine boarded a train coming to this city. He got off here and started for another of the Bradley camps in the Florida Mountains where he had previously worked and was well acquainted. Mr. Baker was close on his trail, however, and sent word to the Foreman at the Florida camp, Mr. Hathaway, to look out for him while Baker followed another direction to make sure he did not escape. The murderer came into the Florida camp about eleven o'clock on last Sunday evening, was apprehended at that camp and was brought to town and turned over to the authorities and is now in jail awaiting action of the Grand jury.

His honor Judge Cooke Chapman went to the scene of the murder early on Saturday and held an inquest on the remains, the facts found by him being in accordance with the above.

Too much credit cannot be given to all parties concerned in the capture. Sheriff Johnson has always had the best of men in his employ since he has been Sheriff and that is the reason that there are no escapes recorded for this county these days.

Deming *Headlight,* Deming, Luna County, December 5, 1907

Looks Like they will hang.

It is now the fifth of the month. There is but eight more days before Sheriff Johnson will be compelled to carry out the mandate of the law regarding the hanging of the two Mexicans who were sentenced to death at the Nov. term of court in this county, unless Governor Curry sees fit to interfere. It is not thought that the Governor will take any cognizance of the petition that has been circulated here for executive clemency in the case of Magdaleno Sabelloz, who killed a baby in this city last 4th of July, but that the law will be allowed to take its course. In that case the sentence of the court will be imposed and these two men will be hanged on Friday, the thirteenth of December.

While Sheriff Johnson may regret that the duties of his office, as Sheriff of Luna County, imposes this task upon him, still he will carry out the sentence in a just manner if compelled to. He is now busy having the scaffold erected in the jail yard and getting all things ready for this gruesome affair.

Deming *Graphic,* Deming Luna County, N. M.,
Friday, January 17, 1908

One Hanged
Other For Life

Martin Amador hanged;
Magdaleno Sabboloz
Commuted

Gov. Curry commuted the death sentence of Magdaleno Sabelloz, the condemned Mexican murderer, but in the case of the other condemned Mexican murderer, Martin Amador, the Governor refused to interfere with the course of the law, and accordingly, the 30 day respite granted having expired last Monday, Sheriff Don Johnson performed the painful obligation of sending Amador to eternity by the rope route.

A strong petition was sent to Governor Curry in behalf of the condemned men, praying that the death sentences be commuted to life. The Governor, however, after thoroughly considering the cases of the two men, decided to give Sabelloz a life sentence and to allow the execution to proceed with Amador.

The execution of Amador took place in the county jail yard here last Monday afternoon, the Sheriff having sprung the trap at exactly 10:30. Amador smoked a cigarette while the death warrant was read to him and walked from the cell to the scaffold with a steady step. He mounted the scaffold without hesitancy and gamely met an ignominious fate. He was attended by Father Morin on the death march, the sheriff and jailor Will Jennings having escorted the condemned man to the gallows. All along Amador had maintained a stolid indifference as to his fate and was about the coolest man present when the blackcap shut off his view of this world for the last time.

The victim's neck was broken by the drop, and after hanging three minutes physicians present announced that life was extinct and two minutes later the body was cut down, and during the day was buried by the county, no relatives or friends having put claim for the remains. Besides the officials and priest, some eighteen of our citizens witnessed the execution.

Amador had been in jail here since the commission last July of the terrible crime which brought his life to an end. He was a quiet, indifferent prisoner and caused the officers no unnecessary trouble.

Sabelloz, who was sentenced to hang with Amador, was taken to the territorial penitentiary at Santa Fe Monday night by Sheriff Johnson to spend the balance of his days. Further comment on the closing chapter of their careers is hardly necessary, other than to say that it is to be hoped their fates will have a salutary effect upon members of their race and all others and be the means of causing a less frequency of murder and crime in general in this country.

The murder for which Magdaleno Sabelloz was commuted occurred on July 4th, 1907. On that day, Magdaleno was drunk and started an altercation with a Mr. Adelfino Palamino. Without provocation Magdaleno Sabelloz pulled out a pistol and shot at Mr. Palamino as he was holding a small child in his arms. The bullet missed Mr. Palamino, but hit and instantly killed the child he was holding.

Sources:

Deming *Headlight*, July 11, 25; November 5, 1907
Deming *Graphic*, January 17, 1908

Francisco Alvarez, Juan Sanchez
June 9th, 1916

Eusevio Renteria, Taurino Garcia,
Juan Castillo and Jose Rangel.
June 30th, 1916

At 4:25 in the morning of March 9, 1916, 485 Mexican men commanded by Francisco "Pancho" Villa crossed the border into the United States. The small army of men entered into New Mexico southwest of the thirteenth Cavalry camp and the small village of Columbus, New Mexico. The town of Columbus was two miles north of the international border and thirty-two miles south of Deming.

A soldier stands guard over the aftermath on the raid on Columbus, New Mexico, March 9, 1916. Photograph by W.H. Horne of El Paso, Texas.

Due to the early morning hour of the raid, both the cavalry and the residents of the town were taken by surprise. Pancho Villa intended on killing men in the town and as many as possible at the army camp. By looting the stores, hotels, bank, and the Golden State Limited train, he would gain the cash and supplies that he was in desperate need of. Once the town was surrounded, the bandits, who were referred to as the "Villistas," rode into Columbus shooting bullets through the windows of the buildings and yelling

"Viva Villa, Villa Mexico and Matarros Gringo." A special coal train ahead of the Golden Limited pulled into Columbus. The Villistas, mistaking the coal train for the Golden Limited, began firing their weapons at it. The engineer quickly backed the train out and Pancho Villa was deprived of robbing the Golden State Limited.

The Mexican bandits first looted the Lemmon & Romney store and took everything that they could carry away. Afterwards, the store was set on fire. Other bandits, at the direction of Pancho Villa, centered on the Commercial Hotel. The Villistas entered the hotel and robbed the men of their cash, and the women of their jewelry. The fire from the store quickly spread to the Commercial hotel. The Villistas shot several of the guests and threw their bodies into the burning building. The Cavalry units not only fought the Villistas from their camp, but were also able to defend Columbus. Pancho Villa, seeing he was losing the battle, quickly retreated back into Mexico, believing the Calvary would not pursue after him beyond the international border. He was mistaken, for the army pursued the Villistas some twelve miles into Mexico, wounding and killing a number of his men.

It was estimated that the Calvary had killed, wounded or captured about 100 Mexican Villistas. Forty of the dead Villistas were cremated in a large pit and covered over. The Mexican bandits had killed 9 civilians and 8 soldiers at Columbus. Only 3 civilians and a total of 6 soldiers were wounded. The bandits who were captured and survived their wounds were imprisoned at the Luna County jail in Deming. All the Villistas were charged with the murders of James T. Dean, Charles D. Miller, Paul Simon, and J. J. Moore.

On Wednesday, April 19, seven of the bandits were dressed in blue denim shirts, and blue overalls to stand trial before Judge E. L. Medler. Tried were Juan Rangel, Eusenio Renteria, Taurino Garcia, Jose Rodriguez, Francisco Alvarez and Juan Castillo. Each of the defendants testified that they had taken part in the raid of Columbus and wounded American soldiers. The men told the jury they were forced to join Villa's army for fear of being killed, and claimed they were unaware they had crossed into the United States when they attacked the American town. Twenty-one-year old Taurino Garcia and twenty-four-year old Eusiero Renteria both claimed they were under a Villa Lieutenant and were just arriving at Columbus when Pancho Villa was returning. Twenty-six-year old Juan Castillo and twenty-eight-year old Jose Rangel both claimed they remained with the horses and did not partake in the fighting. Eleven-year-old Jesus Pias told the jury his father had been robbed of all his money by Pancho Villa and forced to join his Army. Jesus explained his father had hoped for both of them to escape from Villa at the first opportunity. They planned to escape into the United States so he could go to school. Just before the fighting, his father told him to stay clear of the fighting and to remain with the horses. A severe wound to the leg required that Jesus' leg be amputated. The boy was not charged with any crimes, for he turned State's witness. Jesus testified against the other Villistas. The boy rebutted their earlier testimony in telling the jury that the men were promised, by Villa, if they joined, that they would all get a white wife once all the white men were killed. The men would also receive money from the bank, food and clothes from the stores. There was no further record as to what happened to Jesus Pias or what had become of his father.

Before noon on Thursday, the jury went into deliberation for a total of twenty minutes. The jury returned with the verdict of guilty in the first degree for all six defendants. After lunch, the judge and jury returned to hear the murder trial of Juan Sanchez for his part in the Columbus raid. His trial began at 2 o'clock in the afternoon. Juan Sanchez at first testified he had not taken part in the Columbus raid. But upon being cross-examined, Sanchez admitted to firing a shot close range at Charles D. Miller. He contended he only shot in the air. Joshua Hawkins testified he and other soldiers fought against Juan Sanchez and six other Villistas. Mr. Hawkins testified Sanchez was shot through the leg as he mistakenly stepped from behind a water tank yelling "Viva Villa." At 3:30 the jury went into deliberation. At 4 o'clock the jury returned with a verdict of guilty of murder. When Judge Medler passed the death sentence on the defendants, only two of the seven could stand because of battle wounds. The men showed no emotion with the exception of Juan Rangel who wept from his cot when being carried out. Judge Medler scheduled the condemned men to hang by the neck until dead on May 19, 1916, between the hours of 6:00 a.m. and 6:00 p.m.

The defendant's attorney, E. C. Wader Jr. appealed personally to President Wilson. The attorney asked the President to investigate the case, and for him to further make a recommendation to Governor William Mc Donald. Attorney Wade asked that the Governor grant executive clemency by way of having the sentences commuted to life in prison. President Wilson did ask the Governor to carefully investigate the case. Governor Mc Donald did grant a respite until June 9th. The Governor reviewed the court transcripts, interviewed the prisoners after they had been transferred to the state penitentiary, and personally made the trip to Deming. Afterwards, the Governor did grant another 20-day reprieve for all except Francisco Alvarez and Juan Sanchez. He commuted Jose Rodriguez to life in prison. Once Rodriguez recovered from his wounds, he was immediately placed to work within the penitentiary's brick making plant.

Contractors from Rosch & Leupold began building the gallows at the northwest corner of the jail yard. The trap doors were cut from the edge of the platform and allowed to swing on hinges to a depth of 2 ½ feet. This allowed for two men to be dropped at the same time. A strong rope was tied to the corner posts that then passed across the gallows under the doors and over a small block in the middle. This provided the Sheriff with just enough room to stand between the two men as he cut the rope with an axe. Only 20 witnesses were allowed to view the execution by invitation from the Sheriff and approval of the judge.

On the night of June 8th, the two prisoners were said to have slept soundly until the jailer awakened them. Both men were then dressed in overalls and white shirts. Capt. A. W. Brock read the prisoners the death warrant in Spanish. The prisoners requested not to be hanged, but to be executed by a firing squad against an adobe wall as was the custom in Mexico. This request was denied. Francisco Alvarez, being the first selected to be hanged, walked to the gallows along with his two spiritual advisors, Fathers Carnet and Alfonso Romero. He had been shot through the mouth during the battle and still had the bandage wrapped around his face and head. He showed no emotion until the black cap was being adjusted. The condemned man began to tremble and started backing away from the scaffold until Sheriff Simpson bound his legs together and secured the noose.

After Buck Chadborne sprung the trap, the body hung for thirteen minutes until cut down. The body was then carried into the jail yard and covered with a quilt. Juan Sanchez was immediately removed from the cell and marched to the gallows. Sanchez, who had been wounded in the leg when he stepped back from the water tank, claimed his age to be 16. His companions all said his true age was 23. At 7:13, the trap was sprung and the drop broke the man's neck. After 10 minutes of hanging, the physician found no heart or pulse beat and declared the body dead. He was then cut down and placed next to the remains of Alvarez. It was then discovered, that Sanchez had resumed breathing and had a pulse. Although he never regained consciousness, his body was then returned to the gallows and Sheriff Simpson again placed the noose around the neck and the body was dropped through the trap. The body hanged again until the pulse and heart beat both ceased. The Deming *Graphic* had the following headlines and story.

2 COLUMBUS RAIDERS
PAY EXTREME PENALTY

Make no Comment as They Pass
Into the Great Beyond, Except
To Say "I Don't Care."

EVERYTHING PASSED QUIETLY

Sheriff Simpson Had Everything In
Perfect Readiness and there was
Not One Slip in the Cog

Francisco Alvarez and Juan Sanchez paid with their lives early this morning for their part in the raid on Columbus, March 9, by Villistas, in the local jail yard. They were the first to die of seven found guilty of murder in the District Court here. It is expected that the others will be hung later, a stay of execution having been granted by Governor Mc Donald.

Alvarez stepped on the gallows at 6:31 o'clock: at 6:36 the trap was sprung and at 6:45 he was pronounced dead. Sanchez mounted the gallows at 7:10 o'clock: at 7:13 the trap was sprung and at 7:30 his dead body was cut down, carried into the jail yard and covered with a quilt beside the body of his comrade. Both were very indifferent to their fates. Particularly was it true of Alvarez, who answered Capt. A. W. Brock, "Yo no quiero," (I do not care to) when asked if he would like to make a final statement. His attitude has from the first been one of absolute indifference to his fate. The Rev. Father Joseph Carnet, and the Rev. Alfonso Romero, his spiritual advisor were with him from 4:30 o'clock this morning until the black cap and noose was adjusted. Even up to the moment the death march started he was smoking a cigarette and joking as though he was going to a picnic. Juan Sanchez was a little more serious, and for the last three or four hours prior to his execution was engaged in semi-silent prayer. This was the attitude of Alvarez at intervals. A few minutes before starting for the gallows, Alvarez called for a cigarette. Capt. A. W. Brock read the death warrant in Spanish, to which no comment was made.

Alvarez turned his head accommodatingly to have the rope adjusted. Sheriff W. C. Simpson and his assistants performed the work, Dr. R. C. Hoffman and Dr. P. M. Steed pronouncing each body. Deming was absolutely quiet during, before and after the execution. During last night sentries were posted about the jail and provost patrols went on duty with loaded guns and fixed bayonets. Beside these there were veteran peace officers from all along the border.

On Thursday, June 29, Sheriff Simpson swore in 40 special deputies to help stay up during the night to guard the jail. Adjutant General Harry T. Herring brought in Company D to patrol the town and assist any disturbance. The Deming *Graphic* on the day of the execution had the following details.

FOUR MORE RAIDERS
MEET THEIR DOOM

———

There Was Not a Hitch or Break in
The Proceedings This Morning
When Penalty Was Paid

———

One Commuted By Governor

———

General Herring Brought up Company
"D" to be Used in Case of Emergency, But None arose

———

The seven Columbus raiders convicted of murder by a Luna county jury, after a fair and impartial trial, are now all disposed of according to law and it is hoped that the matter is now a sealed book. Deming had had enough of this kind of publicity, right this minute.

Sheriff W. C. Simpson is to be congratulated on the efficient manner in which he conducted affairs, and the valiant and patriotic men who helped have the sincere thanks of he people.

Company "D" of the 1ˢᵗ New Mexico Infantry, reached Deming Thursday morning by truck train, from their station at Columbus. The company immediately went into quarters at the state armory. A provost guard was organized and patrolled the streets of the city performing only such duties as is incumbent upon such organization, and render any such assistance as might become necessary in the event of any emergency, but it is exceedingly pleasant to relate that not the slightest emergency existed.

The first chapter in the story found chief deputy Lee Caldwell, Geo. P. Watkins, T. H. Farmer, Z. U. Mason and C.W. Hoskins, with George II. Thomas, special officer if the Santa Fe, bringing the four doomed men from the penitentiary to Deming.

The party was met at the Borderland crossing by Major Nordhaus and Fred Sherman, the four prisoners riding in the major's car. At six o'clock this morning, Sheriff Simpson invited a small party of his friends, including a score of emergency deputies and Sheriff Felipe Lucero, of Las Cruces.

The prisoners slept well after eating a hearty supper, but all declined breakfast. Taurino Garcia and Eusevio Renteria were the first to mount the scaffold, at 6:20, accompanied by the officers and their spiritual advisor, Rev. Father Jos. M. Carnet. Garcia was still using his crutches, and was a little "trembly." Asked by the sheriff if he had anything to say, he replied: "I hope you people will pardon me like I pardon all of you." His companion tried to cheer him up by saying: "Don't be afraid to die. We all have to die sometime, just as well die now."

Juan Castillo and Jose Rangel went on the platform at 7:14. The latter said he had nothing to say. The former said, according to Sheriff Lucero's translation: "I know I am going to die. I am going to die in justice. I pardon all of you."

Upon their arrival Thursday, Rev. Father Carnet went to confer with them. He found that one was a widower, one had parents living, and the other two had no near relatives. They told their spiritual advisor that they were willing to die and asked him to communicate with their relatives. Señor Garcia, who was formerly an officer in the Mexican army, wrote his people: "I die tranquilly, asking God to forgive me and my enemies."

Gov. W. C. McDonald has commuted the sentence of Jose Rodriguez to life imprisonment, which we hope closes the chapter on the seven, two having been previously executed. Drs. Steed, Hoffman and Milford were the physicians in attendance.

Villa bandits captured at Columbus and Ascencion, Mexico, June 1916. No. 1 was not tried. No. 4 was Jailor Archer. No. 3 was reprieved to a life sentence. Nos. 2, 5, 6, 7, 8 and 9 were hanged on 6/9/16 and 6/30/16.

Sources:

Deming *Graphic,* March 10, 17, 24; April 14, 28; June 9, 16, 30, 1916
Columbus *Courier,* March 24, 30; April 21, 28; May 26; June 9, 1916
Santa Fe *New Mexican*, June 15, 30, 1916
El Paso *Morning Times*, June 10; July 1, 1916
Silver City *Enterprise*, June 9, 30, 1916

Chapter 9

Rio Arriba County

Perfecto Padilla   September 24, 1896

Rosario Ring   September 24, 1896

Perfecto Padilla

John Vipond was a 58-year-old prospector who had been residing at Butte City, Montana. He and his brother William had been prosperous in the mining ventures in Montana and decided to expand their operation in New Mexico. In July of 1895, John Vipond traveled to New Mexico in hopes of locating rich mineral deposits said to be near Copper City in Rio Arriba County. At Bland, New Mexico in the Cochiti mining district, he obtained pack burros and supplies for his prospecting trip. During the first week of August, John Vipond left the small group of prospectors he had been traveling with and headed towards the Gallina mountains. After the group of prospectors returned to Bland, they learned John Vipond had not yet returned. A search party that included William Vipond failed to locate any signs of John and foul play was feared.

Soon thereafter, Perfecto Padilla was seen in Santa Fe placing his daughters in the Presbyterian Mission School. While in Santa Fe, Perfecto Padilla pawned John Vipond's watch and was wearing the victim's hat. The burros owned by John Vipond were also seen in Perfecto Padilla's possession. Once Perfecto returned to Tierra Amarilla in Rio Arriba County, Sheriff Deputies placed him under arrest for the murder. It was believed John Vipond was murdered for his burros along with the $30-watch he was carrying.

On October 4th, the skeletal remains of John Vipond were found 15 miles from Copper City. William Vipond personally investigated his brother's death for almost a year and spent $6,000 dollars of his own money in doing so. His investigation uncovered a witness to his brother's murder. Perfecto Padilla was tried for the murder on November 15, 1895, before Judge Laughlin's court in Tierra Amarilla.

Jose De La Jesus Archibeque testified at the trial as a witness for the prosecutor. Mr. Archibeque related to the jury that he had been riding at the edge of a small park on the afternoon of August 6, 1895, where the remains were found. It was then he saw John Vipond asleep in his camp. Mr. Archibeque witnessed Perfecto Padilla,, whom he had known for nineteen years, carrying a pick handle and quietly sneaking up to Vipond. Mr. Archibeque testified he witnessed Perfecto Padilla striking the victim in the head with the pick handle. Being unarmed and frightened of Perfecto Padilla, he remained in hiding, telling no one of the murder until he learned Perfecto had been arrested.

Prosecuting Attorney Crist strengthened Mr. Archibeque's testimony once the skull of John Vipond, which had a dent to the side, was shown before the jury. When the remains were found, a poll pick handle had been found near by. The prosecutor showed the jury how the octagon end of the handle fit perfectly within the dent of the skull. At the end of the two-day trial, Perfecto Padilla's verdict was guilty of murder in the first degree. Judge

Laughlin set the execution date for December 21, 1895. The execution was stayed while his case was appealed to the New Mexico Supreme Court. The Territory Supreme Court affirmed the District Court's decision and ordered that Perfecto Padilla he hanged by the neck until dead on September 24, 1896, before the noon hour. Perfecto remained in the Santa Fe jail until his execution. It had been rumored an attempt would be made to rescue him while he was being transported for execution in Tierra Amarilla. Rio Arriba County Sheriff Garcia asked the assistance of the Cavalry to provide an armed escort once he arrived with Padilla and Rosario Ring by train at Chamita. Ring was also scheduled for execution on an unrelated crime. At Chamita, the prisoners were transported by a wagon team to Tierra Amarilla. Lieutenant Coleman did lead a squad of six cavalrymen as Sheriff Garcia, William Vipond and deputies escorted Perfecto Padilla and Rosario Ring.

At the gallows, Perfecto Padilla was the first prisoner lead to the gallows to be executed. Perfecto walked to the scaffold and climbed the steps with a firm stride. When asked by the Sheriff if he had anything to say, Perfecto walked to the edge of the scaffold and addressed the crowd in a clear voice. In addressing the crowd, Perfecto first bid them all farewell. He cautioned the people not to take for granted that a man is guilty because he was convicted of a crime in a court of justice. "There are people who, for the sake of revenge and their greed of money, are ready at any time to swear a man's life away. Money is a most powerful agency, you all well know. And gentleman, I am the victim of that agency, for I was convicted by the power of money and false witness of a crime I never committed, and today I am doomed to die here on the gallows.

"When I was in jail at Santa Fe, District Attorney Crist and Sheriff Cunningham offered to help me with their influence and to use money also in my favor, and promised to see that I went free if I would be a false witness and swear that T. B. Catron was implicated with the Borrego's in the murder of Francisco Chavez. But as I had committed no crime, and did not care to send my soul to the Evil One, I refused. Gentleman, this is the truth, as I am about to stand before my God, and let this be a warning to you all, for you may at some future day be convicted of a crime through the power of money and false witnesses, and still die an innocent man. With this, gentleman, I bid you all good-bye."

Afterwards, Perfecto Padilla was placed over the trap door. Being that he was so frightened and could barely stand up straight, the sheriff deputies had to support Perfecto while they placed the noose around his neck.

Sources:

Albuquerque *Weekly Citizen*, September 26, October 10, 1896
Santa Fe *Daily New Mexican*, November 26, 1895
Albuquerque *Daily Citizen*, September 29, 1896
Albuquerque *Morning Democrat*, November 16, 1895; September 23, 1896

Rosario Ring

Rosario Ring was considered a dangerous man after his arrival in Tierra Amarilla, Rio Arriba County, New Mexico. He was new to the area and citizens quickly learned he was the primary suspect in the murder of his wife and child in Colorado. It was believed Rosario arrived to help his friend, Ceiestino Romero, in a long standing feud with Carlos Ulibarri.

During most of the day on September 16, 1895, both Rosario Ring and Ceiestino Romero drank liquor. Once both were liquored up, they set out to find Carlos Ulibarri. Upon locating Carlos in the street, a beer bottle was broken over his head. Carlos' mother, hearing the commotion went outside to investigate. Fearing her son was in trouble, she persuaded him to leave the street by taking Carlos by the hand and pulling on him to the door of her home. While his back was turned to enter his mother's home, he was shot in the back. Thirty-year-old Carlos Ulibarri died in his mother's arms.

Judge Laughlin's trial of both men ended on November 21, 1895. Ceiestino Romero was acquitted, but Rosario Ring's verdict was guilty of Murder in the first degree. The original execution date set for December 21, 1895, was delayed on appeal to the Supreme Court. The higher court denied the request and the execution was rescheduled for September 24, 1896. This was the same date set for Perfecto Padilla's execution at Tierra Amarilla for murder. Requests to the Governor to commute the sentence to life in prison were made by Rosario Ring's attorney. After a strong protest was received by the citizens of Rio Arriba, the Governor refused to interfere. Both Perfecto Padilla and Rosario Ring were held in the Santa Fe jail for safekeeping. From Santa Fe, both men were transported to Chamita by train where a squad of Cavalrymen waited to escort them to Tierra Amarilla. One of the men present with the escort was the father of Carlos Ulibarri. Immediately upon seeing him, Rosario Ring began singing, "Oh where is my wandering boy tonight."

Perfecto Padilla was hung first. After the body was lowered and removed, Rosario was lead out of the jail to the gallows. Without any signs of nervousness and with a firm step, he climbed the steps of the scaffold. Rosario made a speech both in Spanish and English. He told the spectators, "There are no doubt people who thought that I had committed a cold-blooded murder and deserved death, but it was not so for I was under the influence of liquor and out of my head. If I had not drank liquor, I would never have killed Carlos Ulibarri for he had no enmity nor ill will against him. If I had left liquor alone, I would not have to die on the gallows. But it is too late for me to reform. But for you gentlemen, it is not too late, and I caution you to let liquor alone for you may, under the influence commit a crime which if you were sober you would never think of doing. And you will, like me, think of reform when it is to late. So good bye to you all, and may God help me."

Sources:

Santa Fe *Daily New Mexican*, November 21, 25, 26, 1895
Albuquerque *Weekly Citizen*, September 26, October 10, 1896
Albuquerque *Daily Citizen*, September 29, 1896
Albuquerque *Morning Democrat*, September 23, 1896

Chapter 10

San Juan County

Stephen Katonka   October 20, 1922

Stephen Katonka

On October 20, 1922, at the old Aztec fairgrounds, Stephen Katonka was executed by hanging. Stephen and Alice Katonka were both convicted for the murder of two taxi cab drivers on July 31, 1921. Alice Katonka was convicted along with her husband, and she received a sentence of 5 to 30 years in the state penitentiary.

At the trial, the testimony of the married couple was conflicting. The defense attempted to stop any testimony by Alice on the grounds a spouse of the defendant could not be compelled to testify against her husband. The prosecution showed as evidence that the marriage of Alice to Stephen Katonka was invalid for she was never legally divorced from her previous marriage.

On July 31, 1921, both Stephen and Alice Katonka hired the service of the Gallup Taxi service. On the road between Gallup and Farmington, two taxi employees, William Kelly and Sam Groy, were murdered and buried. The couple was arrested in December at Altoona, Pennsylvania when Sheriff Wynn received a letter about the double murder and the Katonka's whereabouts. After Stephen Katonka was returned to New Mexico, he led Sheriff Wynn to an arroyo where the remains of both men were found partially buried.

At the trial, both defendants testified and blamed each other for the murders. Alice Katonka told the jury her husband forced her to kill one of the men at gunpoint. After shooting one of the two men she passed out and when she came to, both men were dead. Stephen Katonka confessed his wife shot and killed one man with a rifle and then pointed the weapon at him. He then shot and killed the second man with a revolver.

Convicted of murder in the first degree, Stephen Katonka was sentenced to hang on June 26, 1922. An appeal to the state Supreme Court acted as a stay. The court upheld the San Juan District Court decision and the execution was reset for September 26. The execution was temporally delayed because Stephen swallowed iodine that had been smuggled to him by other inmates at the penitentiary. The suicide attempt failed and guards were placed on a deathwatch duty until the execution. As a last attempt, petitions were sent to Governor M. C. Mechem who denied to commute the death sentence. Sheriff J. C. Wynn drove Stephen Katonka to the gallows where he immediately stood over the trap door. At precisely 9:00 o'clock, the trap was sprung. The fall broke the murderer's neck and he died without a struggle.

San Juan County had been created in 1889. Stephen Katonka is the only person executed in that County. The Farmington *Times Hustler* had the following story.

Stephen Katonka
Hung At Aztec
On Last Friday

———

Went To His Death Calmly,
Maintaining His Innocence
Of The Crime Of Murder
To The Very Last.

———

"The wages of sin are Death," according to the scriptures, and while many who heard the trial and others who had Katonka's confidence at the last, believed that he was guilty only as an accessory to the crime for which he paid the death penalty, he himself admitted that his sentence was but the proof of the truth of our quotation. Katonka in his last days made various statements to those who tried to question him and who he did not believe to be his friends. But we have his story from those whom he trusted and confided in and whom we also trust and what is more whom we know would not distort the truth for any purpose.

There have been various stories published and circulated in regard to alleged confessions, but we have taken pains to give our readers "the truth, the whole truth and nothing but the truth."

On Thursday night after he had been informed that there was no chance for saving his life and after even the last "good bye" had been said and all were leaving him he called his most trusted friend and counselor and asked him to come back. The friend went back. Katonka then said to him, "Now I want to tell you something I never told before –I saw Alice (his wife) kill Kelly."

This full confession of the truth seemed to give him mental relief and physical strength. When he was told that the time had come for him to leave his cell for the last time, he walked briskly to the car and got into the car himself. When they reached the scaffold down in the old fair grounds at Aztec he stepped out of the car and walked up the steep stairway of the scaffold unassisted and stepped on the trap door without being told to do so. When Sheriff Wynn asked him if he had anything to say, he said, "I feel that an injustice has been done."

When the Sheriff went to adjust the rope around Katonka's neck, the latter asked the Sheriff not to make the rope so tight that it would choke him before the trap was sprung. When the trap was sprung his neck was broken by the fall and he died without a struggle. He maintained his innocence of murder to the end but admitted he was an accessory, claiming his wife did the actual deed.

He attributed his trouble to an occurrence of many years ago when in a fit of anger he struck his father. At the time his father asked God to punish him and he went to his death firmly believing that his father's curse had been fulfilled. He desired that this event of his life be given publicity as a warning to the young people who might benefit from it.

The prevailing opinion in this county is that Steve Katonka got only his just deserts for the part he played in the heinous crime to which he was a part and they just as firmly believe that there was a sad miscarriage of justice in the case of his wife.

Sources:

Farmington *Times Hustler*, October 19, 1922
Albuquerque *Morning Journal*, October 21, 1922
Santa Fe *New Mexican*, October 20, 1922

Chapter 11

San Miguel County

Paula Angel, alias Pablita Martin   April 26, 1861
Roy French, alias Frank   September 12, 1870
Frederick Martin   August 19, 1892
Herman Maestas   May 25, 1894
Julian Romero   April 11, 1918

Paula Angel, alias Pablita Martin
Murder, San Miguel County.

It had been believed for many years that Mary Elizabeth Surratt was the first woman executed in the United States. Mrs. Surratt was hanged at Washington's old penitentiary on July 7, 1865. She was convicted as being part of the conspiracy in the assassination of President Abraham Lincoln on April 14, 1865.

However, On April 26, 1861, near Las Vegas, New Mexico, in San Miguel County, Paula Angel became the first woman executed in the United States, and also in the Territory of New Mexico.

Not much is known about Paula Angel, and few documents have survived from the trial. There is some reference to her name being either Pablita Martin or Pabilita Sandoval. Paula is said to have been between 26 and 27 years old and living in the small town of Loma Parda with her parents. She learned the trade of a seamstress from her mother.

Paula met a man, by the name of Miguel Martin, who was married and had five children. Regardless of the marriage, she had an affair with the man. Soon after their affair began, Mr. Martin told Paula he wished to break off the affair as he had no intention of leaving his family. On March 23, 1861, Paula convinced Miguel Martin to see her one more time. During the meeting, Miguel reiterated to Paula that he had no intention of leaving his wife. Unknown to Miguel Martin, Paula had brought with her a butcher knife, which she had concealed in her dress. What exactly happened is unknown, but it is generally believed she killed her lover while she hugged him good-bye. He died from a stab wound to his back. Paula Angel was arrested for the murder by Sheriff Antonio Abad Herrera on the same day and taken before Judge Kirby Benedict.

On March 28, 1861, Paula Angel was tried for the murder before twelve men. Paula's Attorney was Spruce M. Baird. He argued and used the defense that Paula Angel was "disturbed by her Lovers rejection". In closing arguments Attorney Baird pleaded to the jury in both English and Spanish. Attorney Baird asked the jury, if Paula was to be found guilty, to sentence her only to prison. "Do not be so cold in soul as to demand death of this fair maiden who has been wronged by an uncaring adulterer". The prosecutor felt otherwise by stating "She should pay the entire cost of the action".

Judge Benedict instructed the jury prior to deliberations that the jury must either find Paula Angel guilty of first-degree murder or not find her guilty of any crime. On March 28, 1861, the jury did find Paula Angel guilty of first degree murder. Judge Benedict then passed judgment on Paula Angel. Judge Benedict announced that she be "hanged by the neck until dead on Friday, April 26, 1861, between the hours of 10 o'clock in the forenoon and 4 o'clock in the afternoon". Judge Benedict instructed Sheriff Herrera to locate a suitable place one mile from the church within the town of Las Vegas to carry out the sentence. Paula was further ordered by the judge to pay all court cost and the expense of her hanging.

For the next 29 days, it was said Sheriff Herrera would mentally torment Paula as to how many days she had to live and how he was going to hang her until she was "DEAD, DEAD, DEAD". On the day of her execution, April 26, 1861, Paula was described as "a sack of bone enveloped in Flesh." Apparently her lack of sleep, eating, and her mental anguish during her month in jail had taken its toll on her. Sheriff Herrera prepared a wagon and team and loaded the bed with the coffin. At 10 o'clock in the morning, Sheriff Herrera removed Paula from the jail and had her sit upon her coffin on the way to her execution sight.

The Sheriff drove his team of horses to a grove of cottonwood trees northwest of town. A crowd of spectators waited near a large cottonwood which had already been prepared with the hangman's noose. Sheriff Herrera stopped the wagon directly under the noose and ordered Paula to stand. After slipping and tightening the noose around Paula's neck, he eagerly jumped onto the wagon seat and popped the reins for the horses to go forward. In turning back to look at Paula, he was shocked to see that in his excitement to hang Paula Angel, he had forgotten to tie her arms and legs. As Paula was strangling, and attempting to pull herself up, Sheriff Herrera ran to the helpless woman, grabbing her around the waist and with his body weight attempted to pull her downward.

Strangulation, crying or suffering at an execution was generally frowned on. Several of the spectators rushed in, pushed the Sheriff aside and cut Paula down. The crowd felt Paula had hung long enough and the sentence of the court had been carried out. Sheriff Herrera drew his revolver and reminded everyone he was still the Sheriff. He warned the crowd he would shoot anyone who interfered with the execution. Col. Jose D. Serna who was well respected stood up and read the death warrant out loud from the top of the wagon. He explained the warrant which said that Paula was to hang by the neck until dead by 4 o'clock of April 26, and she was not dead and it wasn't even 4 o'clock.

The wagon was moved back under the limb and Paula again stood on top of the wagon. This time her arms and legs were tied. The horses were driven forward and Paula Angel died after having to be hanged twice on the same day.

Sources:

Bryan, Howard. *Wildest of the Wild West*. Clear Light Publishers, Santa Fe, New Mexico, 1988.

Hertog, Peter. *Legal Hangings*. The Press of the Territorian, Santa Fe, New Mexico, 1966.

Roy French, alias Frank French

Not a lot is known about 23 year old Roy French who was hanged at 10:20 on the morning of September 12, 1870. The *Weekly New Mexican* newspaper dated Tuesday, September 13, 1870, had the following information.

Roy French, the Negro convicted of murder at the last term of the San Miguel District Court, will hang at Las Vegas on next Monday, the 12th inst. The warrant for his execution was issued yesterday by Gov. Pile. We are informed that a petition was forwarded from Las Vegas to the Governor asking that the sentenced be commuted, or a new trial granted the prisoner, but under the present law the Executive can only pardon unconditionally or let the law take its course; there is no provision by which he either can commute the sentence or grant a new trial.

Sources:

Weekly New Mexican, September 13, 1870

Frederick Falkner

In August of 1891, James Lannon was heading for Texas by wagon when he stopped in Trinidad, Colorado. There he met Frederick Falkner, who asked Mr. Lannon if he could hitch a ride with him. Mr. Lannon, not wanting to turn down the opportunity for some companionship on the journey, agreed to his request.

The men traveled past Trinchera, New Mexico, and camp was set up. During the night while James Lannon slept, Frederick Falkner slipped up on him with an axe and struck the body twice. The next morning, the body was found and a Sheriff's Posse was organized. The posse of men tracked Falkner and captured him the following morning. He was still in possession of the victim's watch, his wagon, and team.

Frederick Falkner was tried in Las Vegas, New Mexico, on a change of venue and convicted of murder in the first degree. His attorney immediately appealed the conviction to the Territorial Supreme Court at Santa Fe. Justice Seeds wrote the opinion on August 9th, affirming the lower courts decision. Judge Seeds wrote "The defendant had a fair and impartial trial, his rights were duly protected by court and counsel, the jury acted without precipitation or any evidence of passion, and their verdict was unquestionable right and just. There being no error found in the action of the trial court, the judgment will be affirmed."

The final order of the Supreme Court is as follows:

"On Friday, the 19th day of August, 1892, between the hours of 9 o'clock in the forenoon and 5 o'clock in the afternoon of said day, within a special enclosure secured from public view, in the presence of a sufficient number of witnesses to attest the execution of the judgment, in the area of the yard appurtenant to the common jail situated in Las Vegas, in the county of San Miguel and the territory of New Mexico, the said plaintiff in error, Frederick Falkner, shall be taken by the sheriff of said county, or other duly authorized officer, and by him be hanged by the neck until dead," etc.

As a last attempt to save his client's life, his attorney sent a petition with over 300 signatures to Governor Prince requesting a pardon or commutation to life in prison. The Governor consulted with Chief Justice O'Brien who was familiar with the case. The Governor's reply was received the day before the execution and read to the condemned man in his cell. The Governor wrote that he saw nothing in his investigation which would lead him to take any action.

On August 19th, 1892, Frederick Falkner made no last comment on the scaffold. Sheriff Jose L. Lopez placed the noose around the man's neck and released the trap at 2:51. The drop failed to break Falkner's neck because the noose had been improperly placed. The witnesses watched as Falkner strangled to death for 20 minutes. The *Daily Citizen* had the following story.

Frederick Falkner

He Pays the Death Penalty for His Crime at Las Vegas,

Frederick Falkner was hung at the Las Vegas jail at 2:51 this afternoon, a great number of people had assembled on the outside of the jail, but the proceedings were conducted with promptness inside, and only a few witnessed the act.

The man who expiated his crime of murder on the gallows at Las Vegas this afternoon, was accused of having murdered his friend and traveling companion, James Lannon, in August last, near Trinchera, Colfax county. Falkner met Lannon in Trinidad, Col., and as the latter was on route to Texas, in a wagon, Falkner asked to go along, and the two men started together across Colfax County on the journey to the "Lone Star" state. After leaving Trinchera, Lannon disappeared as suddenly as if the earth had opened and he had been swallowed up. Falkner, however, continued on, driving the team of Lannon and was soon in the Panhandle country. A few days later Lannon's body was found on the prairie, and a posse of officers went in pursuit of Falkner, whom they found in possession of the team of the murdered man, and several articles, including Lannon's watch, were also found on the person of Falkner.

On a change of venue, Falkner's trial came on at Las Vegas, and the circumstantial evidence was so strong that the jury promptly declared him guilty of murder in the first degree. The murderer has a criminal record and it is a terrible one, being noted in Colorado, Kansas, and elsewhere for various crimes, and some of them are murders.

Sources:

The Albuquerque *Daily Citizen*, August 19, 1892
Santa Fe *Daily New Mexican*, August 19, 1892

Herman Maestas

Herman Maestas belonged to a gang responsible for numerous murders, robbery, and cattle thefts in San Miguel and Mora County. The gang was organized by Vicente Silva and headquartered out of his Imperial Saloon in Las Vegas, New Mexico. The gang was known as the Secret Crime Organization, or the Society of Bandits of New Mexico.

In late February or early March of 1894, before a justice of the peace at Los Alamos, Herman Maestas married a woman of the name of Rosa Duran. The marriage certificate was never registered with the county clerk as required by law. Soon after the marriage, Herman Maestas was jailed in Las Vegas for robbery. While in jail, Pedro Romero learned that the marriage of Herman and Rosa had not been registered, thus making the marriage invalid. Pedro Romero then married Rosa Duran himself. Afterwards, to tease him, Pedro and his new wife went to the jail and told Herman of their marriage to each other. In anger, Herman broke out of the Las Vegas jail and immediately set out, with Jesus Vialpando, to find Pedro Romero at his sheep ranch.

Both men found Pedro with a young boy. Herman rode up to Pedro and asked him, "Why did you marry my wife? Didn't you know that she was married to me? Ingrate, why did you when I was in jail, go there yourself with my wife to tease me." Pedro replied boldly, "I was advised to do so by Manuel Gonzales y Baca. He told me to go to the office of the probate judge and find out that your marriage was invalid." Herman Maestas shot and killed Pedro as the boy look on. The boy's life was spared with the understanding if he told anyone what was witnessed he would suffer a painful death. The boy went to a neighboring ranch and reported the murder. Herman Maestas was arrested and tried for murder. Being found guilty of the murder, he was sentenced to hang on May 25, 1894.

The Gallows was built within a small enclosure at the Las Vegas jail. On May 25, the execution was delayed because of a heavy rain and hailstorm. At 12:37, the 150 witnesses who had been issued invitation cards to the execution were allowed inside the enclosure. The condemned man was lead out of his cell at 1:14 and lead to the gallows by Sheriff Cunningham, of Santa Fe, Sheriff Lopez, deputies, and Father Grom, the spiritual advisor.

Once on the scaffold, Maestas declined to make a final statement, but recited his prayers. After he finished his prayer, Maestas was placed over the trap door. At 1:16 the trap door was sprung and Herman Maestas fell to his death at the end of the rope. His pulse ceased after five minutes and five minutes later the doctor pronounced Herman Maestas dead. The body was lowered and the remains released to family members. Jesus Vialpando was never charged for his part in Pedro Romero's murder. His criminal career ended the same as Herman Maestas, for he was executed in Santa Fe on

November 19, 1895, for the murder of Tomas Martinez. The Albuquerque
Weekly Citizen had the following headlines and story about Maestes.

PAYS THE PENALTY.

MURDERER MAESTAS HANGED AT LAS
VEGAS THIS AFTERNOON.

A Drenching Rain Storm De-
Lays the Execution.

He recites His Prayers and Then
Dies Bravely.

Proceedings Perfect.

*Herman Maestas receiving last rites from Father Grom seconds before the
trap door is released. Courtesy Museum of New Mexico, Neg. No.
177014. Unknown photographer.*

Special to the *New Mexican.*

Las Vegas, N.M., May 25. At 1:20 this afternoon Herman Maestas in the
presence of 200 people, expiated on the gallows his crime of murdering Pedro
Romero at Los Alamos two months ago. Led by Sheriff Cunningham, of
Santa Fe, the murderer walked firmly and with a smiling face to the gallows.

He made no public statement or confession from the scaffold. After prayers by the priest to which he answered in a clear voice the rope was drawn around the neck, the black cap placed over the head and Maestas was launched into eternity. His neck was broken by the fall; life was pronounced extinct in five minutes. His body was turned over to his aged father for interment.

A GANG OF CUT THROATS.

Herman Maestas was an active member of an infamous secret society, organized to rob and murder, which has infested San Miguel and Mora counties for over two years. There were originally twenty five members of the organization, and among them were several policemen of old Las Vegas, through whom they were kept posted of every move the law officers made, and thus it happens that the gang so long enjoyed immunity from prosecution. Their crimes consisted of stealing stock, robbing country stores and post offices, intimidating voters at the polls to keep their members in office, fence cutting, barn burning and murder. Eight or ten murders are said to be directly traceable to this society, not particularly for robbery, but also because of personal spite that some influential member may have had against the citizen.

To the work of the present Democratic administration is due the collapse of the society and punishment of its members. The officials now in power have pursued the scoundrels with such relentless energy as to free San Miguel County of its worst enemies, and wipe out the stain upon its otherwise fair name. It is regrettable, however, that the two ring-leaders of the gang, Vicente Silva and Jose Chavez y Chavez, are still at liberty, but the officials express a determination not to let the case rest until these two outlaws pay the penalty of their crimes.

There are now in the penitentiary for complicity in murders and robberies committed by the gang: Librando Polanco, Remigio Sandoval, Martin Gonzales y Blea, Dionicio Sisneros, Eugenio Alarid, an ex-policeman, and Julian Trujillo, all sentenced to life; Procarpio Rael, ten years; Marcos Barela, seven years; Nestor Herrera, seven years; Pedro Baca, five years; Nicacio Rael, five years; Zenon Maes, four years; Jesus Tiburcio Montoya, three years.

BRUTAL MURDERS.

Although Maestas is the only member of the gang to hang yet the crimes of the others were almost as revolting, but there were mitigating circumstances that prompted the court and jury to lighten their sentences. It is safe to say, however, that if Silva is ever found he will be furnished a rope adornment for his neck.

The two most shocking murders of the gang were the hanging of Maes and the stabbing death of a youth named Gabriel Sandoval. The desire to be revenged for personal wrongs prompted the murder of Maes. He was a member of the gang, but is said to have given away one of their secrets. He was tried in Silva's saloon, taken out and hanged to a bridge in the center of the town about 2 o'clock in the morning.

Sandoval was the brother-in-law and was accused of being criminally intimate with his own sister, who was Silva's wife. It was merely a trumped up charge, but Silva issued the edict that Sandoval must die and the innocent youth was consequently killed.

Sandoval was lead to the slaughter by Julian Trujillo, who was a policeman at the time. Silva was concealed behind a bush and as Sandoval and Trujillo passed him jumped out and stabbed Sandoval to death.

WHY HE WAS HANGED.

Maestas was one of the most despicable scoundrels on the entire gang. His murder of Pedro Romero was extremely brutal. Romero was a sheepherder and was accused by Maestas of being too intimate with his wife. About three months ago Romero was tending to his sheep near Los Alamos in company with a small boy, when he saw Maestas and a companion, whose name the hanged criminal refused to divulged, coming toward him. The herder knew the murderous intentions of the two men and informed his youthful companion that they were coming to kill him.

Maestas and his accomplice wasted no time when they came up to Romero, but immediately shot, Maestas firing the first shot. Romero fell and he was shot again while lying on his back. The two murderers held a short consultation and decided to kill the boy, but for some unaccountable reason they permitted him to go free and his testimony caused Maestas' conviction.

The boy was cautioned, upon pain of death not to leave the place where the murder was committed and not to reveal his secret for the pace of twenty four hours. The brave little fellow disobeyed his instructions, and soon as the two brutes left the scene of the murder he made his way to a ranch and told of the occurrence. Maestas was shortly afterward arrested and conviction soon followed.

OTHER CRIMES.

The killing of Romero was not by any means the only one of Maestas' crimes. In a partial confession made a few days ago he told of numerous criminal deeds in which he was implicated. He said that he, in company with another desperado, held up four preachers at one time in what is known as the lower county, on the San Juan River, and relieved the divines of $100 in cash.

He openly confessed that he had been implicated in more robberies and cattle and horse stealing than he could remember. In 1892 a school director named Carpio Sais was killed and robbed of $150. Sais' body was buried and up to this time has not been recovered. Maestas' recital of the murder of Sais is one of the most cold blooded narratives ever published and proves the perpetrators to have been utterly void of feeling.

Maestas came into town from his home on the day of the murder and met Julian Trujillo, Jose Chavez y Chavez and Pablo Lucero. Chavez spoke to Maestas and revealed to him the plot to rob Sais. It was the intention of the men to kill their victim, as they knew too well that if they merely robbed him they would be made to suffer for the crime. Maestas entered into the conspiracy without hesitation. They decoyed Sais to a place where the crime could be committed with safety and then accomplished their hellish designs by stabbing and stoning their victim to death.

Maestas declares that his part of the program was to remain behind the rest in order, it is supposed, to give the alarm in case of detection. He went into a saloon to buy a bottle of whiskey, but delayed too long as when he came out his co conspirators were not in sight. He was unable to find them and went back to a saloon where he waited until Chavez, Trujillo and Lucero returned. When they did return they reproached Maestas for what they termed his cowardice, gave him $9 and cautioned him to keep his mouth shut lest he share the same fate. Maestas denied any complicity in the murder of young Sandoval, but it is thought he was in some way connected with it.

HIS GUILTY CONSCIENCE.

There is one mean trait that Maestas could not be accused of and that was cowardice. He bore his fate with becoming bravery, but the conscience of a guilty man never rests easy, and so it was with Maestas. Although he maintained a stoic demeanor, he nevertheless was afraid to meet death.

When asked what he had to tell his friends and fellow-criminals, he replied that he advised them all to refrain from wrong doing. He averred that a man who is a criminal is always restless and uneasy. He professed religion and shortly before his death acknowledged his faith in God and declared that he believed the Almighty had forgiven him his sins. The hanged man was an unmitigated liar, but a true friend to the man who assisted him in the killing of Romero. He refused to give his companion's name, because, as he said, it would do him no good.

BREAKING UP THE GANG.

The hanging of Maestas was a triumph of justice. Gov. Thornton was besieged with requests from Maestas and his friends for a commutation of the sentence to life imprisonment, but the chief executive refused to interfere with the work of the courts. The execution means the virtual disbandment of the criminal gang of San Miguel County. The criminals had enjoyed their freedom so long that they had about arrived at the conclusion that they were greater then the law and that they could not be brought to suffer for their crimes. In this they were mistaken. Among the first acts of the present administration was the attempt to run to earth the criminals and it has succeeded beyond its most sanguine hopes. At the recent session of the District Court twenty-nine criminals were sentenced to the penitentiary and was sentenced to be hanged.

This is a record for law and order that speaks well for all New Mexico. The hanging of Maestas has taught the rest of the gang a salutary lesson. The only thing that now remains to be done to break up the gang entirely is the capture of Vicente Silva and Jose Chavez y Chavez. That this may soon be accomplished is the earnest wish of every law abiding citizen in San Miguel County.

Sources:

The *Evening Citizen* (Albuquerque), May 25, 1894
New Mexico Review (Santa Fe), May 31, 1894
Albuquerque *Weekly Citizen*, May 26, 1894
Albuquerque *Morning Democrat*, May 26, 1894
Santa Fe *Daily New Mexican*, May 25, 1894

Julian Romero

On the night of May 26, 1917, Julian Romero murdered a woman named Maria Varela de Jaure. Romero shot and killed the woman in a jealous rage in upper Las Vegas. He was tried and convicted for murder in the first degree. The death sentence was appealed to the State Supreme Court, which affirmed the lower court's decision.

At the noon hour of April 10th, Sheriff Delgado in the company of Rev. Father Balland notified Julian that the Supreme Court had denied his appeal and that he must hang the following day. As Sheriff Delgado read the verdict of the court, Julian stood with his arms crossed to brace himself. With an uncontrollable body tremor and water filled eyes, Julian collapsed to the floor kissing the Father's hand. Sheriff Delgado asked Julian if he had anything to say. He begged the Sheriff for more time and was told that was not possible and that he would hang the next day. Julian said he was sorry no clemency had been granted, but where clemency had not been given here, he expected to have if from God.

At 1:00 o'clock the scaffold was completed and the trap was tested. Julian regained his composure and showed courage the next day on the scaffold before the 20 witnesses who had been invited to watch the execution. Julian Romero was described as having a small stature, 5'5 in height, and having a thick neck that extended in a straight line to his chin. The paper wrote that this was "a characteristic of many of the worlds most notorious criminals."

At the end of his short statement, Julian stood over the trap door that was sprung at 7:35. The fall broke Julian Romero neck and he died instantly. County Physician H. J. Mueller and Drs. Marais and G. M. Fleming pronounced the body dead after 10 minutes and then it was cut down. The Santa Fe *New Mexican* had the following story.

TWO YOUNG WOMEN SEE
A MURDERER HANGED

JULIAN ROMERO DISPLAYS
GREAT NERVE WHEN FACING
DEATH IN SAN MIGUEL COUN-
TY JAIL YARD

The Las Vegas *Optic* States that Julian Romero who was hanged in San Miguel county jail yard yesterday, went to his death as bravely as any condemned criminal has faced his executioners. Romero was sustained by the thought that sincere repentance would obtain for him the forgiveness of the Creator. Rev. Father Ballard, pastor of the Church of Our Lady of Sorrows, was with Romero before his death. The priest pronounced a prayer for the man's soul, and the last word Romero uttered upon this earth as he shot downward to his death was the name of God.

Among the 20 official witnesses to the hanging were two young women. A photographer made an effort to get a picture of the hanging but it is believed the cloudy weather interfered. The trap was sprung at 7:35 o'clock. It is believed that Romero died instantly. His body was taken down at 7:45 o'clock, when the county physician and an assistant pronounced him dead.

Before adjusting the black cap, Sheriff Delgado asked Romero if he wished to say anything. With rare courage the young man stepped to the edge of the scaffold and spoke in a clear tone of voice for a few moments, He said:

"Ladies and Gentlemen:

"I, as a man sentenced to death today have the honor to thank you all most sincerely for your good appreciation, and for what you have done for me to the last minute: and I hope that God will repay you. I will ask God for you, as these are favors that are not often received.

"Also ladies and gentlemen and young ladies, I cannot say very much to you at the present time but I have come to my day and my hour to leave this world with honor, because I fell in an awful crime. God and I only know how I did it.

"I thank you all most sincerely for your kind attention. This sheriff of San Miguel county it is his duty to enforce the law. I know that he wouldn't want to do this, but the law makes him do so, and he is obliged to do it and comply with the law.

"And, all my friends: these will be my last words to you. I will take my death, and I am resigned to take the best there is. Goodbye."

Wednesday night crowds of people visited the county jail for a last word with Romero. Sheriff Delgado left word with the jailors that none were to be refused admittance though they were forced to speak to the man through the bars. Romero's mother, Mrs. Melecio Archibeque, visited her son for the last time. Mrs. Archibeque is deaf and though she could not hear the words of her son she read in his face the pitiful confession of his sin and his state of mind preparatory to his coming death. The parting of mother and son was indeed pitiful. Broken-hearted, the mother turned her steps from the jail at a late hour with prayers and weeping for the salvation of the soul of her only son.

A sad incident in connection with the hanging of Romero is the fact that his only sister, Mrs. P. Gallegos, was unable to see her brother at the last. Mrs. Gallegos is dangerously ill at her home and it is feared that the news of the hanging of her brother will result in her death.

Sources:

Santa Fe *New Mexican*, April 11, 12, 1918

Chapter 12

Santa Fe County

Don Antonio Maria Trujillo April 16, 1847
Thaddeus M. Rodgers September 14, 1860
Jesus Vialpondo November 19, 1895
Feliciano Chavez November 19, 1895
Francisco Gonzales y Borrego April 2, 1897
Antonio Gonzales y Borrego April 2, 1897
Lauriano Alarid April 2, 1897
Patricio Valencia April 2, 1897
Jose Telles, alias Alejandro Duran April 3, 1903
Elbert W. Blancett July 9, 1920

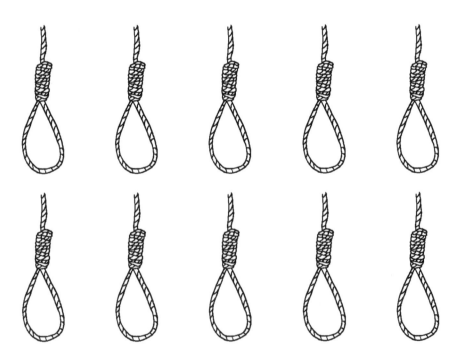

Don Antonio Maria Trujillo

Don Antonio Maria Trujillo may have been the first person executed in the territory of New Mexico. He was charged, sentenced, and hanged for the crime of treason against the Government of the United States. His crime of treason occurred when war was declared by Mexico against the United States in 1847. Don Antonio Maria Trujillo was a native of Santa Fe and appointed by Mexico as Inspector of Arms. In January of 1847, Don Maria Trujillo received a document from Jesus Tafolla. What title or rank Jesus Tafolla held is unknown. The letter reads,

To THE DEFENDERS OF THEIR COUNTRY:

With the end to shake off the yoke imposed upon us by a foreign government and as you are Inspector General, appointed by the legitimate Commander for the supreme government of Mexico, which we proclaim in favor of, the moment that you receive this communication you will place in readiness all the companies under your command, keeping them ready for the 22nd day of the present month, so that the forces may be on the day relentless at that point. Take the precaution to observe if the forces of the enemy advance any toward those points, and if it should so happen, appoint a courier and dispatch him immediately so that diversions may be doubled. Understand that there must not be resistance or delay in giving the answer to the bearer of this official document.

Jesus Tafolla.
Senior Inspector.
Antonio Maria Trujillo
Jan. 20, 1847

This document and the following one written by Don Antonio Maria Trujillo were used as evidence at his trial.

By the order of the Inspector of Arms,
Don Antonio Maria Trujillo: I here – unto send you this order that the moment this comes to your hand you will raise all the forces together with all the inhabitants that are able to bear arms, connecting them also with persons in San Juan Caballeros, by the morning of the 22nd day of the present month, and not later than 8 o'clock in the morning. We have declared war with the Americans and it is now time that we take our arms in our hands in defense of our prostrate country, that we may try if possible to regain the liberty of our unhappy country. You will be held responsible, if you fail in the execution of the above order.

Juan Anto. Garsla.
Sn. Dn. Pedro Vigil.

The letter was sent to both men named above and was accompanied by the first letter by Jesus Tafolla. When the United States intercepted both letters, Antonio M. Trujillo was arrested and placed in an adobe stockade. Judge Joab Houghton was the first judge for the Territory of New Mexico to prosecute a case. On March 16, 1847, Judge Houghton called court to order to hear the case, "The United States of American vs. Antonio Maria Trujillo, Treason." In pronouncing sentence, Judge Houghton made the following sentence:

"Your age and grey hairs have excited the sympathy of both the court and the jury. Yet, while each and all were not only willing but anxious that you should have every advantage placed at your disposal that their highly responsible duty under the law to their country would permit, yet have you been found guilty of the crime alleged to your charge. It would appear that old age has not brought you wisdom, nor purity, nor honesty of heart; while holding out the hand of friendship to those whom circumstances have brought to rule over you, you have nourished bitterness and hatred in your soul. You have been found guilty of seconding the acts of a band of the most traitorous murderers that ever blackened with the recital of their deeds the annuals of history.

"Not content with the peace and security in which you lived under the present government, secure in all your

PERSONAL RIGHTS AS A CITIZEN,

in property, in person and in your religion, you gave your name and influences to measures intended to effect universal murder and pillage, the overthrow of the government and one wide spread scene of blood shed in the land. For such foul crimes an enlightened and liberal jury have been compelled from the evidence brought before them and by a sense of their stern but unmistakable duty to find you guilty of treason against the government under which you are a citizen, and there only now remains to the court the painful duty of passing upon you the sentence of the law, which is, that you be taken hence to prison, there to remain until Friday, the 16th day of April next, and that at 2 o'clock in the afternoon of that day you be taken thence to the place of execution and there be hanged by the neck till you are dead! dead! dead! And may the almighty God have mercy on your soul."

Sources:

Santa Fe *Daily New Mexican*, February 18, 1883

Thaddeus M. Rodgers
Murder, Santa Fe County.

Thaddeus Rodgers was executed on September 14, 1860, in an arroyo east of San Rosario Church in Santa Fe. Mr. Rodgers had been employed as an engineer for Herach's Flour Mill at the south end of Water Street. On Christmas Eve, 1859, Mr. Rodgers had been drinking liquor since early morning and decided to go to Joseph Herach's store.

When entering the store, Mr. Rodgers had a pistol in his hand. He announced to those present in the store that he intended to kill either Mr. Herach or surveyor William White. A teamster named Marcelino Sabiallos was shot and killed while defending Mr. Herach as he ran to get away. Thaddeus Rodgers was jailed in Santa Fe for the murder but later escaped and fled to Colorado. Thaddeus was recaptured and returned to New Mexico to stand trial for murder in the first degree. Being found guilty of the murder, his execution was supervised by Sheriff Jesus Maria Baca y Salazar.

Sources:

Rio Grande *Republican*, November 22, 1895

Jesus Vialpando & Feliciano Chavez

Jesus Vialpando and Feliciano Chavez were executed minutes apart on Saturday, November 19, 1895 in Santa Fe, New Mexico. Both men were executed for the first-degree murder of Tomas Martinez.

Jesus Vialpando and Feliciano Chavez were known cattle thieves. Both men on January 18th, left San Pedro, New Mexico, along with Zenobio Trujillo and Emilio Encinias to return to Las Vegas. During their journey back, the weather had turned cold and snowy. The four men arrived at a corral near Ole de la Baca and started a large fire to warm themselves. Cold, hungry, and seeing cattle, five or six steers were rounded up and locked in the corral. One of the steers was killed and meat from the hindquarter was cut and roasted in the fire.

Thirty–two year old Tomas Martinez had been out looking for stray cattle, belonging to his father, for four days in Cañon Blanco. He was on his way home when he spotted the men and the fire in the corral. Jesus Vialpando upon seeing Tomas riding up commented to his companions, "There is a fine horse coming, that will be a nice chicken for us." The men asked Tomas to dismount off his horse and to join them at the fire to get warm. He did so and was asked if he had any coffee. Tomas replied he did, and retrieved a bag of coffee from his saddlebags. While the men were drinking the coffee Tomas provided them, he turned his back and hands towards the fire to warm them. Jesus Vialpando gave a signal to Chavez who jumped up and bear hugged Tomas from behind pinning his arms. Jesus drew his revolver and ordered Tomas to throw his hands up and for Trujillo and Encinias to disarm him.

Vialpando told Trujillo and Encinias to ride on out and that Chavez and he would catch up with them. After riding about a half mile, Trujillo and Encinias heard three or four gunshots. Soon Vialpando and Chavez caught up to them. Chavez was riding the horse with the saddle and bridle Tomas had been riding. Encinias asked Vialpando, "what did you do with the man that came into the corral on the horse Chavez is now riding?" Vialpando told him, "We killed him, you *cabron*, do you want me to kill you too? I'll do it if you say anything about this."

Vialpando was arrested at his mother's home and was still in possession of Tomas's saddle and bridle. After Chavez was arrested, he took officers to the location where he had killed Tomas's horse. He told officers, he killed the horse to avoid any connection to the murder after he had read in a newspaper that the remains of Tomas Martinez had been found. Both Vialpando and Chavez confessed that Trujillo and Encinias had left the corral before the murder. Vialpando and Chavez had cut some more meat off the steer when Tomas saw the brand. He told both men that the steer belonged to his father. Vialpando, angered by this, drew his weapon and told Tomas to take off his overcoat. After doing so, Vialpando shot Tomas in the left temple and Chavez fired two more bullets into the body. The body was then picked up and placed on top of the fire. The men gathered wood fence posts from the corral and placed that wood on top of the body and fire. Vialpando, seeing Tomas's dog, shot the animal between the eyes. Before he had the opportunity to place the dog in the fire with his master, the dog recovered and took off running. Amazed by what he saw, Vialpondo didn't realize that the bullet had glanced off the dog's head and lodged behind the ear.

Both Vialpando and Chavez were tried for the murder on March 26 before Judge Laughlin. On the 30th, both men were found guilty of murder in the first degree. Judge Laughlin sentenced them on April 12 to hang by the neck until dead. Trujillo and Encinias were released on a $1,000 bond for cattle theft. The murder conviction was appealed to the Supreme Court which affirmed the lower courts decision. The Supreme Court ordered the sheriff of Santa Fe to hang the condemned men on November 19, 1895, between the hours of 6 and 10 in the morning. The only action the Governor took was to sign the death warrant on November 14th.

Prior to their execution, Jesus Vialpando wrote a statement to Sheriff Cunningham for publication. In the statement, Vialpondo wrote he was 30 years old, born on May 5th, 1865 in Valencia County, New Mexico. During his life he had been elected as a Constable of precinct 58 in San Miguel County. In 1890, he was elected Justice of the Peace, and in 1892 elected School Director. He further wrote he had been with Herman Maestas when Pedro Romero was shot and killed for marrying Maestas wife. At the end of his statement he asked that his friends look over his wife and children. He thanked Sheriff Cunningham for his kind treatment. Feliciano Chavez did not make any written statement or brief history of himself.

In preparation for the execution, the County Commissioners ordered the hanging rope from Kansas City. The gallows was built in a sandy arroyo a half-mile north of the county jail and to the back of the federal building. On execution day, the guards were issued Winchester rifles and shotguns. Jesus Vialpando was the first man removed from the jail and driven to the scaffold where an estimated 3,000 people had gathered to watch. Vialpando was so unnerved that he was unable to talk to make a last statement. While he was being prepared for execution, the deputies returned to the jail to get Feliciano Chavez. The trap was sprung at 6:47 and thirteen minutes later cut down. The neck was so stretched by the drop that Vialpando's feet were two inches above the ground. Chavez walked up to the scaffold and spoke to the crowd for eighteen minutes. He told the crowd he was present when Jesus Vialpando killed Tomas Martinez and did nothing. Chavez was then executed and eight minutes later cut down. The rope had cut deep into the neck, and it was speculated that had the drop been any further, Chavez would have been decapitated. The *Daily New Mexican* dated November 19, 1895, had the following story.

AWFUL SEQUEL TO AN AWFUL CRIME

Vialpando and Chavez Executed
Law and Justice Vindicated

PAID THE DREADFUL PENALTY

In compliance with the decree of the District Court, affirmed by the territorial Supreme Court, and in obedience to the command of the death warrant duly signed by the Governor, Sheriff Cunningham this morning hanged Jesus Vialpando and Feliciano Chavez by the neck, until they were dead, for the brutal murder of Tomas Martinez, on Saturday, the 20th day of January, 1895.

Deputy Sheriff Tucker stayed with the condemned men at the county jail last night as a death watch, and reports that Vialpando slept one hour and Chavez slept about three hours. Both were exceedingly nervous, but quiet. Neither would taste any breakfast this morning. Vialpando begged the sheriff for whiskey but this petition was firmly refused. Neither of the men were given a drop of stimulating liquor either last night or this morning.

About 6 o'clock this morning Sheriff Cunningham with a sufficient force of deputies, Sheriff Hubbell and Romero, of Bernalillo and San Miguel counties, Father Antonio Fourchegu, and a number of others went to the jail. The scene there was pathetic when the doomed men handed to Sheriff Romero packages containing about $3.25 each, the money having been given to them in nickels by visitors to the jail, and requested him to give the same to their respective families. They also returned the prayer books that they had kindly been loaned to them and both kissed the crucifix.

VIALPANDO TAKEN FIRST

Vialpando was led to a carriage in waiting and quickly transported to the scaffold in the arroyo north of the gas works and about a half mile north of the plaza. There a large crowd of people estimated at from 1,000 to 1,500 had already assembled.

Vialpando ascended to the platform of the scaffold supported by Sheriffs Cunningham and Hubbell and followed by Sheriff Romero, Pedro Delgado, A. P. Hill, Antonio Borrego, Pablo Martinez (brother of the murdered man), Officer Carson, of Albuquerque, and Antonio Cajal, of Las Vegas. He looked pale and frightened, but stood erect on the death trap. He did not utter an audible word. The noose was swiftly placed around the neck, his arms and legs were securely pinioned and the black cap placed over his head.

At 6:50 Sheriff Cunningham pulled the lever and the drop fell. By the time the quickest observer caught a glimpse of the suspended body, with its feet only about six inches from the ground, life was practically extinct. The cervical vertebra was dislocated by the fall and death followed without a struggle or contortions. Dr. Diaz, who held the pulse of the hanging unfortunate, says that the man lost consciousness in thirty seconds and that a quicker or more merciful death could hardly have been inflicted. During the first minute the pulse beats were 65, during the second 42, during the third 20, and during the fourth they were hardly recognizable. The body was cut down by Deputy Sheriff Tucker in thirteen minutes, the boots were removed, and it was immediately placed in a coffin and carried to Undertaker Gable's wagon.

RETURNED FOR FELICIANO CHAVEZ.

The sheriff and his assistants promptly returned to the jail for Feliciano Chavez. Chavez reached the place of execution at 7:40 and he at once ascended to the fateful platform accompanied by the same persons who had so recently stood there with Vialpando. Chavez appeared to face the ordeal with stronger nerve than his predecessor. He made a rambling talk of eighteen minutes to the crowd in Spanish, Mesers. Hill, Cajal and Delgado taking turns as interpreter. He admitted and then virtually denied that he participated in the killing of young Martinez; laid the burden of responsibility for the crime upon Vialpando; implicated Zenobio Trujillo as one of the principals in the horrible affair; professed that he endeavored to prevent the deed; thanked Sheriff Romero and Cunningham for their kindness to him; pathetically referred to his wife and little children; warned all his hearers to beware of the evil association that had been his destruction; said that he was resigned to his fate and ready to meet his God, and concluded by bidding all good bye.

He was then led to the trap and prepared for execution in the same manner, as was Vialpando. After the black cap was over his head he exclaimed, "*Adios todos.*" Just at 8 o'clock the sheriff pulled the lever, the trap fell and Feliciano Chavez was hurled into eternity. His neck was broken and it is probable that a foot more of fall would have severed his head from his body. After he dropped a slight tremor passed over him, but otherwise he died without a struggle. The doctors say he lost consciousness instantly. During the first minute his pulse beats could not be felt, during the second minute they were 65, during the third 47 and during the fourth 20. He was cut down in fourteen minutes, his body was placed in a coffin and then in the undertaker's wagon by the side of Vialpando.

BODIES GO TO ROMERVILLE.

In compliance with request the bodies were turned over to Sheriff Romero by Sheriff Cunningham. They were taken to the depot at 8:30 this morning, and will tonight be shipped to Romeroville, San Miguel County, where the families of the deceased reside. Vialpando and Chavez were each about 30 years old. The former leaves a widow and two children and the latter a widow and five children.

Story of the Crime.

Don Lorenzo Martinez, of Santa Fe, owns and operates an extensive cattle and horse ranch at Ojo de la Baca (Cow Springs) in the southeastern part of this county, and last January his sons, Tomas and Maximiliano, were there looking after their father's interest. On Thursday morning, January 17, Tomas, the oldest of the two young men, started away from the ranch on horseback in quest of missing cattle. He was mounted on a good horse, had a first class saddle and bridle, was well armed and had an excellent equipment of blankets and warm clothing. A faithful and favorite dog of the bull-dog species accustomed to such trips eagerly followed his master. As the young man rode away he told Maximiliano that he would be back on Sunday afternoon. But he never returned.

THE NOBLE AND SAGACIOUS DOG.

About 10 o'clock on Tuesday morning however, the noble and sagacious dog returned to the ranch in a most pitiable condition. He was completely exhausted from exposure, hunger and loss of blood from a ghastly gun-shot wound in the head, but after being fed, the poor dog showed by unmistakable sign that something serious had happened and that action must be taken at once. After examining the dog's injury and reflecting that the loyal animal never would have deserted his master except under most extraordinary circumstances, Maximiliano instantly concluded that the evident anxiety of the animal to be moving meant something and should not be disregarded. So he quickly saddled a horse and started to ride south, the direction in which he supposed his brother to be, but the dog obstinately refused to go that way, whining mournfully and running almost due east. Finally Maximiliano decided to follow the dog, and after riding about eight or nine miles, he reached his father's round up corral at La Muralla. The dog ran in ahead, went straight to the remains of what had evidently been an unusually large camp fire and began barking and digging in the ashes with his paws. Maximiliano was soon on the ground and in the corral. There he saw the tracks of a number of horses, the fresh footprints of a number of men and noticed part of the carcass of one of his father's steers.

Found His Brother's Foot.

As the dog persisted in barking around the spot where the fire had been and indicating in many other ways that was the place to explore, the young man began raking in the heap of ashes and lifeless embers, and almost immediately discovered a human foot still encased in a heavy shoe and overshoe, which, although partly charred, he recognized as belonging to his brother. He also found part of the large pelvis bones. The rest of the body had been consumed by an intensely fierce fire. Having made this discovery he at once realized that his brother had been murdered and he therefore, as soon as he could find one, sent a runner to Santa Fe to apprise the sheriff of what had happened.

Sheriff Cunningham was engaged in eating supper at the Palace Hotel when the runner got to Santa Fe and saw him. The sheriff and Deputy Sheriff Juan Delgado immediately started for the scene of the tragedy, forty miles distant, riding nearly all night. When it was sufficiently light next morning to make an examination, they found that the snow, which had fallen since the occurrence of the tragedy, had so far obliterated the tracks in and leading from the corral as to leave them practicably indistinguishable. The sheriff followed the faint signs which the snow had spared, however, toward Las Vegas, finally reaching a village called Gusano, which he knew to be inhabited by some very tough characters. Here he could not discover anything, as the inhabitants refused to sell him food either for himself or his horse, so he rode to a way station on the railroad for the purpose of remaining over night with an acquaintance. While there

A One-armed Arab Peddler

Came in and said that he had been robbed a short time previously and further stated that he could identify the parties that had robbed him. Sheriff Cunningham accompanied the peddler and succeeded in arresting four men whom the Arab identified. The sheriff also found the goods which had been taken from the peddler. Mr. Cunningham took his prisoners before a local justice of the peace in San Miguel County, and brought them to Santa Fe, where he lodged them in jail.

Important Admissions.

By working on the prisoners whom he had in custody, the chief of whom was Orecensio Martinez, at whose father's house in Gusano Vialpando had headquarters, the sheriff finally secured admissions from them that, on Sunday night, January 20, Jesus Vialpando, Feliciano Chavez and two other men with five horses passed through Gusano and that Vialpando had told the elder Martinez not to tell anyone that they had been there. The latter soon after came to Santa Fe to help his son out of trouble and he confirmed this story. The sheriff then gave the prisoners some money and turned them loose, they promising to locate one or all of the parties implicated in the murder and telegraph him as arranged by signal. After several days, and when he was about to give up the hope of any assistance from his prisoner assistants, the sheriff received a telegram as agreed on. He took the first train for the point from whence the telegram had been sent, which was in San Miguel county, south of Las Vegas. There he met one of his quondam prisoners who guided him to where a boy named Emilio Encinias was hiding. The boy was at once arrested, and being thoroughly frightened, gave the sheriff information which led to the arrest of Vialpando, Chavez and Trujillo. It has since been proved that this trio had determined to kill young Encinias, fearing that on account of his youth he would, of his own accord, or in case of arrest, be forced to divulge his knowledge of the whole horrible transaction. Having some suspicion of this the boy left the neighborhood where the others lived and was really in hiding from them when arrested. Thus it is surely retributive justice that another of their intended victims was one of the principal agents in bringing the brutal murderers of Tomas Martinez to the gallows.

Sources:

The *Daily New Mexican*, November 19, 1895
Albuquerque *Weekly Citizen*, November 16, 23, 1895
Santa Fe *Daily New Mexican*, November 18, 1895
Albuquerque *Morning Democrat,* November 20, 1895
Rio Grande *Republican*, November 22, 1895

Francisco Gonzales y Borrego, Antonio Gonzales y Borrego, Lauriano Alarid, and Patricio Valencia

Sheriff Francisco "Frank" Chavez served as Sheriff of Santa Fe County from 1886 to 1891. In 1890, Sheriff Chavez attended a dance where Frank Borrego appeared, shot, and killed Jose Silvestre Gallegos. Frank Borrego was arrested and held in the Santa Fe County jail to await trial. While imprisoned, a jailer named Juan Pablo Dominguez, frequently beat and abused the prisoner. Frank Borrego complained to Sheriff Chavez of cruel treatment and requested protection from the jailer who had a long-standing grudge against him. Jose Gallegos was a close and personal friend of Sheriff Chavez. The Sheriff told Borrego that he had "been treated with greater mercy than deserved." An altercation erupted between the two when the Sheriff beat Frank Borrego over the head with the use of his pistol. Frank swore vengeance on the Sheriff and said he would kill him once he was free, even if it took 50 years to do it.

Somehow the charge against Frank Borrego did not stick and he was released from the jail. His friends feared trouble would brew over his treatment and convinced him to leave for Colorado. Frank Borrego remained there for a year and half. Immediately after Borrego returned to Santa Fe, Frank Chavez, who was no longer Sheriff, was murdered on his way home on May 29, 1892. The following night, jailer Juan Dominguez armed himself and announced out loud, "The city of Santa Fe was not large enough to contain himself and Frank Borrego." Dominguez, along with two friends who had accompanied him, found Frank Borrego in front of the archbishop's house. Jailer Dominguez drew his revolver, but Frank Borrego was quicker and a better shot. The jailer died of a bullet wound and Frank Borrego was again back in jail, and along with his brother Antonio Borrego and Lanriano Alarid, charged with murder. The men were tried and acquitted on a plea of self-defense.

In January of 1894, Santa Fe County Sheriff Cunningham swore out warrants before Judge Seeds for the arrest of Frank Borrego, Antonio Borrego, Chino Alarid, Francisco Rivera, Marcus Valencia and Hipolito Vigil, who were known as the Button Gang. All six men were charged with the murder of Frank Chavez. On January 10th, Sheriff Cunningham and three deputies arrested Frank Borrego in front of the capitol. While Borrego was being handcuffed and placed within a carriage, officers spotted Hipolito Vigil walking towards them. Sheriff Cunningham ordered Hipolito to throw up his hands as he was wanted on a warrant. Hipolito jumped behind a telegraph pole and drew a pistol. Sheriff Cunningham and the deputies immediately fired their pistols, Winchester rifles and shotguns at the wanted man. Both Hipolito's body and the telegraph pole were filled with lead and buckshot. Sheriff Cunningham received no other resistance from the other four men when arrested.

Once all were arrested, the men were held in jail, without bond, to wait the action of the Grand Jury. Indictments on the charge of murder were handed down and trial was set for April 23, 1895. The trial lasted for 37 days and concluded on May 29th, three years after the murder. The jury found all the defendants guilty of murder and the death sentence was passed. The case was appealed to the territory Supreme Court which affirmed the lower courts decision. The execution date was scheduled to take place on September 24, 1896. The Supreme Court granted a stay of execution on the motion for re-trial. The motion was denied and the execution was rescheduled for October 15th. The United States Supreme Court next delayed the execution and then rescheduled for February 23, 1897. Governor Thornton had denied all requests and petitions for the sentenced to be communed or delayed any longer until ordered to do so by United States Attorney General at the direction of President Cleveland. The 30-day respite expired on March 23rd. On that day, the prisoners had been removed from the penitentiary and escorted to the gallows by a cavalry unit when President Mc Kinnley blocked the execution for 10 days so he could review the case. On the tenth day, President McKinley sent word there would be no further interference or delays in the execution.

The execution was lastly scheduled for April 2, 1897, one day before Frank Chavez's 46th birthday, had he survived. Sheriff Kinsell received assistance in guarding the four prisoners by a total of 45 men from troops E and B of the cavalry. On April 2nd at 7:30 in the morning, Sheriff Kinsell entered the cells and read the death warrant to them. Father Fourchegn remained with the men, as their spiritual advisor, until 9:00 when they were told their time was up. At 9:07 the procession of prisoners was lead out of the cells to the gallows where all mounted the scaffold with a firm step. The prisoners were directed as to what positions to take over the trap door. Patricio Valencia was ordered to take the west end of the gallows, Louriano Alarid, Antonio Borrego and Frank Borrego followed him and took up the east end. The men were restrained at the ankles and elbows by ropes. Sheriff Kinsell asked if any of them wished to make a last statement. The offer was refused. At that point the halter and black cap was adjusted. "At 9:09 o'clock the trap bolt was drawn, and the four bodies shot through the six feet of space to death." With the exception of Valencia, the necks were broken by the fall. Valencia died in three or four minutes from strangulation and was the first to be pronounced dead. Antonio Borrego died after six and a half minutes, Frank Borrego after seven minutes and Alarid at nine and a half minutes. The bodies remained hanging until 9:31 when they were cut down and placed in coffins to be released to family members.

The Albuquerque *Weekly* dated April 3, 1897, had the following headlines and story.

FOUR MEN HANGED!

Murderers Of Ex-Sheriff Chavez
Die on the Scaffold.

The Execution Took Place in Santa
Fe County Jail.

End of a Remarkable Series of Crime at
The Territorial Capital.

SCENES AT THE EXECUTION.

Santa Fe, April 2. – Francisco Gonzales y Borrego, Antonio Gonzales y Borrego, Lauriano Alarid and Patricio Valencia, condemned for the murder of Frank Chavez, May 29, 1892, were hanged at 9:10 o'clock to-day.

Thursday night ten special guards were placed in the jail by the sheriff and this morning a draft of forty men was made on the cavalry and infantry companies by the Governor, with instructions to act under orders of Sheriff Kinsell.

The scaffold was 12 by 21 feet, with a six foot drop through a single trap six feet long and three feet wide. The prisoners passed a restful night, the guards saying that not one even turned in his sleep.

The death warrant was read to them at 7:30 and was received by the Borrego's with some facetiousness. The vicar general remained with the doomed men until they were lead to the scaffold, attended by the sheriff and three deputies and the vicar general and disappeared from the view of the limited number of spectators within a tent which surrounded the scaffold.

None of them showed the slightest weakness. They made no statement except to request the sheriff not to fail to remove all traces of the cause of their death before their bodies were turned over to their families. The ropes and caps were adjusted, and at 9:09 the trap was sprung. The necks of all were broken except that of Valencia, the lightest in weight, who died from strangulation. At 9:31 the men were all pronounced dead by attending physicians, and at 9:30 the bodies were placed in plain black coffins furnished by the county. The funerals will take place on Sunday forenoon from the cathedral. The hanging was a perfect mechanical success.

PARTICULARS OF EXECUTION.

Special to the Citizen.

Santa Fe, April 2 – On the night of May 29, 1892, ex-Sheriff Frank Chavez was assassinated. This morning at 9:09 Francisco Gonzales y Borrego, Antonio Gonzales y Borrego, Lauriano Alarid and Patricio Valencia atoned for the crime by hanging on the scaffold until dead. Sheriff Kinsell pulled the trigger.

Upon being advised that further clemency was out of the question, the men seemed very much unconcerned, still asserting their confidence in their attorney, T.B. Catron, who has made a great fight to save his clients. One company of cavalry did guard duty at the jail last night, and this morning another company of cavalry and the militia was on duty. The condemned men slept well last night and was up early this morning and had a hearty breakfast.

A dead line was drawn around the jail yard, and a surging crowd of several hundred anxious to see the execution was kept back. Housetops and windows in the neighborhood were full of persons anxious to know if the men would have any statement to make in reference to their crimes.

The four men have large families, and the parting scene was pathetic, indeed. About seventy-five witnesses were inside, but as the gallows was canvassed over they could not see the men until the drop was made. The men marched from the jail to the gallows unattended. At 9:28 Drs. Sloan, Brady and Crosson pronounced the men dead. The bodies were cut down and turned over to friends at 9:35.

On being asked if they had any statement to make every man absolutely refused to talk except in regard to the disposition of their bodies. The men showed no signs of nervousness whatever, and met their death bravely. There was not a hitch in the entire proceeding. Father Facheau was the spiritual advisor for the men.

Sources:

Santa Fe *Daily New Mexican*, September 24, 1896; April 2, 3, 1897
Las Vegas *Daily Optic*, April 2, 1897
Albuquerque *Weekly Citizen*, April 3, 1897
Santa Fe *New Mexican*, April 3, 1903

Jose Telles, alias Alejandro Duran

Jose Telles felt his life was ending as he was a "victim of circumstances of bad luck that has followed him." After shooting a road section boss between Bowie and Wilcox Arizona, Jose Telles fled Arizona for Springer, New Mexico. There, he found work and got drunk with a friend on the job. Both men attempted to enter the mess tent to eat, but were refused admittance because of their intoxication. Telles got into a fight with the ticket taker who pushed Telles out of the entrance and outside onto the ground. Jose Telles became mad, and in a drunken rage pulled his revolver. In his drunken state of mind, he shot and killed his friend in confusion. While being held in Santa Fe jail on that killing, Jose Telles and Alfred Hampe planned their escape. Their plan ended with the killing of a jailer for which Telles was executed. The Santa Fe *New Mexican* had the following headlines and story.

HIS LIFE PAID
THE PENALTY

Jose Telles or Alejandro Duran was Executed
This morning for the Brutal Murder of
Epitacio Gallegos.

FORMER STATEMENT PUB-
LISHED FOR THE FIRST TIME.

At ten seconds of 9 o'clock this morning, not a dozen yards from where he shot Epitacio Gallegos in cold blood, just 75 days ago, Jose Telles or Alejandro Duran was executed for that crime.

It was 8:55 O'clock, when Sheriff Kinsell and Deputy C. R. Huber entered the condemned man's cell where he had since early morning been in the company of Father Vincent Thomas and Rev. Father C. Joseph Hintzen, his spiritual advisors. The prisoner was lead forth by deputy Huber who was preceded by the Sheriff and the two priests. Telles or Duran was smoking a cigar and exhibited remarkable nerve though visibly a little bit affected. On ascending the scaffold, the condemned man was placed facing the audience and Sheriff Kinsell announced that Telles had a statement to make before dying. He spoke in his native tongue and his statement was interpreted to those assembled by John V. Conway. Telles said: "Please excuse me if I have offended you. I want you to pardon me and help me by praying for me. I pray everybody to be forgiven." He then knelt and repeated the act of contrition after Father Hintzen. After he arose to his feet he was embraced by the priests who then descended from the scaffold.

Jose Telles standing in the Santa Fe County Jail doorway on the day of his execution, April 3, 1903. Published in the Santa Fe New Mexican. *Note the leg shackles.*

The condemned man was then lead to his place on the trap door. He continued to smoke his cigar while being bound. When Deputy Huber placed the noose around Telles' neck, he spit this cigar out and said: "Good-bye boys." He closed his eyes as the black cap was adjusted. "All right" said Deputy Huber, and Sheriff Kinsell pulled the lever. The murderer was given a 3-foot and 11 inch drop and his neck was broken by the fall.

The body swung half around four times and then remained motionless save for a raising knee and clutching of his hands in the death struggle. Dr. J. Diaz held the pulse of Telles' left hand and Dr. J. H. Sloan the right. His pulsation ceased four and one-half minutes after the trap was sprung and Sheriff Kinsell cut the rope two minutes later. The physicians on examination stated that the murderer's neck had been broken by the fall.

Telles retired at 10 o'clock last night and while he did not leave his cot and death watch believed him to be asleep, he stated this morning that he had spent a sleepless night. He was called at 5:30 o'clock, and barely touched the food placed before him for breakfast. The priests arrived early and the morning was spent in prayer. Just before he was taken from his cell a few friends who wished to bid him good-bye were permitted to enter. He greeted all with a smile.

Telles was clean shaven and was dressed in a dark gray suit of clothes with a white stiff bosomed shirt and no collar. His remains were taken to the undertaking establishment of Charles Wagner to be prepared for burial. The funeral will occur at the Cathedral at 8 o'clock tomorrow morning. Interment at Rosario Cemetery.

DURAN'S STATEMENT TO MARTIN

Telles or Duran, was worried to the last lest his father had been held for trouble which Telles caused in Arizona. About four weeks ago he sent for W. E. Martin, deputy warden at the territorial penitentiary; and stated that he would like to see him. Mr. Martin went to the jail to see him and a have short talk with him. He did not recognize him and Telles then did not have much to say. He made the request of Mr. Martin that if his sentence was not commuted and when it became certain that he had to die, he should be permitted to make a statement to him that was not to be made public until after the execution. In accordance with this request, Mr. Martin went to the jail a few days ago and after a few minutes' chat, Telles made himself known to him. When a boy, Telles, or as his right name is Alejandro Duran, was employed by Mr. Martin's mother to herd her cows. He remembered Mr. Martin and, after recalling the circumstances, Mr. Martin remembered him perfectly. Duran was born at Mesilla, Doña Ana County and was about 28 years old when executed. He was a son of Sabastian Duran and his mother's maiden name was Catarina Telles. An uncle, Gregorio Duran, is now living at Chamberino, Doña Ana County.

Duran stated that he was never in any trouble in Doña Ana County. About ten or eleven years ago he left there and went out on the Southern Pacific railroad to work on the California division. While working on the road he married and in 1901 he returned to Las Cruces to get his father. His mother had died in the meantime, and Duran was accompanied on his trip by his wife and three children. They traveled in a covered wagon which he owned and he had a team of good horses. After getting his father, the entire party went to Morenci where Duran expected to secure work, but in this he failed.

During the winter of 1901 he started to secure work on the Bisbee road. While on the way there, he secured work on the section between Bowie and Wilcox at a place called Lucino. The party moved into a dug out and Duran worked on the section for seven days. The eighth day he did not go to work as he wanted to shoe his horses. The section boss demanded that he go to work and Duran refused, giving the above reason. The section boss, Duran says, lost his temper and abused him. Duran says he lost his temper and high words passed between them. The section boss then ran into the house nearby and came out with a double-barreled shotgun. Duran had run into the dugout and taken from the trunk his revolver. Duran says as he came from the dugout, the section boss shot at him, but missed. He then shot at the section boss with his revolver and hit him. The section boss fell and Duran says he ran forward, picking up the shotgun and broke it across the rail. As he did so, the second barrel was discharged.

Duran complained bitterly of his "Luck" to Mr. Martin. He stated he had not intentionally wronged or hurt any man and that not in a single instance was any murder he committed intentional, but that he had been in each case, a victim of circumstances. He stated that he does not know to this day whether the section boss died or not. He does not know whether or not the shot from his revolver killed or only wounded him and he does not know whether or not the charge from the second barrel of the gun struck him. He did not stop for an instant, he said, but at once struck out for the hills and left his wife, children and father there. The section boss was down on the ground when he left, but he does not know if he is living or dead. From that moment to this, Duran said he has not heard nothing of his father, his wife or his children, and he does not know where they are.

He asked Mr. Martin to give the fullest publicity to his statement of the trouble lest it was thought at the time that his father might have something to do with it and that he was arrested or punished for it. He said that his father had absolutely nothing to do with it, that his father is an honest man who never got into any trouble and that he alone was responsible for anything that may have happened in this shooting affray. If his father had been held for it, he desires that his statement be accepted and that he be released. Duran was quite wrought up when discussing this matter, but Mr. Martin could give no information on the point Duran said that if he did kill this man, it was unintentional and he did not aim to do so.

Duran said that after fleeing from this place, he went to El Paso and there heard of the railroad building on the Dawson branch of the Rock Island system and went there to secure work. In this he did not succeed and he went to Springer where he heard of the construction of the Santa Fe Central, so he came to this city and went from here to Kennedy.

The murder he committed there he said was another instance of the bad luck that has followed him constantly. He stated to Mr. Martin that he had become very friendly and "chummy" with the man he killed. Each of them had a meal ticket that was good at the mess house there and before supper on the day of the murder, he and his friend had been drinking. Duran said he was intoxicated when they reached the door of the mess house. The man who punched the meal tickets at the door refused to let him in on account of being intoxicated and they had a few words. The ticket taker finally pushed him from the entrance, seized him by the throat and threw him to the ground. Duran said as he arose from the ground he drew his revolver with the intention of firing at the ticket taker, but became confused and shot and killed his bosom friend instead.

Coming to the time of the murder of Epitacio Gallegos, Duran stated to Mr. Martin that this was a further instance of circumstances being against him. He insisted that he begged Hampe to leave many times before Gallegos returned to the jail but that Hampe declined on the ground that it was to all right for them to escape. Hampe claimed there would be no trouble and all that would be necessary would be to order Gallegos to throw up his hands and the order would be obeyed. Instead of obeying, Gallegos grappled with Hampe. Duran said three shots were fired, two by Hampe with his revolver, and one by himself with the rifle. Gallegos, said Duran, was not armed and it was his belief that the shot he fired with the rifle is the one that struck Hampe in the arm. Duran stated to Mr. Martin that he was prepared to die and that he was satisfied he had never done any man an intentional wrong. He stated he entered a plea of guilty because he and Hampe were equally guilty of the crime and, as they were both in it, he thought they might as well say so. Duran maintained he was never in any trouble other than the scrapes named. Mr. Martin questioned him closely about the Fountain, Alexander Bull and Pedro Du Alde murders, all of which took place in Doña Ana County. Duran stated he did not know of the Fountain murder until three years after it had taken place, and that he was working on the California division of the Southern Pacific when the others took place. He denied having anything to do with them or having knowledge of them.

THE CRIME

The crime for which Telles' eventful and sinful life was today ended by law was murder – the heartless shooting down of Epitacio Gallegos, at the time jailer at the Santa Fe county jail. The crime was committed on the evening of Sunday, January 18, at or about the hour of 6 o'clock.

On that evening, Gallegos had occasion to go across the Santa Fe river and while he was away, Victoriano Casados, the night watchman at the jail, undertook to put the prisoners in their cells for the night. In an unguarded moment he was overpowered by Telles and Alfred Hampe. The latter was a prisoner charged with robbing a railroad car, while Telles was awaiting trial on the charge of having murdered a man at Kennedy, this county. Casados was relieved of his keys and himself locked in a cell. The two men then made their way up the stairs to where there were some firearms. Possessing themselves of a revolver and rifle, the former property of the man who was afterwards murdered, and the latter belonging to Sheriff Kinsell, they descended the stairs and went to the cell wherein they had confined Casados. They inquired whether or not Gallegos was armed and were assured that he was not. Casados told them that they had all of the keys and that there was nothing between them and liberty. He asked them to go, but they refused, saying they would wait for Gallegos. Their subsequent explanation was that they wanted to lock him up in a cell too, so that they could get a good start before their escape was discovered. They went up the stairs again and there waited the return of the jailer. When Gallegos got back, he went up the stairs to where they were and was attacked at the head of the stairs by Hampe, according to Hampe's statement, Telles failed to come to assistance as had been agreed, but stood back. Seeing that the jailer was getting the better of him, Hampe fired his revolver. He says he did it to frighten Gallegos. The latter's face was powder burned by this shot. It did not have the effect of bluffing the jailer for he bent Hampe's hand back so that when he pulled the trigger a second time the bullet entered Hampe's other hand. It was at this juncture that Telles fired the rifle. The bullet crashed through the officer's heart, producing instant death.

A passing boy who was attracted by the shots, reached the jail in time to see the prisoners scale the wall. He was covered with the rifle by Telles and ordered to "git." He complied with the order but stopped later and observed their flight. He notified citizens and an unsuccessful attempt was made to affect an entrance to the jail. Sheriff Kinsell was sent for and went in over the jail wall. He ascended the steps leading to the office and stumbled over the body of the murdered jailer at the head of the stairs. He soon discovered the absence of Telles and Hampe and found Casados where he had been imprisoned by the jail breakers.

The bloodhounds from the penitentiary were pressed into service. They took the trail for a short distance only, when they returned. The two men afterwards said that they had to fight the dogs off that night so this probably accounts for the animals' failure to follow the scent very far. The hunt was finally abandoned for that night and the dogs worked better the next day.

It was several days however before the pursuers met with success. On Friday the 23rd, Hampe was captured in the vicinity of Thornton. His feet were frozen and this together with the wound in his arm were bothering him. Telles had left him that morning.

Telles was at large until February 7, when he was arrested in Grant County. He was making for the Republic of Mexico. He hoped to escape over the international boundary line and remain in seclusion there until the excitement caused by his crime had died down and the vigilant search made for him had been given up. Upon his arrest he denied that he was Telles, declaring that he was Alejandro Duran, which it is now believed is his real name. He finally admitted that he was Telles, but declared that he was not the one that had fired the fatal shot. He begged his captors to shoot him rather that return to Santa Fe, saying he feared he would be lynched.

When arraigned before Judge John R. Mc Fie at the March term of the 1st Judicial District Court on March 5, Telles entered a plea of guilty. He was warned that he was as liable to be given the death sentence upon entering a plea of guilty as he was if found guilty. The prisoner said that he understood and so the plea was accepted by the court. Sentence was pronounced on the confessed murderer the following Saturday. Hampe's plea was not guilty and when arraigned for trial he asked for a change of venue which was granted. He will be tried in Rio Arriba County during the present month.

THE SENTENCE PASSED.

Judge Mc Fie then stated that there seemed to be some discussion among the people and even the lawyers as to whether it was in the power of the court to assess the death penalty upon a plea of guilty of murder in the first degree. He stated that the law of New Mexico gave him no alternative even if he were inclined to pronounce a lighter sentence. He said that he had inquired into Telles' past history some of which came from the murderers own lips and other parts from the court records; the prisoner seemed to have entered upon a life of crime years ago; that Gallegos life was not the first he had taken. "In taking his life," Judge Mc Fie said, "You took the life of one of the best native citizens of Santa Fe County and probably of the whole territory. Epitacio Gallegos was a law abiding citizen, a good citizen, an inoffensive man, one who had committed no crime against you, and who went to his grave guiltless – because of your murderous desires. Ordinarily the duty that this court is called upon to perform would be an exceedingly disagreeable one. It would tax this court severely in many cases to perform this duty but feeling as I do in your case, that the punishment is just, that you have taken more than one life before you took the life of Epitacio Gallegos, in a dastardly manner, takes all sentiment from the court in passing this sentence. I feel sorry for you Telles that you must end your life in this way. But the law is supreme. It must be obeyed. The lives of citizens must not be taken by the criminal class; there must be protection; and sad it is for you, that in order to guarantee that protection that the law intends every law abiding citizen shall have, it becomes necessary that your life must be taken." The court stated that the prisoner seemed to feel that he had gone far enough in his life of crime, that he had entered a plea of guilty to murder in the first degree understanding the consequence. "You seem to realize," said the judge, "that you have reached that point in a criminal life where there is nothing left for you that is worth living for, and it is a sad thing that you have arrived at that time in your life when you feel that it is just that your life shall be taken for the blood you have shed." Judge McFie then pronounced the death sentence on the confessed murderer.

Sources:

Santa Fe *New Mexican*, April 3, 1903

Elbert W. Blancett

Elbert W. Blancett was executed for the murder of his traveling companion, Clyde D. Armour. On the night of October 22, 1916, the two men stayed the night at the Troy hotel at Las Vegas, New Mexico. The next morning the two left by car for Santa Fe, but Elbert Blancett arrived alone.

In Santa Fe, Elbert purchased a round of drinks for the saloon customers and then registered at the Motezuma hotel under the name of Clyde D. Armour. During the next seven days, Elbert assumed the identity of Clyde Armour and enjoyed himself at the different saloons and gambling halls. Running short of money, Elbert left Santa Fe, and traveled to Albuquerque and sold the car. Afterwards, the impersonation of Armour continued by wiring Clyde Armour's mother in Los Angeles asking for more money. With this money, Elbert continued buying drinks for saloon patrons. On October 30th, Elbert purchased a one-way train ticket to Friday Harbor in Washington State where his mother resided.

Meanwhile Clyde Armour's mother became concerned after having no further word from her son, in addition to his failure to arrive in Los Angeles. For these reasons she sent her other two sons to New Mexico to investigate. Soon after the sons' arrival, local law enforcement was notified of their suspicions. While law enforcement investigated and began discovering the impersonation by Elbert, search parties were organized at Las Vegas and Santa Fe and searched the hills from Valley Ranch to Glorieta in hopes of finding Clyde Armour.

The Santa Fe County Sheriff notified the Friday Harbor Sheriff's Department that it was believed Elbert Blancett was there and asked their assistance in apprehending him. On December 30th, Elbert was placed under arrest as a fugitive from justice from New Mexico. Elbert asked the arresting deputy for permission to visit his mother at Richardson, Washington. The officer agreed and after arriving at his mother's home, Elbert ran into another room and grabbed a shotgun. Not wanting to tell his mother of his arrest for murder, he attempted suicide by placing the shotgun to his neck and firing the weapon. After several weeks in the hospital and a legal battle to fight the extradition, Elbert Blancett was returned to New Mexico for the suspicion of murder. After his return and up to the trial, Elbert remained silent as to the whereabouts of Clyde Armour. Then on the morning of January 14, 1917, the remains of Clyde Armour were found near Glorieta, New Mexico.

The remains were discovered after a dog returned home carrying a large bone with a shoe dangling from it. The pet's owner followed the dog tracks and the dragging marks of the shoe to the scattered remains. The remains had been located about 3 miles from Glorieta and 400 yards off the main highway within an arroyo. Papers found in the pockets and the sewn name tags in the clothing identified the remains as being that of Armour. Next to the body was a rusty shotgun and skeletal evidence indicated the deceased died from a shotgun blast to the back of the skull and neck. A wristwatch on the remains had stopped working at 3:25, which suggested the time of death on October 23, 1916.

Elbert Blancett's trial for first degree murder began on April 13, 1917, in Santa Fe. The trial was the biggest sensation for the town in many years. At the trial there was standing room only with spectators arriving early, with their lunches, to get a seat. Woman brought in their sewing material and sewed during the entire day and into the night. Up until the trial, Elbert remained silent, not speaking a word as to what happened in the woods when Clyde Armour was killed. At trial, Elbert told the jury he had been drinking during the day. Just outside Glorieta they both decided to go hunting. After stopping the car, Clyde lead the way into the woods as Elbert followed with the shotgun. He testified he had stumbled and the shotgun accidentally discharged striking Clyde. He at first thought of running for help, but not knowing the area feared he would be suspected of murder and charged.

Elbert was cross-examined as to why he assumed Clyde Armour's identity and wired the victim's mother for money. Elbert replied he only did that to forget the tragedy and that he needed money to get away. At the end of the twelve day trial on April 24th, Judge Edmund C. Abbott instructed the jury to return one of the following verdicts: Murder in the first degree, Murder in the second degree, Voluntary Manslaughter, Justified Homicide or Not Guilty. When the jury returned at 1:30 the next morning, Elbert broke down crying after the foreman read a verdict of "Guilty of Murder in the First Degree." The conviction was appealed up to the United States Supreme Court, which affirmed the lower court's conviction. The Supreme Court set the execution for July 9th, 1920, between the hours of sunrise and sunset.

Santa Fe County Sheriff George W. Armijo told the public the execution would take place "as soon as the sun appears over the tops of the Santa Fe Mountains." The execution would further take place on the gallows, which had been erected, three years prior, on the county jail yard grounds. To seal off view from the public, a high board fence surrounding the gallows was erected. Only twenty witnesses were to be admitted with prior approval by the judge.

Prison Chaplin, Father Henry le Guillion, wired Governor Larrazolo at Las Vegas, New Mexico, on an eleventh hour appeal for commutation. The Chaplin wrote, "In my opinion there is a serious doubt that justice has been done." Governor Larrazolo wired back an immediate reply to the Chaplin that read, "I have studied this case conscientiously and religiously. I am sorry, but let justice have its course. God save Blancett and forgive him." Signed O. A. Larrazolo, Governor.

On the night of July 8th, Elbert Blancett ate a large supper and remained awake during the entire night writing letters, reading a book by Zane Grey, and the Holy Bible. The letters written included goodbyes to his mother, and attorney, A. B. Renchen. He wrote to his attorney to not feel bad for he had done all he could. In a written statement, Blancett wrote, "I told the truth on the witness stand. I am going before my maker. What I told the court was the truth and I have nothing else to say. Good bye."

Early the next morning, Santa Fe Deputies arrived to transport Elbert from the penitentiary to the awaiting gallows at the jail yard. Elbert's right hand was the only one handcuffed since he had no use of the left hand after his suicide attempt in Washington. Sheriff Armijo read out loud the death warrant as Blancett listened in a military attention posture. At the end of the reading, Elbert's spiritual advisor accompanied him in the car for the short ride to the gallows and to provide last minutes of strength. Upon arriving, Elbert mounted the 13 steps to the top of the platform. There, Elbert picked up the end of the hanging rope and said, "When I am at the end of this, it will all be over." Sheriff Armijo began reading the death warrant before the twenty witnesses when Elbert told the Sheriff, "We might dispense with that, it will only delay the same."

After the execution, the body was removed to Watt's Mortuary Chapel for a funeral. Before the casket was lowered into the ground, Father le Guillion blessed the casket. The following headlines and story was printed in the Santa Fe *New Mexican*.

Elbert W. Blancett Goes to Death on Scaffold with a Smile; Confessor
in Vain Makes Last Appeal to Governor
for Clemency.
"I HAVE NOTHING TO SAY," LAST WORDS

Murderer of Armour Faces Executioners
Calmly; Dead in Ten Minutes After
Trap Falls, At Sunrise.

Elbert W. Blancett answered the state's demand of a life for a life in the yard behind the jail this morning at 5:22 o'clock.

He went to his death as a man would go to breakfast. He gave no sign of mental stress and ascended the steps to the scaffold unaided except that Father Henry le Guillion, the prison Chaplin and his confessor, who walked beside him, laid his hand lightly on his arm.

On the scaffold they knelt in prayer – the priest and the prisoner. They remained kneeling a few minutes and the priest then embraced the prisoner. As Blancett arose Sheriff George W. Armijo asked him if he had any statement to make. He stood with his shoulders thrown back and faced squarely the witnesses gathered below. He spoke slowly and clearly.

"I have nothing to say," he said, enunciating each word distinctly, and turned toward the deputy sheriff as if to say he was ready when they were. Deputy Warden Pat Dugan, of the penitentiary, sprang up the steps and grasped his hand. He spoke a few low words and descended. The canvas curtain then dropped and the scaffold was hidden from the witnesses.

The trap was sprung at 5:22 o'clock, shortly after sunrise, and 10 minutes later Dr. E. W. Fiske, prison physician, and Dr. David Knapp, county physician, pronounced him dead. The drop apparently failed to break his neck, although no examination was made, but the prisoner was unconscious and death was painless. The snapping of the heavy knot of the noose against his head, behind the ear, produced unconsciousness at the instant of the drop and he knew nothing after that.

Sources:

Santa Fe *New Mexican*, April 25, 1917; July 4, 7, 9, 1920
Las Vegas *Optic*, July 9, 1920

Chapter 13

Socorro County

John Henry Anderson

John Henry Anderson, like many men before him, traveled west after the Civil War. After arriving in New Mexico in the 1870s, he worked at a Socorro quarry as a laborer. On June 21, 1885, John Anderson and Alfonso Williams argued and fought. There were heated words of death exchanged. Alfonso Williams, who had not been feeling well, returned to his company bunk to lie down. John Anderson procured a pistol from another worker and quietly snuck up to the window next to Alfonso Williams and shot him to death. For this murder, John Anderson was tried, convicted of Murder in the First Degree, and sentenced to die on May 6, 1887. His execution was witnessed by only a dozen spectators, half of those persons being reporters. The Albuquerque *Daily Democrat* described John Henry Anderson's last moment: "The doomed man met his fate without a tremor, taking the fatal leap as cool as though he was going to a meal." The *Daily Democrat* dated May 7th, 1887, had the following headlines and story.

GONE TO GLORY

———————

John Henry Anderson Steps into Eter-
Nity with Words of
Hope on his lips.

———————

His Special Pleating of a Hair
Splitting Defense on
The Scaffold.

———————

Sheriff Charles Russell's
Well arranged and orderly Execution.

———————

Special to the *New Mexican.*

Socorro N.M., May 6 – John Henry Anderson was executed in the jail yard here today at 11:25 a. m. for the murder of Alfonso Williams in 1885. The execution was strictly private. Sixteen minutes after the fatal drop he was pronounced dead by the attending physicians and seven minutes later the body was cut down and placed in a coffin.

Photographs were taken of the unfortunate man as he dangled at the ropes end between heaven and earth. Anderson betrayed no emotion whatever as he stood on the scaffold just prior to the fatal moment. Previously Anderson begged the sheriff not to proceed with the execution until the last hour,

STIPULATED IN THE DEATH WARRANT,

which was 4 p. m., but the sheriff justly declined to grant his request. Sheriff Russell read the death warrant and the doomed man listened to it with a nonchalance that froze the blood of the handful of spectators that stood in the jail yard to witness the execution.

Father Lestra, Sheriff Russell and Deputy Sheriff A. L. Robinson and Cook escorted the victim to the scaffold. Father Lestra made a brief address, stating to Anderson that he belonged to the Catholic Church besides on earth, and was soon to leave the world and appear before his Maker, where there was peace and happiness.

Father Courssey visited the unfortunate fellow just before he was brought from his cell, as did also three colored women, but they remained only a short time.

PERFECT SYSTEM

characterized the execution, and all pronounced it a neat peace of work on Sheriff Russell's part, disagreeable as it was.

Anderson made a short speech just before the fatal plunge, in which he stated he had not been fairly dealt with on his trial, but still he was fully prepared to go. He continued: "It seems hard that I have come to this, but I hope to meet my redeemer in peace. I leave this world with no ill will towards any one. I have been kindly treated by Sheriff Russell and his assistances. I do not believe that my hand caused Williams death – it was the doctors fault that he died; the wound I inflicted was not necessarily fatal. I did not have

THE MONEY

to carry on my trial nor could I get Charlie Owens down here from Las Vegas to testify in my behalf, else I believe I would not be standing here to-day. I don't think the Governor has given me justice. I thank Mr. Russell for all his kindness.

Anderson then shook hands with the officials and the reporters and physician and ministers, the black cap was adjusted and the flap door fell from under him.

ANDERSON'S CRIME.

Anderson's crime is a tame affair as compared with that of Baker, through none the less black and brutal. Anderson is a burly Negro who had been employed with a gang of laborers quarrying luck near Socorro. Alfonso Williams was also a laborer there, and on the morning of the 21st day of June, 1885, the two men engaged in a quarrel and fought, Williams coming off victor. In the heat of the excitement Williams made some casual threat which Anderson claims to have construed to mean that his life was in danger, and when the noon hour came Anderson went about among the men making counter threats and swearing he would kill Williams. His companions endeavored to pacify him, and kept Williams out of his way, but this seems only to excite the bully still more; he declared his intention more boldly than ever and made numerous attempts to

BORROW A WEAPON

for the purpose but without success, and finally in his frenzy for blood he openly boasted of his determination to murder Williams, and even went so far as to offer $25 for the loan of a revolver with which to carry out his threat. At the time Williams lay sick upon one of the sleeping bunks of the quarry lodging house. Anderson finally succeeded in procuring a weapon, a six shooter, and with this in hand he started out in search of his antagonist. During the afternoon he found Williams lying near an open window, on a bunk where he slept, with many of the work-hands present, and stepping up to the window he thrust his arm in and began firing upon Williams. The firing was continued until five chambers of the revolver were empty and Williams was

FATALLY SHOT.

"Nothing occurred as any just legal provocation to the act," says Chief Justice Long in rendering the Supreme Court's opinion in the case, "or to cause hot blood. It was a cold-blooded murder, in open day, in the presence of witnesses."

For this crime Anderson to-day paid the death penalty. For several weeks he has prepared himself for the ordeal by prayer and supplication. His spiritual adviser was R.V. Father Lestra. Yesterday Anderson spent the day reading the bible and in prayer, and last night ministers of the gospel remained with him throughout the night. Among his last requests he asked that his brother, a resident of Kansas, be sent for to transport his body to Missouri for burial.

ANDERSON'S CAREER.

Socorro's victim of the law was a native of Jackson County, Mo., being born on George Hudspeth's farm nine miles out of Independence. In 1838, when four years old he and his twin brother were sold to one Issac Pearce of Duckport, La, whence they were taken from Missouri. His mother had sixteen children besides the twins. During the war of the rebellion the twin brothers became separated and Anderson went through the army serving as body servant to his young southern master, who was an officer in the Confederate army. At the close of the war he returned to Louisiana, and in 1866 visited Independence in search of his family, whom he found scattered through Missouri and Eastern Kansas. In 1874 he again returned to Louisiana and then immigrated to Kansas, coming hence to New Mexico. His mother is still living, aged 84 years, and her home is near Valley Falls, Kas. He has also six brothers and sisters residing in that state.

Sources:

Santa Fe *Daily New Mexican*, May 6, 1887
The *Daily Democrat*, May 7, 1887

Carlos Sais

John Billingslea was a telegraph operator who lived in Colorado. He had discussed with his wife the idea of prospecting in New Mexico. The prospecting would be an adventure and their vacation of camping and seeing the beauty of New Mexico. In late summer of 1906, John and his wife left Colorado, by train, to prospect in the Manzano Mountains. They had camped in the mountains for two months when they met William McLaughlin.

William McLaughlin had lived in the Manzano Mountains for three years. He was considered to be experienced in mining, hunting and camping. A partnership between both men was made. Mr. Billingslea would fund the partnership, while Mr. McLaughlin would set the camps and provide food by hunting wildlife. It had been decided to set out for the Oscura Mountains to investigate the reports of rich mineral there.

The first night the trio spent the night at the village of Mountainair. On the second day, two Mexican men named Carlos Sais and Eliseo Valles came upon the prospectors and told them they were familiar with the mountains and knew the locations of mineral deposits and water. Both men were hired as guides to lead them into the mountains. The first night, the guides slept in the same tent with Mr. McLaughlin. On the second day, camp was set up at noon on a location called "Red Hill" because the water supply had run out.

Both guides told the prospectors they knew the location of water on top of the mountain. It was suggested that in order to bring enough water back, all four men needed to go, taking the horses. As the men set off to get water, Mrs. Billingslea remained behind to set up camp. A short time later, she heard several gunshots. She did not think much about it at the time, but later recalled her husband had allowed one guide (Carlos Sais) to carry his luger pistol. Mr. McLaughlin had also allowed the other guide to carry his rifle when they left for the water. At 1:30 p.m. both guides returned asking Mrs. Billingslea if the other two men had returned. After both men ate lunch, they left the camp on foot with the empty canteens and returned within ten minutes with water. At 4:00 p.m., the men departed the camp taking the remaining horses with them. Mrs. Billingslea remained at the camp for two days waiting for her husband to return. Believing her husband may have been injured and needing assistance, she set out on foot and walked to the small settlement of Sais. Once there, warrants were issued for both Carlos Sais and Eliseo Valles for horse theft. A search party was assembled and set out for the camp. From there they would start looking for Billingslea and McLaughlin..

The bodies of both men were found less than a half-mile from their camp. McLaughlin had been shot first in the back of the head. The bullet had exited above the left eye. Mr. Billingslea apparently took off running after Mr. McLaughlin was shot. While running to escape, he was first shot in the shoulder. After running some, he sat down to rest, and was shot in the back of the head with McLaughlin's Winchester rifle.

Both Carlos Sais and Eliseo Valles were arrested and charged with murder in the first degree. Eliseo Valles, not wanting to take his chances at trial, pled guilty to murder in the second degree before Judge Frank W. Parker. Carlos Sais stood trial in Socorro on December 5 and 6th, 1906. The Jury deliberated just over an hour to bring back a verdict of guilty of murder in the first degree. Judge Parker ordered both men to be brought before him on December 17th for sentencing. On that day, Judge Parker ordered Eliseo Valles to be confined at the Territory Penitentiary in Santa Fe to serve a sentence of ninety-nine years. He ordered Carlos Sais to be hung by the neck until the body is dead on January 11, 1907. No appeal was made to Governor Hagerman for a stay of execution or a plea of commutation. Carlos kept his nerve until the last few days when he could hear the carpenters erecting the gallows. He was then described as being terror stricken, crying and refusing all water and food. On the gallows Carlos Sais confessed to his crime and said the only sorrow he felt was his relatives had not visited him while in jail. He asked that his body be sent home to San Juan across the Rio Grande near Sabinal. After the black cap was adjusted, Sheriff Abeyta then pulled the lever to the trap door. The fall broke the murderer's neck. The Socorro *Chieftain* had the following story.

Carlos Sais Hanged

He Thus Pays the Penalty for the Murder of John Bellingslea and William McLaughlin in the Manzano Mountains Last September. His Ac-Complice is in the Penitentiary.

Carlos Sais was hanged in this city yesterday afternoon at 3:50 o'clock. Five minutes later the attending physicians, Doctors C. G. Duncan and C. F. Blackington pronounced life extinct. At Sais own request on the gallows, his body was shipped to San Juan to be buried near his old home.

Sheriff Aniceto C. Abeytia and his assistant jailer Silvestre Abeytia, are entitled to very great credit for the perfection with which all arrangements for the execution were made, and for the accuracy and perfect success with which the execution itself was conducted. The gallows had been erected under the elevated passage way between the court house and jail. He was accompanied by his spiritual advisor, Reverend Martin, and his assistant as far as the jail door, where he was met by Sheriff Abeytia and his assistant. Sais walked firmly and without assistance, mounted the steps, and placed himself under the fatal noose. He was then asked if he had anything to say. He spoke about two minutes to the twenty or more witnesses assembled, saying that he had done wrong and warning all young men not to follow in his footsteps.

His last words were the request, "Send my body to my old home at San Juan for burial." The black cap was adjusted, the condemned man's arms and legs were bound, the trap was sprung, the body shot down ward, there were a few very slight tremors, and all was over. The execution had been conducted without the slightest mishap to mar its success.

Carlos Sais and Eliseo Valles were arrested, given their preliminary hearing, indicted by the grand jury and arraigned for the trial at the last session of the District Court for Socorro County. Valles pleaded guilty to murder in the second degree and was sentenced to serve a term of ninety-nine years in the Territory Penitentiary. Sais was tried, found guilty of murder in the first degree, and has expiated his crime as the laws of the Territory of New Mexico prescribed. The body was accompanied to San Juan by Remegio Pena.

Sources:

Socorro *Chieftain*, October 13, December 22, 1906; January 12, 1907
Santa Fe *New Mexican*, January 11, 1907

Ivory Frazer, alias John W. Gates

On the night of November 7, 1911, a lone masked man climbed over the Luna County Jail stockade wall. Armed with a Winchester rifle, he disarmed Sheriff Dwight B. Stephens and two deputies of their guns and jail keys. The masked man demanded the release of John W. Gates, who had been held on burglary charges since July 21st.

Outside the jail, a second masked man waited with three saddled horses for use in their escape. Sheriff Stephens notified Grant County Sheriff McGrath to organize a posse of men to cut off the outlaws should they head towards Silver City. Sheriff Stephens, and his men, which consisted of Deputies Thomas H. Hall, Al. L. Smithers, Mounted Police Officer W. C. Simpson, and Cattle Sanitary Officer Johnnie James, pursued the outlaw's trail into the Black Range Mountains. Having a head start on the posse, the three men stopped long enough to burglarize a ranch house for supplies of food, ammunition and additional firearms. The posse of lawmen had trailed the outlaws for eight days, when a rancher reported to the Sheriff that he had seen three heavily armed men earlier in the morning. At 4 o'clock on the same afternoon of November 17th, the posse trailed the three men to a house on the VXT Ranch located 85 miles west of Engle, Socorro County, New Mexico.

Luna County Sheriff, Dwight Stephens, part of the posse who tracked and recaptured Ivory Frazer after his escape from the Luna County Jail on November 7, 1911. He was shot and killed while attempting to recapture escapees from his jail in February of 1916.

The lawmen surrounded the house at once. The three wanted men appeared unconcerned by the officer's presence or that they were taking positions around them. The three men saddled their horses, and in single file rode directly towards Deputies Thomas Hall and Al Smithers, who were also horseback. . As the men approached within 75 yards of the two officers, they were ordered to throw up their hands and surrender. Without any warning, the three outlaws fell to the ground from their horses and opened fire on the officers. Deputy Smithers was killed instantly from a bullet to the left side. Deputy Hall emptied his Winchester rifle before he was shot off his horse with a bullet to the head. The remaining horses of the posse and outlaws became frightened by the battle and bolted leaving all the men on foot. Sheriff Stephens and Johnnie James ran from the opposite side of the house where they had been positioned and joined in the battle. Sheriff Stephens shot one outlaw in the hip and neck, while Johnnie James shot at John W. Gates, whose real name was Ivory Frazer. After the shooting stopped, and the smoke cleared, both Deputies Hall and Smithers lay dead along with one outlaw. The dead man, killed by Sheriff Stephens, was identified as the well-known and dangerous John Greer. Within the pockets of the outlaw was a colt revolver belonging to a deputy, as well as the jail keys. Evidence showed Ivory Frazer, alias Gates, had been wounded and dragged himself on his hands and knees down an arroyo for 400 yards before making his escape. The third outlaw, who escaped with Ivory Frazer, was identified as Reynold Greer, the brother of John.

Officer Johnnie James traveled 25 miles to obtain a wagon to transport the three bodies. With the wagon the posse traveled to Belen, New Mexico, to board a train to take them back to Deming. The following Monday, Deputy Hall was buried in Deming, while Deputy Smithers body was returned to family members in Amarillo, Texas. John Greer's body was released to family members who returned the remains to Lincoln, New Mexico for burial.

All three outlaws were excellent riflemen and experienced fighters. John Greer was already wanted by authorities in El Paso, Texas, for the robbery of a Southern Pacific train on December 22, 1910, and the murder of Charles E. Graham. After the murder, Ivory Frazer, John and Reynold Greer crossed into Mexico and joined Francisco I. Madero and General Pascual Orozco's army. Ivory Frazer was commissioned a second lieutenant and is said to have fired the first shot at the battle of Juarez. During the fighting at Casas Grandes, the rebel fighters were defeated and had to retreat leaving their wounded where they fell. Ivory Frazer saw John Greer fall from his horse after being shot through his body and head. Frazer returned for John, holding off the federal troops with accurate gunshots from his Winchester rifle. Frazer then lifted John Greer up upon his horse and carried him to an abandoned house near the border. Frazer remained with John until he was fit to ride. In return, John swore to Frazer he would repay the debt even if it meant with his own life. While robbing Saloons and mail stagecoaches near the mining town of Mogollon, John learned of Frazer's arrest in Deming for burglary. Not forgetting his promise, John planned the unlawful rescue of Frazer with his brother, Reynold.

After the VXT gunfight, Frazer in desperation for money attempted to pawn a fancy engraved revolver that he had taken from the jail during his escape. The pawnbroker noticed that the butt strap on the gun contained the engraving of a Grant County officer's name, and alerted the police. Frazer was arrested, this time using the alias I. M. Gray. Sheriff Stephens and Grant County Sheriff McGrath both traveled to El Paso and identified the man as Ivory Frazer. After being returned to Socorro, Frazer stood trial on April 5, 1912, before Judge Mechem for the murder of the two lawmen. The next day, the jury convicted Frazer of both counts of murder in the first degree. With the findings of the jury, Judge Mechem set the execution date for May 3rd. While the execution was stayed on an appeal to the Supreme Court, Frazer was transferred to the state penitentiary in Santa Fe for safekeeping. Once the Supreme Court affirmed the lower courts conviction, the execution was rescheduled to take place on April 25, 1913.

As the execution date became closer, Frazer smuggled a letter, intended for Reynold Greer, out of the penitentiary. Unknown to Frazer the letter was intercepted and brought to the attention of Governor McDonald. The letter directed Reynold Greer to begin making last minute plans for Frazer's rescue. Frazer suggested Reynolds have one man board the train at Albuquerque and for the rest of the gang to board at the La Joya station north of Socorro. There the gang was to hold up the officers and rescue him regardless of the cost. Governor Mc Donald agreed there was a need for extra security when Frazer and another outlaw named Granado were transported to Socorro. On the night preceding the execution, Mrs. Anna Meadows,, Frazer's sister, arrived at the state penitentiary to bid her brother goodbye and return his body to San Antonio, Texas for burial. At 2:55 a.m, Sheriff James and several lawmen arrived at the penitentiary to take custody of Frazer and Granado. Both men were heavily shackled and 18 lawmen served as guards to insure both men arrived at their appointed execution. Captain Fred Fornoff of the New Mexico Mounted Police, Chief Special Agent Ben Williams of the Santa Fe Railway, along with Deputy Sheriff's, Mounted Policemen, and Railway agents made up the 18 officers.

The private car blinds were pulled down, and the only civilians allowed were the spiritual advisors for the two condemned men. Once the train left Santa Fe, it did not make any scheduled stops, especially not at La Joya. It quietly arrived at Socorro. Both men were then marched past the gallows and into the courthouse to eat their last breakfast. After eating the meal, the two men were taken to the gallows, and both stood on the double trap door. The Santa Fe *New Mexican* had the following headlines and story.

AVENGING ROPE SENDS
FRAZER AND GRANADO
TO GREAT BEYOND

AT DAWN TODAY BOTH MURDERERS PAY EXTREME
PENALTY ON GALLOWS IN SOCORRO COUNTY JAIL, DEATH
BEING INSTANTANEOUS.-"MAY THIS BE A LESSON TO
YOUNG MEN OF NEW MEXICO," WERE FRAZER'S LAST
WORDS.

GOVERNOR M'DONALD TELLS WHY
HE LET LAW TAKE ITS COURSE

Special Correspondent of *"The New Mexican."*

Socorro, N. M., April 25. –"May my death on the gallows be a warning to all young men in New Mexico." With these words on his lips, Ivory Frazer, alias Gates, went to death by the rope, his body dangling next to that of Francisco Granado, who also paid the extreme penalty for murder, leaving no message behind.

All through the night and up to the first rays of dawn, the last they were ever to see, the two men showed the same iron nerve and fiery courage which had characterized their lives. They died as they had lived, eyeing the gallows with the same calm gaze that was used behind a Winchester or pistol aimed at their fellow men.

Death was instantaneous, both necks breaking in the six foot drop. The officers of the law had done their duty and had done it in a extremely, efficient manner. The hanging took place in the county jail in the presence of eighteen persons, many of them officers of the law. The trap was sprung by Sheriff Emil James of Socorro County. Both men went to death the same instant. The bodies were cut down after thirteen minutes and Dr. Duncan and Dr. Parvis, of Socorro, pronounced them dead.

Then the bodies were given in charge of undertaker Borrowdale who would prepare them for interment. Granado will be buried in Socorro and Frazer's in San Antonio, Texas, where his sister, Mrs. Meadows, resides.

TRIP FROM SANTA FE.

The prisoners were taken from the New Mexico pen by Sheriff James and his deputies shortly after 3 p. m., and were placed in a car which was made "private" by pulling down the blinds and locking the doors. A riding guard included Captain Fred Fornoff, of the New Mexico mounted police and accompanied the men. The journey to Socorro was uneventful. No one in the car slept. Granado was taciturn through once he spoke, giving addresses of certain relatives who were to be informed of his death.

Frazer was more talkative, though he did not say a great deal. On the way to Socorro he looked at the officers of the law and said: "You all will be sorry for this." It was presumed that he meant he did not feel guilty of the murder in the first degree. Near Frazer sat the Rev. J. M. Shimer, pastor of St. John's Methodist Episcopal church, who traveled as his spiritual adviser. The Rev. Mr. Shimer was with the doomed man to the last, exhorting him on the scaffold. Father Stoffen and Father Tiessler were with Granado as his spiritual advisors.

The arrival of the car in Socorro did not arouse great curiosity for the public believed that the hanging would take place about noon. The sheriff and his assistants arranged it cleverly so that it was all over before many were stirring in Socorro's streets.

(By *Associated Press*.)

Socorro, N. M., April 25.-Ivory Frazier and Francisco Granado were hanged at 4:52 this morning in the Socorro county jail. Just at sunrise the men were led to the court house, where they had been confined under heavy guard until 3 o'clock this morning, across from the jail, where the scaffold had been erected. As they stood on the trap, Frazer asked for the officers to make the execution as nearly painless as possible.

The usual precautions were taken to prevent any attempt to rescue the men and the time of the execution was kept secret. These precautions were due to the fact that the officers discovered that Frazer, while confined at the penitentiary at Santa Fe awaiting execution, sent a letter to friends, urging them to hold up the car at La Joya, a small town eighty miles south of Albuquerque, and take him from the officers as they were driving him here for execution.

Fearing that the friends of the condemned man might try to carry out the request, the officers brought the prisoners here in a special car with a guard of 18 officers, all heavily armed. The train which is scheduled to stop at the La Joya, dashed through the village full speed, while officers stood on the platform with rifles in their arms.

THEIR CRIMES.

Socorro, N. M., April 25.- Ivory Frazer was tried and convicted for the murder of Deputy Sheriff Thomas Hall and Al Smithers of Luna County. A few weeks later Frazer was captured at El Paso and his identity discovered when he attempted to pawn a revolver stolen from the sheriff at Deming when he broke jail with the aid of the Greers. Frazer was returned to New Mexico, tried at Socorro, convicted of murder and sentenced to be hanged. On appeal, the state Supreme Court affirmed the finding and ordered the hanging to proceed.

Ben Williams, Chief Deputy under Pat Garrett for Doña Ana County, Deputy U.S. Marshal, Constable, Cattle Detective and first Chief Special Agent for the AT&SF Railroad. He was called on to insure that Ivory Frazer and Francisco Granado did not escape from the train on the way to the gallows in Socorro.

Francisco Granado shot and killed William S. Clark, manager of the Mogollon Mercantile Company store at Mogollon, February 19, 1912, in an attempted hold-up of the store. He escaped with his pal, who was shot in a subsequent flight with a posse. Granado was severely wounded and later surrendered. He was found guilty of first degree murder and appealed to the Supreme Court, that tribunal refusing to interfere with the ordered execution.

Summarily appeals were made in each case to Governor W. C. McDonald for a commutation from a death sentence to one of life imprisonment, but the Governor declined to interfere.

GOVERNOR'S STATEMENT.

Governor McDonald who returned last evening was seen by a representative of the New Mexican this morning. In speaking of the two men who were hung today at Socorro, the Governor said that he had not given out anything regarding the hanging for various reasons, chief among which was, that he desired to avoid the possible creation of any false or morbid sentimentality regarding the affair for in all the pleas for clemency there has not been anything to show that the evidence in court against the men has been in any way controverted. He takes the position that a chief executive should not be a final court of judgment.

The people of this state are in favor of capital punishment for murder in the first degree. The men in these cases had been found guilty of murder in the first degree and there were not such extenuating circumstances as to justify executive interference. It was his duty not to interfere with the findings of the lower court as affirmed by the Supreme Court of the state and he had in these cases tried to do only his duty. It was a hard position to be placed in, but he could not see his way clear to do otherwise than not to interfere, where the evidence was clearly and overwhelming against the accused. Some of the pleas for clemency had been made on suppositions only and were not backed by the facts shown in the evidence anywhere. One man had asked for commutation of Frazer's sentence on the grounds that Judge Mechem was in favor of it.

The Governor said that Judge Mechem had not shown himself to be so in any declaration that had come to him. The men had been given a fair trial, had been found guilty by all the evidence, and duly sentenced by Judge Mechem to be hanged, and the decision of the lower court was fully sustained by the Supreme Court. The Governor takes the ground that it has been wise not to give out any statement tending to encourage the belief that there was hope of commuting the sentence, or lend, by publicity, an impetus to such public discussion as would create a weak sentimentality regarding the matter. The Governor, with due regard for the feeling of the friends and relatives of the condemned men gave the cases exhaustive consideration, and was led to but one conclusion, and that was that his duty to the people and to the decisions of the court was not to interfere in these cases, and the men were therefore hanged today.

Note: Other newspapers reported that the gallows consisted of the trap door being cut out from the 2nd story floor inside the county courthouse, and the men were hanged by dropping them through the floor.

Sources:

Albuquerque *Morning Journal*, Nov 14, 20, 21, 1911; April 25, 1913
Deming *Headlight*, November 24, 1911; April 12, 1912
Deming *Graphic*, November 24, 1911
Santa Fe *New Mexican*, April 24, 25, 1913
El Paso *Morning Times*, November 20, 21, 1911

Francisco Granado

On the evening of February 19, 1912, Mr. C. A. Freeman walked from the store he managed to the Mogollon Express Office to pick up a package. The package contained the payroll for a mining operation near the town. At 7 o'clock, Mr. Freeman returned to the Mogollon Mercantile Company store to place the $3,500 within the store's safe. Just as Mr. Freeman was turning around after closing the safe door, two Mexican men entered the store with Winchester rifles. The two men ordered everyone inside the store to put their hands up in the air. As Mr. Freeman raised his hands high, he was shot and killed by a bullet to the heart. Mr. William Clark, the store clerk ran to the end of the store counter where he also was shot and killed. The only other person in the store was the bookkeeper who begged that his life be spared. The bookkeeper told the men he knew where the money was kept and directed the robbers to the store's safe. In return for his cooperation, the robbers agreed not to kill him. The murderous robbers then emptied the safe of the $3,500 and a package of silver. Upon exiting the store, the robbers where confronted by townsmen who had gathered outside after hearing the gunshots. Both robbers kept the men at bay with their rifles as they slipped back into an alley. Realizing that the silver was too heavy to carry and that it would slow down their escape, it was discarded in the alley.

Once Sheriff Emil James was notified of the murder and robbery, he studied the route he would take to Mogollon from Silver City in hopes he would cross the tracks of the two killers. While the Sheriff and Deputy Scott Heapley traveled to Mogollon, they came across two fresh tracks which they believed to be left by the two wanted men. In the tracking of the two men, the Sheriff determined they had hidden in the hills during the day and traveled at night to avoid detection. The lawmen trailed the men for 22 miles, over four days, and arrived at noon on February 23rd at an adobe house at Gila Farms, being 30 miles northwest of Silver City. The Sheriff was confident the tracks of the men had ended at the adobe house and here he confronted a Mexican woman. The woman denied that any men were present or in the home. Just then two Mexican men approached the officers from inside the home. The woman quickly grabbed her two children and ran out of the house. Once she was out of the line of fire, the two wanted men fired upon the officers from the doorway. The lawmen returned fire, killing one of the robbers with a bullet to the left eye. The second suspect retreated back into the home shooting at the officers from the window. Over 50 bullets had been fired when the owner of the adobe house returned home after hearing the gunshots. Sheriff James confronted the man and ordered him to approach his house and convince the wanted man to surrender. Believing he would be shot, the homeowner at first refused. Sheriff James told the owner he could either convince the man to surrender or he prepared to see his house blown up with dynamite. The owner, not wanting to see his home destroyed, approached from the rear yelling into the home. He called out to the man inside that he had no chance of escape and that it was hopeless to resist the officers any longer. A short time later, 19 year old Francisco Granado emerged from the house with his hands above his head.

The body of the dead man was identified as Gregorio Torrango. Within the pockets of the dead man was over $2,000 and most of the remaining $1,500 was found scattered throughout the house. When questioned by the Sheriff as to the murders, Francisco Granado confessed to his participation. Francisco said when he and Torrango entered the store, he ordered everyone to put their hands up. Seeing everyone unarmed, he and Torrango each shot and killed a man "merely to get them out of the way." He related the bookkeeper was just about to be killed when he vigorously pleaded with them not to kill him. After the bookkeeper showed them where the money was located, Torrango and he both decided to spare him his life. After fleeing the store, he and Torrango camped four miles outside of the town and remained hidden there up until the following day.

Francisco was tried in Socorro, New Mexico, before Judge R. P. Barnes on April 12, 1913. The jury deliberated a short time the next day and returned a verdict of guilty of murder in the first degree. Convicted of murder, Francisco was transported to the State Penitentiary in Santa Fe and lodged in a cell on the second floor until his execution date. Ivory Frazer was convicted of murder, in Socorro, directly after Francisco's trial and his execution date was set for the same date as Francisco Granado. Ivory Frazer was lodged on the first floor of the penitentiary. The two men who were going to share the double trap door at their execution did not meet until they were both removed from their cell at 3 o'clock in the morning of April 25, 1913 and heavily shackled. Both men changed out of their prison stripe uniforms into their funeral clothes. Afterwards the two men sat next to each other on the train for the return trip to Socorro.

On the train, Francisco remained quiet other than to provide names of relatives to be notified of his death. During the rest of the journey, Francisco was caught up in his own thoughts about his approaching execution. At 4:50 a.m., Francisco Granado and Ivory Frazer stood next to each other on the double trap doors of the gallows. Once Francisco refused to make a last statement, the trap was sprung at 4:52. Both bodies remained hanging for thirteen minutes until Doctors Duncan and Parvis pronounced life extent. The body of Francisco Granado was then cut down and placed in a coffin for burial in Socorro.

Sources:

Santa Fe *New Mexican*, April 24, 25, 1913
Albuquerque *Morning Journal*, April 25, 1913
Socorro *Chieftain*, February 24, March 2, April 6, 13, 1912

Chapter 14

Taos County

Jose Maria Martin,
 alias Jesus Maria Martinez

John Conley

May 13, 1864

February 1906

Jose Maria Martin

Jose Maria Martin murdered a blacksmith by the name of Julian Truillo in Taos, New Mexico. Directly after committing the murder, Jose Martin fled from New Mexico to Colorado to escape arrest. After time had elapsed, Jose believed it was safe enough for him to return back home to his wife at Taos. Upon his return home, he was immediately placed under arrest for murder in the first degree. Attorney General Clever prosecuted the case for the Territory, before Chief Justice Kirby Benedict, during the April term. Jose Maria Martin was found guilty and sentenced by Judge Benedict who showed no sympathy for the convicted man. Judge Benedict was first appointed in 1853 by President Pierce, reappointed by President Buchanan and then appointed Chief Justice of the Court by President Abraham Lincoln. It was for the colorful death sentence passed upon Jose Maria Martin by Judge Benedict in April of 1864 that he is best remembered:

"Jose Maria Martin, **stand up!** Jose Maria Martin, you have been indicted, tried and convicted by a jury of your countrymen of the crime of murder, and the court is now about to pass upon you the dread sentence of the law. As a usual thing, Jose Maria Martin, it is a painful duty for the judge of a court of justice to pronounce upon a human being the sentence of death. There is something horrible about it, and the mind of the court naturally revolts from the performance of such a duty; happily, however, your case is relieved of all such unpleasantness, and the court takes positive delight in sentencing you to death.

"You are a young man, Jose Maria Martin, apparently of good physical constitution and robust health. Ordinarily you might have looked forward to many years of life, and the court has no doubt you have, and have expected to die at a green old age, but you are about to be cut off as the consequence of your own act. Jose Maria Martin, it is now the spring time; in a little while the grass will be springing up in this beautiful valley, and on these broad mesas and mountains sides, flowers will be blooming; birds will be singing their sweet carols, and nature will be putting on her most gorgeous and most attractive robes, and life will be pleasant and men will want to stay; but none of this is for you, Jose Maria Martin; the flowers will not bloom for you, Jose Maria Martin; the birds will not carol for you, Jose Maria Martin; when these things come to gladden the senses of men, you will be occupying a space about six by two beneath the sod, and the green grass and those beautiful flowers will be growing above your lowly head.

"The sentence of the court is that you be taken from this place to the county jail; that you there be kept safely and securely confined in the custody of the Sheriff until the day appointed for your execution. Be very careful, Mr. Sheriff, that he have no opportunity to escape, and that you have him at the appointed place at the appointed time; that you be so kept, Jose Maria Martin, until . . . `Mr. Clerk, on what day of the month does Friday, about two weeks from this time, come?'" `March 22, your honor'. "Very well – until Friday, the 22d day of March, when you will be taken from your place of confinement to some safe and convenient spot within the county, (that is your discretion, Mr. Sheriff; you are only confined to the limits of the county), and that you there be hanged by the neck until you are dead, and – the court was about to add, Jose Maria Martin may God have mercy on your soul, but the court will not assume the responsibility of asking an all wise Providence to do that which the jury of your peers has refused to do. The Lord could not have mercy on your soul! However, if you affect any religious belief, or are connected with any religious organization, it might be well for you to send for your priest or your minister and get from him such consolation as you can, but the court advises you to place no reliance upon anything of that kind. Mr. Sheriff – remove the prisoner."

Judge Kirby Benedict is best remembered for his colorful sentencing of Jose Maria Martin in 1864.

Jose Maria Martin was not executed as first scheduled on March 22, 1864, but was executed on Friday, the 13th of May 1864.

Some articles show Jose Maria Martin also as Jesus Maria Martinez as printed in the Santa Fe *New Mexican*, Santa Fe, dated May 7 and 21, 1864.

EXECUTION OF JESUS MARIA MART-
INEZ, AT TAOS.

The terrible sentence of death was executed upon this man on Friday, the 13 of the present month. We have seen and conversed with Don Aniecto Valdez, the sheriff of Taos. We are informed that the best order prevailed at the execution. A great number of people were present at the gallows. Since the sentence, the conduct of the county officers and people seem entitled to much credit. The judge of probate, Santes Estevan, gave the sheriff every assistance in his power. A guard was kept at the jail. The people, as they were summoned to serve as guard, served with cheerfulness. For the day of the execution, the sheriff asked of Don Pedro Valdez, Brigadier General of Militia, the assistance of a company of soldiers. They were promptly upon the ground, with their officers, and all well armed.

The prisoner was attended to the gallows by a priest. When he came within sight of the frame, all the bravado he had shown upon his trial, and afterwards, forsook him. All his spirit seemed to give away, and desert the victim. At the gallows he had to be lifted, so completely was he unnerved. After he fell, he hung over half an hour. So has perished another murderer. So has ended the life of more who practiced his brutal bravados upon the living. We give our sincerest thanks to the people and officers of Taos, who have stood so faithfully in aid of the executions of the laws in their midst.

Sources:

Santa Fe *New Mexican*, May 7, 21, 1864
Las Cruces *Citizen*, June 23, 1906

John Conley

John Conley was convicted and sentenced to hang for the murder of James Redding. On the day of the murder January 16, 1904, John Conley had killed another man during a violent incident at a mountain camp near Questa, New Mexico. John Conley made a statement that two men, one of them James Redding, were drunk and attacked him with axes. Therefore, he killed both men in self-defense and as a last resort. This story of self-defense did not hold up in court. The Santa Fe *New Mexican* on February 26, 1906 had the following headlines and story.

Conley Cuts Throat
TO CHEAT GALLOWS
HANGED WHILE INSENSIBLE FROM WOUNDS
INFLICTED WITH OLD POCKET KNIFE - - -
CARRIED TO SCAFFOLD BY GUARDS.

Special to the *New Mexican*.

Taos, via Embudo, 3:30 o'clock p.m. Feb 26 – At 7:30 this morning, while the birds were singing and the sky was clear and beautiful, John Conley, convicted of the murder of James Redding and sentenced to hang to-day, cut his throat from ear to ear and severed his wind pipe, but did not cut deep enough to cut the main artery.

This was done while he was in the steel cage. In a few minutes the floor of the cage was covered with blood; the guards noticing this, rushed in and the old pocket knife with which Conley slashed his throat was taken away from him. The deputy sheriff in charge went for Dr. T. P. Martin, who hastened to the jail and arrived there twenty minutes after Conley had made his attempt at suicide. The doctor stopped the flow of blood and dressed the wound inflicted by Conley on his throat. The parish priest was summoned, who immediately responded for Conley's soul.

Conley, in an apparently unconscious condition, was carried to the scaffold at 9:22 a.m. The guards held him in an upright position while the black-cap was adjusted over his head, and the body was dropped from the gallows. He made no sign of consciousness and the body was quite limber. This was 9:27. The body dropped four feet. Deputy Pablo Gomes operated the mechanical contrivance. The body slipped through the hole and Conley's neck was evidently not broken. He stopped bleeding entirely at 9:37; at 9:42 Dr. Martin pronounced life extinct.

BODY BURIED

The body was taken down and today was buried in the public cemetery near this place. No friends or relatives attended the funeral. Seventeen persons witnessed the hanging. The pocket knife which Conley used in his endeavor to commit suicide had evidently been concealed by him for months and had not been detected, although he was searched several times very carefully before being placed in the steel cage and while an occupant of it. His attempt to end his life was a surprise to everyone concerned with the jail management. He left a letter which was opened after his death, in which he again denounced his enemies and reasserted his innocence of the crime for which he was convicted.

Among those who witnessed the hanging was ex-sheriff Harry C. Kinsell, of this city, who went to Taos last week as the Governor's agent. In accordance with the executive's order, the affair was robbed of as much publicity as possible. The gallows was built within the adobe walls of the jail yard so that only those admitted by ticket could witness the hanging. Guards were placed upon the walls and nearby buildings overlooking the scene to prevent the un-welcome presence of morbidly curious spectators.

The gallows was crudely constructed, but answered the purpose. Two upright posts with a crossbeam supported by the rope and its victim. There was a narrow platform upon which officers and prisoner stood. The trap was supported by two stout oak pegs, which were quickly withdrawn when the executioner, stationed behind Conley, pushed a small iron lever. Ex-sheriff Kinsell tested the trap several times before the hanging and it was in perfect working order.

THE CRIME.

The crime for which John Conley was executed today at Taos was committed on January 16, 1904, at the Guadalupe Placers, four miles from Questa in northern Taos County. The two victims were James Redding, son of E. S. Redding, hotel and saloonkeeper at Questa, and Charles Purdy of Red River.

Young Redding would have been 20 years old in the month following his death, and Purdy was 68 years old, but despite his age, was strong and active. Conley had been given a contract by E. N. Jordan, of Minneapolis, to do the assessment work on the Guadalupe Placers and had hired E. S. Redding, his son James, and his son-in-law Jesus Herrera and Charles Purdy to do the work with him. Conley had charged only $100 for the contract and claimed that he was upbraided by the others for not charging $600.

This quarrel resulted in a bitter feeling which was augmented by Conley discharging Jesus Herrera after a day's work, and by a claim of Purdy that Conley had not paid him for some work done on a mining claim for a man named Hawk in Indian Territory. Purdy had been drinking heavily previous to the day of the murder, and on that morning was under the influence of liquor. James Redding, too, as the evidence showed, appeared intoxicated. Conley was also a drinking man, but on the day of the murder, both before and after the deed, was sober.

The three men started from Questa for the Placers, and upon arrival there prepared a meal and ate it. After the meal, Conley said, "let us go to work." Both Redding and Purdy refused to go to work and told Conley to leave the Placers. Conley turned toward his horse when, so Conley claims, Purdy threw a heavy steel skillet at him, which was found afterwards in the snow. Conley dodged it and continued toward his horse. Purdy and Redding each seized an axe and Conley shot down Redding in his tracks, firing two shots, each sufficient to cause death. He fired one shot at Purdy who retreated to the tent. Conley followed and fired a second shot into Purdy, killing him instantly. Both men were found with axes at their sides. Conley then tied the flaps of the tent and rode into Questa and from there to Red River, where he gave himself up the following morning before daylight.

Upon his trial, Conley's plea was "Self Defense," while the prosecution convinced the jury that Conley's deed had been murder in the first degree, the trial being for the murder of James Redding.

The jury went out after supper and returned a verdict about 3 o'clock in the morning. One juryman reported that at first the poll stood seven for a verdict of first degree and five for second and third degree.

A motion for new trial was overruled. An appeal to the Territorial Supreme Court was granted but Conley, not having the means of paying for a transcript of evidence, the Supreme Court could not review this and could do naught but confirm the verdict and set the execution for February 16. In the meanwhile, the court stenographer and district clerk furnished a transcript of the testimony free of charge, but efforts to reopen the case proved futile, Governor Hagerman refusing to grant a reprieve of thirty days for that purpose. A petition for a writ of habeas corpus, raising constitutional questions, was denied by Judge Ira A. Abbott of the Second Judicial District. A day before the first day set for the execution, representations being made to Governor Hagerman that Conley had become violently insane, a reprieve of ten days was granted, but the report of Conley's insanity was unfounded and therefore the hanging took place today….

Conley's Statement.

Conley, after giving up all hope for a reprieve or commutation of sentence, made a statement to a representative of the Daily New *Mexican* reviewing briefly the events that brought him to the gallows. It was his request that his dying declaration not to published until after the execution. It is as follows.

"On the morning of January 16, 1905, I arose at 6 o'clock. On my way to the hotel of E. S. Redding, about half way, I met his son, James Redding, who asked me whether I was going to work. I answered that I was and asked him: "Where are you going?" He said he was looking for a horse and would go to work with me, although he had been up all night at a wake, drinking and drunk, but that he would be all right.

"When I got to the hotel, I took off my overcoat and left it in the office and then went to get Charles Purdy out of bed. I saw that he was drunk and laid on the bed with his coat and vest on. When I called him, he rolled over, reached under the pillow and offered me a whiskey bottle, saying: "Have a drink?" I refused. He said it was good whiskey and insisted upon my taking a drink, but I would not do it. He took a drink and then sat the bottle on the floor.

"I went to the barn, fed my horse and returned to the hotel office, but just on the outside I met E. S. Redding. I bid him good morning and told him that I had met his son up the road. He replied: "Yes, we were up all night with him, he was sick". I told him that his son had been up all night at a wake, drunk.

"I made another effort to persuade Purdy to get out of bed. I told him that breakfast would soon be ready. A few minutes later he came into the office with his bottle in his hand. Taking a drink, he remarked that he felt tough. I told him he looked as if he had been out all night. He said that he had been up with old Redding and then went around with Jim, who was drunk, and therefore would probably not show up for work. I told Purdy that I had met Jim Redding on the road and that he had promised to go to work. Purdy went in to the bedroom for a moment, then returned and sat down by the fire asking: "How long will work last?" I replied, that I thought that we would get through in a week or so, He said that, that was just the thing he and old Redding had been discussing during the night, and we felt that you should make the outfit put up $100 a claim instead of $100 for the entire six claims.

WANTED MORE MONEY.

"Redding said that the outfit would have to put up $500 any way if he was doing the work, or he would take the property and show Jordan that it did not belong to him. I answered that I did not care to whom the property belonged, that I only knew Jordan is the auditor and that we would work for him while the money lasted; that I knew that Redding was sore and I was told that Redding had written to Jordan. I said that Redding was continually nagging about the job, that he needed the money.

"Continually I said: You both know that Jordan has written me to do this work cheaply, as he had to pay for it; that if he had made a sale, then the company would have to put $500, but that he alone could not afford it. Redding says that the property is not worth working that he would not have it, that we panned the different prospect holes and could hardly get any color after a week's panning. Purdy replied that this was all right, but that Purdy was going to make him dig up the money or know why. Purdy then got up, reached for his bottle, offered it to me; I told him I wanted none of it, and he then threw the bottle under the washstand.

"About that time E. S. Redding came into the office; then Henry Young. The first named, led the way to breakfast. Purdy took up a cup of coffee, but could not eat. After breakfast I went to the barn and got my horse and returned to the hotel. E. S. Redding brought over a horse for Purdy, and about the same time Jim Redding rode up. Purdy asked me to get him a bottle of whiskey and I told him that he should know that the saloon was closed, as he had just come from there. E. S. Redding asked what Purdy wanted and Purdy told him, a bottle of whiskey. At that moment he saw Rael, the saloonkeeper, coming and requested him to open up and Rael replied that he would go for the key. I gave Purdy a dollar, who, upon the request of Jim Redding, passed it to him to get the whiskey. Jim Redding returned with the whiskey, they took a drink, mounted and started away. I waited and told Rael that Jim Redding had gotten the Whiskey. I then asked R. S. Redding whether he was coming along, and he said no.

DID NOT WANT TO WORK.

"I soon overtook Jim Redding and Purdy on the way to camp. On the way they drank twice out of the bottle and insisted that I should drink, but I refused. When about half a mile from camp, I heard two shots fired. One of these whistling right by the front of me. The sound came from the far right side of the road. I called Purdy's attention to the unusual incident and he replied that I might or would hear more of them.

"On reaching camp they tied their horses to a tree. I took the bit out of the mouth of my horse and let the reins drop to the ground. At the tent we took off our overcoats and I said "Let's go to work." Purdy said that he was first going to cook up some thing to eat, at the same time taking the lids out of the stove. Jim Redding went to the stream with the bucket to fetch water; I cut kindling wood for the stove. Purdy started the fire and then he and Redding took another drink.

"After the meal, we all stepped outside, leaving the dishes unwashed at the foot of the bunks, where they had been used. I then said: 'Boy's let us go to work'. Purdy said that he wasn't going to work. Jim Redding said, no more work for him. I asked them what was the matter, and they simply said that they were not going to work. I put on my overcoat and again asked what was wrong. Purdy told me, 'Get off and stay off!' They both commenced cursing. I started toward my horse. Purdy grabbed a bog steel skillet from the stove and threw it at me, at the same time calling me all kinds of names. Jim Redding picked up an axe and followed me, and Purdy reached for the second axe. I called to Redding to keep away. But he kept on approaching through the deep snow cursing and crying: 'I kill you, you _____.' I was reaching down for the bridle when I saw Redding was close upon me. I again told him to keep away, to come no further, but in reply he raised his axe as if about to strike, when I fired, hitting him in the forehead. He appeared stunned, but his axe was still raised threateningly, and I stepped forward, firing a second time, when he fell backwards.

SHOOTS PURDY.

"In the mean while, Purdy was coming toward me, cursing. I told him to throw down the axe, but to no avail for he kept coming right for me with the axe uplifted and I fired, hitting him in the cheek, under the eye, and wounded him. I again commanded him to throw down the axe and to go to the tent. Finally he obeyed, but taking the axe with him.

"In a few minutes I went to the tent and called him, but received no answer. I went closer and saw him standing with the axe-raised ready to strike me. Realizing that I could not get away, being very close to him, with one tent to my side, one in back of me and the deep snow on the other two sides, I fired, striking him in the neck. He fell backwards and partly on his side, between the bucket of water and the bunk. The axe dropped in front and partly under him.

"I bridled my horse and returned to the tents and loosely tied the top string of the flap as it might flop against the stove. I then mounted my horse and went to Questa. I rode into Redding's barnyard, intending to put up my horse. I changed my mind and rode to Young's store. There I met J. T. Heathman, who was saying that he was going home. I said that I would go with him. I went into Young's store, purchased a box of cartridges and then Heathman and I led our horses along the road to Red River, the stream, for about one half of a mile. He had his horses packed, so I mounted and left him but stopped at his house to tell his mother that he would be home late. I remained a while and had lunch, then rode to Red River, put my horse into the barn un-saddled and fed him.

"I then went to Cartwright's and with him to Mr. Paxton's office. I met J. M. Phipps and with him went to my house, asking if he had received his commission as deputy sheriff. He said that he had not. He asked if anything was up. I told him that I had some trouble. Two men on horseback had come into Red River in the meanwhile and Phipps, who had gone up town, returned and reported that they were after me and that one of the two men was Pedro Barela, and that I had better go to his house. I refused to do so, saying that I had some writing to do and would stay at home. I asked him to go and see Justice of the Peace W. J. Cartwright for me. He came back with the tidings that Cartwright refused to come, that he was scared and did not know what to do. I told him that I wanted to see Cartwright as I would not give myself up to Barela. He went again and when he returned he reported that Barela had sent another man after a posse and that they would shoot the home up, adding that Barela was getting drunk. We had some more words and then he went away.

Surrendered.

"In the meantime I noticed that a guard had been placed around the house. It was very dark by this time. I made a fire and lit a lamp. In an hour or more Phipps returned. He got me some coffee and said that Barela was very drunk; that he could not get Cartwright. He left and returned once more, saying that Barela was at Cielland's and had promised to be friendly and to see to it that I was not harmed in going to Questa. Phipps promised that he and Burns would accompany me. I then gave myself up to Phipps and Burns. Half an hour afterwards they turned me over to Barela, who three hours afterwards surrendered me to H. Gonzales, who had a warrant for my arrest.

"I was taken to Questa and at the preliminary hearing pleaded not guilty and waived an examination. But I saw that the feeling and surrounding circumstances were such that it was absolutely necessary to make a statement; because the house was drunk, packed and things looked blue. One of the guards was drunk and asleep in the chair. I again pleaded not guilty but made a statement of self-defense. I was then brought to Taos, Voluntarily surrounded myself to J. M. Phipps. I had not felt justice to give myself up to Barela because ten days before he had threatened to kill Henry J. Young and myself in his store."

Harry C. Kinsell told the New Mexican reporter, "The court's sentence was carried out in the best manner possible after the man had tried to end his life. There was nothing to do but hang him and we had to do it as expeditiously as possible."

Mr. Kinsell related to the reporter what had occurred with Conley. "Shortly after 7 o'clock a guard ran and told me that Conley had cut his throat. We went hurriedly to the jail and found Conley lying upon the bunk with blood flowing from a wound in his neck which had severed his windpipe. He still clasped a bloody pocketknife in his hand. Two blades opened.

"Four deputy sheriffs threw themselves upon him and he fought desperately, although unable to get to his feet. He struck out blindly with the knife, stabbing Deputy Abron Trujillo and another officer in the hands. Blood flew in every direction. The guards were covered with it and I got my share".

SUBDUE MAN.

"We at length subdued Conley, who lay upon his back gasping. He could not speak. A surgeon was called and the wound was dressed. The guards then supported the prisoner to the scaffold and seated him upon a stool placed on the trap. They quickly bound him, adjusted the black-cap and upon the signal, the lever was jerked and Conley fell to his death. He was not unconscious as stated in press dispatches, but knew what was taking place to the end. His neck was not broken because he did not drop straight down".

"After reaching the end of the rope, Conley struggled for some time, but soon began to weaken. At the end of ten minutes his pulse was lifeless, but we let him hang for a short time longer to make sure that he was dead. His body was then cut down and prepared for burial. It was placed in a wagon and taken to the public cemetery by guards for burial. Had Conley met his death bravely, I do not believe he would have experienced half the suffering he did by cutting his throat. I was with Conley on several occasions during the week proceeding and never saw a man take death so hard. He cried several times and apparently could not serve himself for the ordeal."

Sources:

Santa Fe *New Mexican*, February 26, 28, 1906

Chapter 15

Torrance County

Ysidor Miranda	July 28, 1922
Carlos Renteria	July 28, 1922
Luis Medrano	July 28, 1922
Francisco Vaisas	April, 1923

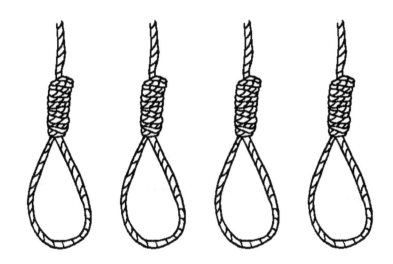

Ysidor Miranda, Carlos Renteria, Luis Medrano, & Francisco Vaisas

Anton Coury owned and operated a small general store in the town of Duran, New Mexico. Mr. Coury lived above the store along with his wife and son. On the Saturday night of September 3, 1921, Mr. Coury had locked the store for the night and gone up stairs. While eating dinner with his family, five men arrived at the store and knocked on the door. The men asked Mr. Coury if he would open the store as they wished to make some purchases.

Mr. Coury unlocked the door. Three of the five men entered the store, while the other two remained outside as lookouts. One of the men asked for a drink of water, a second man asked Mrs. Coury for some cheese and crackers, while the third man lowered the curtains of the store window. Two of the men drew revolvers and told Mr. Coury to put his hands up. When he refused to do so, he was shot three times. The three bullets struck him in the forehead, mouth and heart, killing him. Mrs. Coury fought with one of the men and wrestled the pistol away. The man who had killed her husband then shot her on the right side of the abdomen. Twelve year old Fred Coury threw a can of sweet potatoes at the killer. The can knocked the man down and he was dazed as he staggered to his feet. In the process the killer dropped his pistol and hat. Fred Coury retrieved this pistol and the three men fled into the darkness. One of the men ran directly into a cactus. Help arrived and Mrs. Coury was carried to the railway and transported by train to a hospital in El Paso, Texas. It was discovered the corset she had been wearing deflected the bullet, saving her life.

Using the hat left behind as the scent, bloodhounds from the prison were called to assist the Sheriff in trailing the killers. The bloodhounds trailed the suspects for three days. On the third day, the scent was lost and it was believed the killers had escaped using a car. Nearby ranchers told the Sheriff of seeing three men in a car heading towards Roswell. Sheriff Brock and his small posse arrived in Roswell and learned from Chavez County Deputy Emil Sandoval that he had earlier arrested two men matching the description of the men being trailed. Both men at first denied involvement until the Sheriff observed one of the men needed treatment by a doctor for cactus thorns to his leg. The two men were identified as being Francis Viaza and Carlos Renteria. Both men confessed to their involvement and named Ysidor Miranda as the man who shot the storekeeper in the mouth. Ysidor Miranda was also known as Bernardo Miranda and had already served five years of a twenty-year sentence for murder, and eighteen months for forgery. The men said it was Miranda's idea to rob the store as he said he knew a place where they could get plenty of money. The town of Duran did not have a bank and all the money was kept in the store's iron safe.

Sheriff Brock arrested a third suspect at Estancia, New Mexico. This man was identified as Luis Medrano and was arrested for suspicion of murder after being seen hiding a pistol in weeds. A fourth suspect, Ysidor Miranda, was also captured and it was believed the fifth man, known only as "Muchacho," had escaped to Mexico. Muchacho was never brought to trial. The four men were convicted of first-degree murder and sentenced to hang on July 28, 1922. Francisco Vaisas was granted a last minute reprieve and therefore did not join his conspirators on the scaffold. The gallows was built within the courtyard. It had a canvass surrounding it that kept the execution from view. The execution time was set between six in the forenoon and six in the afternoon. The three men were said to have walked to the scaffold with a firm step. Father Gauthier served as spiritual adviser for Luis Medrano and Carlos Renteria. Ysidor Miranda refused any services from the priest and waved him away.

On the scaffold, Miranda made a speech to the witnesses: "Money is supreme in this country and a poor man has no chance to prolong or save his life, rehearing or appeal. In this country and in this court a poor man has no show. Because I have no money therefore I had no chance. Had I had money I could buy the court and go free. There is no justice in hanging a man because he had killed another. Because I have to die and there is no chance for me, I am happy my end is near." Renteria's only statement was that he agreed with Miranda. Medrano said, "A man with no money is a criminal and they might as well go ahead and hang him." Both Sheriff John Block and Deputy Carl Custer pulled the trap lever at 7:00 o'clock. The body of Ysidor Miranda was claimed by his sister to be buried at Vaughn. The remains of Carlos Renteria and Luis Medrano were buried in the Catholic section of the Estancia Cemetery.

The Santa Fe *New Mexican* dated July 28, 1922 had the following story.

THREE HANGED
ONE SAVED

———

Vaisas, One of Convicted Slayers
Of Coury, Reprieved; 100
See Estancia Executed

———

Widow of Dead Man
Sees murderers die

———

Estancia, N. M., July 28. -
Three men were hanged here at 7 o'clock this morning for the murder of Anton Coury, a merchant of Duran, N. M., last September.

Francisco Vaisas, a fourth man who was convicted, was granted a reprieve at the last minute pending an appeal of his case to the Supreme Court.

Mrs. Coury, widow of the slain merchant, was a silent watcher at the hanging. The three men, Carlos Renteria, Ysidor Miranda and Luis Medrano, were put on scaffolds and the three traps sprung simultaneously. A crowd of about 100 persons witnessed the execution. Francisco Vaisas will be returned to the state prison pending the final disposition of his case.

HANG MEN LIKE GOATS,
DECLARES MIRANDA

Ysidor Miranda, one of the two men who fired the two shots that struck Anton Coury, the Duran merchant for whose death the three were hanged, mounted the steps to the scaffold smiling and was still smiling when the noose was adjusted, followed by the black cap, according to a witness. It was said however, the other two, Carlos Renteria and Luis Medrano, "broke down:" but no details were given.

All three were hanged at one time on a large scaffold built with four traps; but the fourth trap, intended for Francisco Vaisas, was unoccupied when the lever was pulled. An eleventh hour appeal to the Supreme Court was taken for Vaisas. This acted as a stay of execution and saved him from going to death with his companions, although he was convicted along with them of first-degree murder.

Taking advantage of the privilege seldom used by men about to die, all three made brief statements when asked on the scaffold if they had anything to say in the customary form.

"There is no justice in this country," said Miranda in a calm voice. "They hang men like goats." The other two were said to have voiced practically the same sentiment, but witnesses did not remember their words closely enough to quote them.

The drop broke Renteria's neck and Medrano's neck and they were officially pronounced dead 10 minutes after the traps were sprung, but Medrano's neck evidently was not broken as the doctors did not announce his heart has stopped beating for fully 25 minutes. The man, however, was unconscious from the time of the drop.

On April 6, 1923, Francisco Vaisa became the last man legally executed by hanging in New Mexico after statehood.

COOL ON
GALLOWS

Francisco Vaisa Hanged at Estan-

Cia for the Murder of Coury;
Glad of Finish.

Albuquerque, N. M., April 6.

Francisco Vaisa was hanged at estancia, N. M., at 5:30 o'clock this morning, the fourth man to pay the death penalty for the murder of Anton Coury, a merchant of Duran, N. M.

Vaisa went to the scaffold calmly and made no statement. Last night he merely said he was glad to "get it over with." It was 20 minutes after the trap was sprung before he was announced dead.

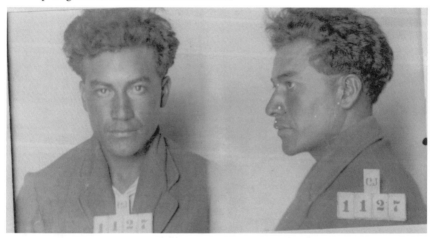

Francisco Vaisas became the last man in New Mexico who was executed by hanging, April 6, 1923. Courtesy of the New Mexico State Records and Archives, Neg. 1341 USJ.

Chapter 16
Union County

Thomas E. Ketchum   April 26, 1901

Thomas E. Ketchum, alias "Black Jack"

Of all the outlaws executed by hanging in New Mexico, Black Jack Ketchum is undoubtedly the best known in Western history. Thomas Edward Ketchum was born on October 31, 1863, in San Saba County, Texas. Thomas' father died when he was five and his mother was blind for several years prior to her death. Thomas and his younger brother, Sam, grew up working as cowboys. The first trouble Thomas got into was his part in the killing of John N. "Jap" Powers on December 12, 1895, in Green County, Texas. When the authorities begun looking for Thomas, he fled to New Mexico. Not long after arriving in Liberty, New Mexico, in 1896, Thomas and Sam robbed the Liberty Post Office and store of $44.69. A posse pursued them, and when they did catch up to the Ketchum's, two of the posse members were killed in the gun battle.

On May 14, 1897, Thomas Ketchum, along with his brother and gang members, went from robbing Post Offices to robbing their first train. On that day, the gang robbed a Southern Pacific train at Lozier, Texas, in Terrell County. During this period, in April 1897, an Arizona bandit by the name of Will Christian, alias "Black Jack," was killed in Graham County, Arizona. Soon after Christian was killed, Thomas and Sam Ketchum were at the Brewery Gulch Saloon in Bisbee, Arizona.

While Thomas was drinking, a bar patron looked at him and said, "If I didn't know better I'd shore swear you was Black Jack Christian. You shore look alike, any kin?" Tom replied that he had never heard of the man. Another patron said, "Well, anyhow, you might look like him but you're shore a mite better off. Because the poor fellow is dead as a doornail." The two men told Thomas about Christian's outlaw history and how a posse near Clifton, Arizona had killed him. The men told Thomas that Christian got his name while working at a round up. There was another man named Jack and because the foreman could not tell them apart, called Christian "Black Jack" for his dark hair. Thomas Ketchum said, "Sounds like a perfect name and fits me perfect. Seeing as how that Christian fellow has no more use for it, I hereby dub myself Black Jack Ketchum."

The gang of robbers held up several trains from September 3, 1897, until July 1, 1898. The gang soon split up and Thomas went his own way. On July 11, 1899, Sam Ketchum and gang held up the Colorado and Southern Flyer near Folsom, New Mexico. Posse members on the train were prepared and a fierce gun battled ensued. Sam Ketchum and Elza Lay were wounded and Sheriff Farr of Huerfano County, Colorado was killed. Sam Ketchum was soon captured, but died of blood poisoning at the New Mexico Territory Penitentiary in Santa Fe.

Then on August 16, 1899, near the same spot where Sam Ketchum had attempted to rob the train, Black-Jack Ketchum tried to rob the same train, single handed. The San Francisco *Chronicle* wrote, "Black Jack held up a Colorado and Southern passenger train. He ordered the engineer and fireman to uncouple the engine and leave the train. The conductor and mail agent opened fire on him, which he promptly returned. He received the contents of a double-barrel shotgun in his right arm, but, quickly changing the rifle to his left shoulder, he succeeded in wounding both the conductor and mail agent. He then escaped in the darkness, but was captured the next day. He was tried for assault upon a United States Mail agent and sentenced to ten years in the penitentiary. In September of 1900, he was tried on the more serious charge of assault upon a railroad train with intent to commit a felony. The jury returned a verdict of guilty in less than ten minutes. Judge William J. Mills sentenced Thomas Ketchum to hang by the neck until dead.

The hanging of Thomas E. Ketchum "Black Jack", hanged, April 26, 1901. Courtesy Museum of New Mexico, Neg. No. 12886. Photograph by W.A. White.

Black Jack Ketchum's arm was so mangled by the shotgun blast that it had to be amputated at the penitentiary. On April 23, 1901, Thomas Ketchum was removed from the penitentiary and placed on a Santa Fe railway train. As the crime was committed in Union County, he was taken to the County Seat at Clayton for his execution. The train arrived on the morning of April 24th. Upon Ketchum seeing the scaffold, he commented it looked like a good piece of work, but that they ought to test it on Harrington, the conductor who shot him. Ketchum again yelled out to the carpenters from his cell window, "You did a fine job boys, but why not tear down the stockade so the fellows can see a man hang who never killed anyone?" While awaiting his execution, Black Jack did ask Sheriff Salome

Garcia for some female companionship as a last request, but was denied this, for there were no public funds to pay for her. Another request he made was to "be buried face down so Harrington can kiss my ass." On the day of the execution, 150 admission tickets had been issued to allow witnesses within the enclosed execution stockade. The Santa Fe *New Mexican* described what the witnesses observed.

Santa Fe *New Mexican*, Friday, April 26, 1901

KETCHUM PAYS
THE PENALTY

HE Writes a Letter to President Mc-Kinley and Makes a Startling Confession.

HE DIES A HORRIBLE DEATH.

The Rope Broke and His Head Was Sev-Ered From His Body – His Last hours He Blasphemed and Asked For Music.

Denver, Colo., April 26. – A special to the *Times* from Clayton, N. M., says: Ketchum passed a quite night, ate a hearty breakfast, took a bath and put on a new suit of clothes this morning. Twenty deputies were on the ground last night. A priest from Trinidad was with him midnight till dawn. In an interview with John R. Guyer, his attorney, yesterday he asked him to write a letter to President Mc Kinley, which was done.

As his attorney was leaving he said: "Say, tell Harrington I'll meet him in hell for breakfast." Harrington is the conductor who shot his arm off. The town is well guarded and quiet. Ketchum made the strange request that he be buried face downward. Upon awakening this morning he remarked it was nice and asked Sheriff Garcia to hurry up the hanging so he could get to hell in time for dinner.

CONFESSION BY KETCHUM.

Denver, Colo., April 26. – A special to the Denver *Post* from Clayton, N. M., says: Thomas E. Ketchum, who was to be hanged there at noon today, mailed the following letter to President Mc Kinley this morning.

Sir: Being now at the town of Clayton, awaiting my execution set for this day and realizing the importance to the liberty of other men and the duty

I conceive to be incumbent upon myself, standing in the presence of death where human aid can't reach me, I desire to communicate to you by means of this letter, facts I deem would be of interest to the people through their president and perhaps be the means of liberating of innocent men. There are now three men in the Santa Fe penitentiary serving a sentence for the robbery of the U.S. mail at Stein's Pass, N.M. in 1897, viz.: Leonard Albertson, Walter Huffman, and Bill Waterman. They are innocent of the crime as an unborn babe. The names of the men who committed the crime are Dave Atkins, Ed Cullin, Will Carver, Sam Ketchum, Bronco Bill and myself. I have given my attorney in Clayton the means by which the articles taken in said robbery may be found where we hid them, also the names of witnesses who live in that vicinity who will testify that myself and gang were in the neighborhood, both immediately before and after the robbery. The fact that these men are innocent and suffering impels me to make a confession. While you cannot help and while I realize all efforts to secure me a commutation of sentence have signally failed, I wish to do this much in the interest of innocent men who, so far as I know, never committed a crime in their lives. I make this statement, fully realizing that my end is fast approaching and I must very soon meet my maker.

Very respectfully, your servant,
THOMAS E. KETCHUM.

At 11:30, Ketchum asked for music. A violin and guitar were sent for. Ketchum talked over an hour with visitors, cooler than anyone who met him. He declared that death is preferable to imprisonment. Ketchum told of the robberies in which he was concerned, but declared he never killed a man, and only shot three. He said he was not Black Jack and that the bandit still lived. Ketchum refused to give the names of friends still at liberty.

THE ROPE BROKE

Clayton, N.M., April 26. - Ketchum mounted the scaffold at 1:17 P. M.; the trap was sprung at 1:21; the rope breaking, but the fall jerked his head off.

TOO BIG A DROP

Clayton, N. M., April 26.- Ketchum was very pale as he mounted the platform, but showed no fear. A priest stood by his side. He declined to make a speech and merely muttered: "Goodbye, please dig my grave very deep," and finally "All right, hurry up." His legs trembled, but his nerve did not fail him. When the body dropped through the trap the half-inch rope severed his neck as cleanly as if a knife had cut it. The body pitched forward, the blood spurting from the headless trunk. Many spectators turned away in horror. Dr. Slack pronounced his life extinct in five minutes. The drop of seven feet was too great for so heavy a man.

THE EXECUTION

Special to the *New Mexican*

Clayton, N.M., April 26.- Thomas E. Ketchum, alias Black Jack, spent the morning talking to friends, his attorney and newspaper reporters. He was cheerful and treated those he liked with marked courtesy. Those against whom he felt ill he would not notice. During his conversation he made statements implicating himself and others in crimes for which innocent men have been convicted and are now suffering imprisonment. He said he thought it was his duty. He said to his attorney: "Tell Harrington I'll meet him in hell soon." After eating a hearty dinner he was told to prepare himself for death.

The death warrant was read to him early this morning. A priest went to him after starting to the scaffold and accompanied him on his death march. At 1:15 he began his march to the scaffold, after having his last request for music, which was granted, complied with. He had given his attorney directions for disposing of his effects. Sheriff Garcia on his right, Harry Lewis of Trinidad, on his left, accompanied by Detective Chambers of Denver, he marched coolly and calmly to the gallows. Coming to the stairs leading to the noose he kept his eyes on the ground. He stepped firmly on the trap door and his legs and arms were pinioned. Then he asked for the black cap which was put on. For some reason it was taken off and Tom shook hands with the sheriff and several deputies. Then was the cap adjusted again.

By this time he was getting nervous and finally became impatient at the delay and said: "Let'er go, boys, let'er go." Sheriff Garcia, at 12:17 P. M. cut the rope and the body shot down. The fall severed the head from his body. He alighted on his feet and the headless trunk stood for an instant upright, then swayed, then fell and great streams of blood spurted out from the severed neck. The head, remaining in the black cap, rolled to one side and the rope, released, flew high in the air. No physician was needed to tell that life was extinct. There was a small stockade, but people could look through the cracks. Quite a crowd was present to witness the horrible spectacle. Thirty minutes before the drop fell, Ketchum said he would meet Captain Fort, counsel for the Wells-Fargo Express company, J. Leahy, district attorney, who prosecuted him, and W. H. Reno, Colorado and Southern Railway detective, there also within a year.

He said he wrote a letter to the "boys" and smuggled it out of the Santa Fe penitentiary telling them to send these parties after him soon. He says they are "Marked." He expressed himself very bitterly against those who engaged in prosecuting him. He retained his nerve to the last and died game, like he said he would. He failed to make the speech promised, but included all he had to say in his statement to his lawyer. He said he would advise all boys not to steal sheep, cattle, or horses, but if they must steal, to rob a bank or a railroad train. He said he began his career of crime in 1897, and never had murdered anyone. The priest attending was Father Dean of Trinidad. His head was sewed on and the body prepared for burial by E. J. Sibert of Trinidad. Thus closes the history of one of New Mexico's notorious bandits. His remains were buried here.

———————— · ————————

Several factors caused Black Jack to be decapitated. Sheriff Salome Garcia purchased a new rope for $20.70 for the execution. The rope was stretched overnight, and the extra length was not added into the 7-foot drop for such a heavy man. Sheriff Garcia was drunk and had difficulty cutting the rope with the axe. After the execution, the head was sewn back on the body by the undertaker from Trinidad before being placed in a pine coffin. The body remained buried in the old cemetery in Clayton until September 10, 1933, when the coffin disinterment took place to remove the remains to the new cemetery. The coffin was opened and to everybody's surprise, the remains of Black Jack looked very much the same as the day he was buried. His hair and mustache had turned to a reddish color and the suit had the sheen of age. Black Jack's last request was also denied for he had not been buried face down. The famous outlaw's 30-30 caliber Winchester rifle was later given to President Theodore Roosevelt as a souvenir.

Sources:

Santa Fe *New Mexican*, April 26, 1901
San Francisco *Chronicle*, April 26, 1901

Appendix A

List of Lynchings in New Mexico.
1851-1893

Name	Place	Date
Young	Socorro	1851
1 man, Texan	Santa Fe	June 14, 1851
Jose de la Cruz	Mora	Sept. 1852
Gabriel Lujan	Mora	Sept. 1852
1 man	Doña Ana Co.	Dec. 1852
Gillion Scallion	Santa Fe	Nov. 12, 1853
2 Indian men	Nambe Pueblo	Mar. 1854
4 Mexican men	Doña Ana Village	Mar. 10, 1855
Matias Ribera	Santa Fe	Mar. 1857
John Miller	Albuquerque	July 4, 1857
Carlos Martinez	Albuquerque	April 1858
1 Mexican man	Mora	May 1858
Joseph Cummings	Lincoln	Nov. 1859
1 Mexican man	Lincoln	Nov. 1859
"Colonel" Sterten	Mesilla (Doña Ana Co.)	Dec. 30, 1860
Charles Hampton	Mesilla	Dec. 30, 1860
1 Mexican man	Mesilla	Mar. 22, 1861
1 Mexican man	Mesilla	April 10, 1861
William Watts	Socorro	April 19, 1861
J.W. Hager	Socorro	April 19, 1861
2 Mexican women	Socorro	April 19, 1861
James Adams	Sapello (San Miguel Co.)	1864
Thomas Means	Taos	Jan 2, 1867
Dan Dimon, alias, Ben Diamond	Pinos Altos (Grant Co.)	July 28, 1867
"Pony" O' Neil	Elizabethtown (Colfax Co.)	1869
1 Mexican man	Elizabethtown	Sept. 13, 1869
Charles Kennedy	Elizabethtown	Oct. 7, 1870
2 men	Los Lunas (Valencia Co.)	Feb. 1871
Jesus Pino	Los Lunas	Feb. 1871
Diego Lucero	Albuquerque	April 14, 1871
Pablo Padilla	Peralta (Valencia Co.)	Dec. 30, 1871
Juan Sandoval	Peralta	Jan. 5, 1872
4 men	Loma Parda (Mora Co.)	July 1872

Lynchings in the New Mexico Territory were not uncommon. From 1851 to 1893, 155 illegal hangings occurred. Many of the names of the unfortunate are unknown. Pictured is the lynching of Thomas Walsh at Lordsburg on April 29, 1883. Courtesy Museum of New Mexico, Neg. No. 112532. Photographer unknown.

Wiley	Ft. Union	Nov. 13-16, 1872
Hill	Ft. Union	Nov. 13-16, 1872
John Cowley	Cimarron (Colfax Co.)	Dec. 28-30, 1873
1 man	Cimarron	1874
Zachariah Compton	Lincoln	Feb. 1874
Still	Lincoln	Feb. 1874
Pas Mes	Doña Ana Co.	Aug. 1875
Thomas Madrid	Doña Ana Co.	Aug. 1875
Jermin Aguirre	Doña Ana Co.	Aug. 1875
Cruz Vega	Cimarron	Oct. 30, 1875
Manuel Cardenas	Cimarron	Nov. 10, 1875
Charles von Kohler, alias Alex C. Collier	Abiquiu (Rio Arriba Co.)	Dec. 27, 1875
Juan Miera	Albuquerque	June 23, 1876
Jose Miera	Albuquerque	June 23, 1876

Meliton Cordova	Albuquerque	June 23, 1876
Jose Segura	Lincoln	July 18, 1876
Jesus Largo	Lincoln	Aug. 1876
Joe Asque	Hillsboro (Grant Co.)	1877
Juan Largo	Bonquilla	Aug. 1877
Metcalfe	Mora	Nov. 1877
1 man	Albuquerque	Jan. 18, 1878
Beckwith	Las Vegas (San Miguel Co.)	June 1879
Manuel Barela	Las Vegas	June 4-5, 1879
Giovanni Dugi, alias Duque, Louis Torbillo	San Miguel Co.	June 4, 1879
Romulo Baca	Los Lunas	June 12, 1879
George Washington	Lincoln	June 28, 1879
J. P. Fish	Albuquerque	Nov. 12, 1879
Dick (Tom) Hardeman, alias Dick Turpin	Lincoln	Nov. 23, 1879
Thomas Jefferson House, alias Dutchy, Tom Henry	Las Vegas	Feb. 7-8, 1880
John Dorsey, alias Jim Dawson	Las Vegas	Feb. 7-8, 1880
Anthony Lowe, alias Jim West	Las Vegas	Feb. 7, 1880
3 men	Albuquerque	Feb. 20, 1880
Paz Chavez	Lincoln	March 1880
Juanito Mes	Seven Rivers (Eddy Co.)	March 1880
Joseph Murphy, alias One Armed Joe	Lincoln	July 1880
Herriman, alias Harrison	Lincoln	July 3, 1880
1 man	Lincoln	July 4, 1880
1 man	Lincoln	July 5, 1880
Jim Dunnigan	Santa Fe	July 18, 1880
Washington	Raton (Colfax Co.)	Dec 1, 1880
Pantaleon Miera	Bernalillo	Dec. 28, 1880
Santos Bernavides	Bernalillo	Dec. 28, 1880
Sandy King	Shakespeare (Grant Co.)	Jan. 1, 1881
William Tattenbaum, alias Russian Bill	Shakespeare	Jan. 1, 1881
Porter Stockton	Farmington (Rio Arriba Co.)	Jan. 10, 1881
California Joe	Albuquerque	Jan. 31, 1881
Escolastico Perez	Albuquerque	Jan. 31, 1881
Miguel Barrera	Albuquerque	Jan. 31, 1881
Jose Lopez	Rio Arriba Co.	Feb. 1881
Juan Chaves	Rio Arriba Co.	Feb. 1881
Faustino Gutierres	Albuquerque	Feb. 24, 1881
2 Mexican men	Lincoln Co.	March 1, 1881
Tom Gordon	Socorro	March 10, 1881
Enofre Baca	Socorro	March 31, 1881

Jim Flynn	Mogollon (Socorro Co.)	April 1881
James Devine	Colfax Co.	April 16, 1881
Narcisco Montoya	Taos	June 10, 1881
Ike Hazelitt	Eureka	June 15, 1881
Bill Hazelitt	Eureka	June 15, 1881
Frenchy Elmoreau	Socorro	Oct. 1881
Bush	Socorro	Oct. 1881
William "Flap Jack" Nicholson	Sanders	Oct. 1, 1881
Aristotle Noranjo	Los Lunas	Oct. 6, 1881
Fernando Chavez	Valencia Co.	Oct. 6, 1881
Selzo Espinoso	Valencia Co.	Oct. 6, 1881
J. F. Jennings	Tierra Amarilla (Rio Arriba Co.)	Oct. 26, 1881
Ed "Kid" Coulter	Tierra Amarilla	Oct. 26, 1881
Slim Kid	Tierra Amarilla	Oct. 26, 1881
Francisco Jordan	Cuchillo Negro (Socorro Co.)	Nov. 25, 1881
Frank Mc Hand	Las Vegas	1882
Dan Swany	Cerrillos (Santa Fe Co.)	Feb. 1882
Charles Shelton	Los Lunas	March 7, 1882
Henry French, aka Simpson	Los Lunas	March 7, 1882
Johnnie Redmond	Los Lunas	March 7, 1882
Jackson	Lincoln	May 25, 1882
Gus Mentzer	Raton	June 22, 1882
Jose Mares, alias Frank	Las Vegas	June 25-26, 1882
Frank "Navajo" Tafoya	Las Vegas	June 25-26, 1882
Juan Alvarid,aka Elvard	Socorro	Aug. 16, 1882
1 man	Deming	Aug. 27, 1882
W. Wiggin	Socorro	Sept. 1882
Guadalupe Archuleta	Bloomfield (Rio Arriba Co.)	Oct. 31, 1882
1 Mexican man	Loma Parda	Nov. 1882
Gilmore	Bernalillo Co.	1883
William S. Pearl	Lincoln (Ft. Stanton)	Jan. 23, 1883
Thomas Walsh	Lordsburg	April 29, 1883
Cristobal Romero	Los Lunas	1884
John Dorsey	San Miguel Co.	Jan. 22, 1884
Joe Fowler	Socorro	Jan. 22-24, 1884
Hank Andrews	Lincoln	Feb. 1884
Mitch Lee	Silver City	March 13, 1884
Frank Taggart	Silver City	March 13, 1884
1 man	Tularosa (Lincoln Co.)	April 1884
Juan Castillo	Raton	Aug. 1884
1 woman	Chimayo	Sept. 1884
Henry Thomas	Las Vegas	Jan. 1885
James Lowe, aka James West	San Miguel	Feb. 7, 1886
John Janes	Lincoln	June 18, 1886
Dewitt C. Johnson	Lincoln	Nov. 19, 1886

Goldenson	Lordsburg	Sept. 21, 1888
Joseph Chaca	Wallace	Aug. 26, 1889
Leandro Gonzales	Cebolleto	Feb. 3, 1893
3 men	Los Lunas	May 5, 1893
Cecilio Lucero	Las Vegas	May 29, 1893

Gus Mentzer was lynched on June, 26, 1882 in Raton, New Mexico. In all, five men were killed and two wounded in the affray. Armed and drunk, Mentzer assaulted one Deputy Sheriff with a pistol and temporarily escaped. During the night, Mentzer killed two men and wounded one. Later, a deputy protecting Mentzer while in custody, killed one man who in turn shot and killed the officer. Then Mentzer, pictured here, was hanged by the townsmen. Courtesy Museum of New Mexico, Neg. No. 14781. Photographer, W.A. White.

Sources:

The Raton *Guard*, June 30, 1882

Appendix B

Early Executions

Documents of early execution in New Mexico are very difficult to locate; some of the best sources of information are the Territorial newspapers. The Santa Fe *New Mexican* dated February 10, 1883 had bits of information of several early executions, all of which bear further inquiry and documentation. Readers with further information on legal hangings in New Mexico are invited to contact the author through High-Lonesome Books.

At Las Vegas, in 1857 (other sources say 1861), a woman named Pablita murdered a man, was tried, found guilty and executed on the gallows. (see Paula Angel – San Miguel County).

Also in 1857, a discharged soldier from Fort Craig went to Isleta and there hired an Indian to take his blankets on a burro to Albuquerque. The soldier murdered the Indian en route and stole the burro. He was captured, tried and convicted and hung at Albuquerque.

Pedro Ranado, who lived at "Fighting Corral," Albuquerque, caught a discharged soldier in his wife's bedroom in 1855, and killed him with an axe. He was found guilty and hanged on the site where Hunning's Mill now stands.

When General Carleton was stationed at Albuquerque, in 1857, a soldier of the Third infantry slipped up behind Francisco Garcia at a *baile* and cut his throat with a razor. He was executed by order of the courts.

In 1854, two Americans and one "half breed" were hung after trial and conviction at Tome. Their crime was murder of three Mexicans who owned a store near Casa Salazar. The murderers attempted to rob the store and in doing so killed the Mexicans.

The *New Mexican* dated November 28, 1849 had the following information on Andrew Jackson Sims. "At the last term of our court, A. J. Sims was convicted of the murder of Johnson Jackson. He is to be executed on the 30th of the present month."

Sources:

The *New Mexican*, November 28, 1849
Santa Fe *New Mexican*, February 10, 1883

Sources

Note: The primary source materials for *Death on the Gallows* are the contemporary newspaper accounts of the period. These sources are listed at the end of each story of crime and punishment within the main body of the text. In addition, the following books and magazines were consulted.

Abbott, Geoffrey. *The Book of Execution*. Headline Press, 1995.
Ball, Larry D. *Desert Lawmen*. University of New Mexico Press, 1992.
Beck, Warren A. & Ynez D. Haase, *Historical Atlas of New Mexico*, University of Oklahoma Press, 1969.
Breihan, Carl. *The Day they Hung Black-Jack Ketchum*. Old West Magazine.
Bryan, Howard. *Robbers, Rogues and Ruffians*. Clear Light Publishers, Santa Fe, New Mexico, 1991
Bryan, Howard. *Wildest of the Wild West*. Clear Light Publishers, Santa Fe, New Mexico, 1988.
Bullis, Don. *New Mexico's Finest: Peace Officers Killed in the Line of Duty*. New Mexico Department of Public Safety, 1996.
Coonfield, Ed. *The Fine Art of Hanging*. Real West, December 1986.
Hertog, Peter. *A Directory of New Mexico Desperados*. The Press of the Territorian, Santa Fe, New Mexico, 1965.
Hertog, Peter. *Legal Hangings*. The Press of the Territorian, Santa Fe, New Mexico, 1966.
Hurst, James W. *The Villista Prisoners of 1916-1917*. Yucca Tree Press, Las Cruces, NM, 2000
L'aloge, Bob. *Ghost's and Mysteries of the Old West*. Yucca Tree Press, 1990.
L'aloge, Bob. *Knights of the Sixgun*. Yucca Tree Press, 1991
Metz, Leon C. *The Shooters*. Mangan Books, 1976
Nash, Jay Robert. *Blood Letters and Bad Men*. M. Evans and Co, 1973.
Nash, Jay Robert. *Encyclopedia of the Western Lawmen & Outlaws*. Da Capo Press, 1994
P.C. News, Vol. 10 #12, December, 1992
Pearce, T.M. *New Mexico Place Names*. The University of New Mexico Press, 1965.
Peterson, Barbara Tucker. *Double Hanging in Lincoln*. True West, April 1999.
Richardson, Sue. *The Black Jack Story*, 2001.
Simmons, Marc. *When Six-Guns Ruled, Outlaw Tales of the South West*. Ancient City Press, Santa Fe, New Mexico. 1990
Sonnichsen, C.L. *Tularosa, the Last of the Frontier West*. University of New Mexico Press, Albuquerque, New Mexico, 1960.
Torrez, Robert. *Wild West Hanging Judges*. New Mexican Magazine, November 1999.
Williams, Oscar. *Witness to a Hanging*. True West, March 1992.

Published Research

The Espy File, Executions in the United States, 1608 – 1987, by: M. Watt
Espy and John Ortiz Smykla

ABOUT THE AUTHOR

West Gilbreath was born and raised in El Paso, Texas. After serving in the United States military, West joined the Doña Ana County Sheriff's Department in Las Cruces, New Mexico. On February 1, 2001, West retired as the Lieutenant of the Criminal Investigations Division to start a second career. He and his family relocated to Denton, Texas where he is a criminal investigator for the University of North Texas Police Department. West is a graduate of the F.B.I. National Academy, and received a Heritage Award for preserving the history of the Doña Ana County Sheriff's Department through the creation of the Historical Museum of Lawmen. *Death on the Gallows* is his first book.

HIGH-LONESOME BOOKS

"Published in the Greatest Country Out-of-Doors"

At **HIGH-LONESOME BOOKS** we have a great variety of titles for enthusiasts of the Southwest and the great Outdoors -- new, used, and rare books of the following:

Southwest History
Wilderness Adventure
Natural History
Hunting
Sporting Dogs
Mountain Men
Fishing
Country Living
Environment

Our catalog is FREE for the asking. Write or call.

HIGH-LONESOME BOOKS
P. O. Box 878
Silver City, New Mexico
88062
505-388-3763
High-LonesomeBooks@zianet.com
Also, come visit our new bookshop in the country
at High-Lonesome Road near Silver City or on-line at
www.High-LonesomeBooks.com